The Reminiscences

of

Vice Admiral Murrey L. Royar

U. S. Navy (Retired)

U. S. Naval Institute
Annapolis, Maryland

Preface

This volume comprises a series of six tape recorded interviews with Vice Admiral Murrey L. Royar, U. S. Navy (Retired). The interviews were obtained by John T. Mason, Jr. for the U. S. Naval Institute and were held in the apartment of Admiral Royar in Vinson Hall, McLean, Virginia. They span a period from July, 1972 to June 1973.

Admiral Royar's memoirs deal with a very full and successful naval career during which time he became Chief of the Bureau of Supplies and Accounts and later Chief of Naval Materiel. His service covers a wide range - from World War I through World War II and the Korean conflict.

Admiral Royar corrected the original typescript as it was made from the tapes. The corrected version was later re-typed and indexed for the convenience of the reader.

VICE ADMIRAL MURREY L. ROYAR
SUPPLY CORPS, U. S. NAVY, RETIRED

Murrey Levering Royar was born in Los Angeles, California, on November 22, 1894. He attended the Los Angeles High School and was graduated from the University of California with the degree of Bachelor of Science. Appointed Ensign in the U. S. Navy on June 29, 1917, he progressed in rank until he was appointed Vice Admiral, Supply Corps, on October 2, 1954. On February 1, 1955 he was transferred to the Retired List of the U. S. Navy.

After completing instruction at the Naval Pay Officers' School, Washington, D. C., in September 1917, he was ordered to the USS COLUMBIA, employed in convoy duty between New York and Europe. He served as her supply officer until January 1919, when he was transferred to duty as supply officer in the USS NEW ORLEANS on the Asiatic Station. Service in that vessel included seven months when she was station ship at Vladivostok, during which time he outfitted men for a newly organized Czech Navy. From February 1920 until November 1921, he had duty as accounting officer at the Navy Yard, Cavite, P. I., followed by a tour as supply officer at the Naval Station, Olongapo, P. I.

After his return to the United States in the summer of 1922, he reported to the Harvard School of Business Administration, Cambridge, Massachusetts, for instruction. He graduated there in June 1924, receiving the degree of Master of Business Administration. Following that duty he was assistant accounting officer in the Mare Island Navy Yard, California, from July 1924 until September 1925, and served as supply officer in the USS RELIEF for two years afterwards.

He was assistant supply officer, Twelfth Naval District, from December 1927 until December 1930, when he was ordered to the Mare Island Navy Yard, for duty in connection with fitting out the USS CHICAGO. He served in that vessel from her commissioning on March 9, 1931 until June 1934. He was in charge of the Clothing Division, and later was assistant to the Officer in Charge of Stock Division, Bureau of Supplies and Accounts, Navy Department, from July 1934 to June 1938, and served as supply officer of the USS SARATOGA from that time until April 1940.

He served as senior assistant to the supply officer in the Navy Yard, Washington, D. C., from May 1940 until May 1942, when he reported for duty in the Bureau of Supplies and Accounts as officer in charge of the Maintenance Division with the responsibility for the plans and operation of the budget and over-all administrative control over civil personnel in the field under the cognizance of the Bureau of Supplies and Accounts. In February 1944 he assumed duty as officer in charge of the Accounting Group of the Bureau, consisting of seven divisions having the responsibility for keeping and auditing the money and property accounts of the Naval Establishment, including manufacturing and operating expenses at yards and stations, lease-lend, and inventory records relating to plant property.

DECLARATION OF TRUST

The undersigned does hereby appoint and designate as his (her) Trustee herein, the Secretary-Treasurer and Publisher of the United States Naval Institute to perform and discharge the following duties, powers, and privileges in connection with the possession and use of a certain taped interview between the undersigned and the Oral History Department of the United States Naval Institute.

1. Classification of Transcript.

    ( )a. If classified OPEN, the transcript(s) may be read or the recording(s) audited by the qualified personnel upon presentation of proper credentials, as determined by the Secretary-Treasurer of the U. S. Naval Institute.

    (X)b. If classified PERMISSION REQUIRED TO CITE OR QUOTE, the user will be required to obtain permission in writing from the interviewee prior to quoting or citing from either the transcript(s) or the recording(s).

    ( )c. If classified PERMISSION REQUIRED, permission must be obtained in writing from the interviewee before the transcribed interview(s) can be examined or the tape recording(s) audited.

    ( )d. If classified CLOSED, the transcribed interview(s) and the tape recording(s) will be sealed until a time specified by the interviewee. This may be until the death of the interviewee or for any specified number of years.

2. It is expressly understood that in giving this authorization, I am in no way precluded from placing such restrictions as I may desire upon use of the interview at any time during my lifetime, nor does this authorization in any way affect my rights to the copyright of my literary expressions that may be contained in the interview.

Witness my hand and seal this 1st day of February 1974.

Murrey L. Royar

I hereby accept and consent to the foregoing Declaration of Trust and the powers therein conferred upon me as Trustee:

Interview No. 1 with Vice Admiral Murrey L. Royar, U.S. Navy

(Retired)

Place: His apartment in Vinson Hall, McLean, Virginia

Date: Wednesday morning, 12 July 1972

Subject: Biography

By: John T. Mason, Jr.

Q: Admiral, I'm grateful to you - grateful in advance - for consenting to do your recollections for us at the Naval Institute. I recall I had a brief conversation with you some weeks ago and I learned at that time of the broad interest of you naval career. Since that time, I've looked into it a little more thoroughly and am convinced that you have a real contribution to make to the historical record.

Would you begin, Sir, in the proper way be giving me the date of your birth and the place of your birth?

Adm. R.: Yes, indeed, I'd be happy to. I was born on November 22nd 1894 in Los Angeles, California. I was born in a house on West 6th Street, close to where the Biltmore Hotel is now. Shortly afterwards my parents moved out to the western part of the city, to 741 South Coronado Street, and I grew up in Los Angeles.

Q: What was your father's business?

Royar #1 - 2

Adm. R.: My father was in business with my uncle in a little shop called Royar Brothers "We Frame Pictures." They also carried pictures and supplies. He and my uncle were very much interested in many of the artists that came out to California and they sold them artists' material, traded supplies for pictures, and in fact helped organize quite an artists' colony around Los Angeles.

Q: There's some reflection of that in all the handsome photographs you have here and frames very artistically arranged.

Adm. R.: Thank you.

Q: Tell me about your early education.

Adm. R.: I went to the Hoover Street Grammar School, which was at 9th and Hoover Street in Los Angeles, and graduated from there in 1908 in the 8th Grade. At that time, the high schools were greatly overcrowded in Los Angeles. There were only two at the time, Los Angeles High School and the Polytechnic High School, and it was very hard to get in. Anticipating trouble, I went to work on The Times scholarship contest. Now, The Times scholarship contest was organized by The Los Angeles Times. They had this contest primarily for getting new subscriptions or renewals, and so on and there were, I guess fifty or sixty very active contestants.

Los Angeles was pretty competitive so I spent a great deal of time in Redlands, California, where an uncle of mine ran the Redlands News and Stationery Company.

Q: That's in the northern part of the State?

Adm. R.: Redlands is about 69 miles west of Los Angeles. I got so many subscriptions and did so well up there that The Times nicknamed me and gave me a story and called me "The Redlands Rustler." Well, I did very well and I earned a scholarship to a school which is now closed - a prep school - called Yale School.

Yale School was founded and run by a gentleman by the name of Mr. Adams, who was a graduate of Yale. I spent my freshman year at Yale School, working afternoons selling or delivering papers, inasmuch as my father died when I was about twelve years old. I also, the following year - the following two years, was in The Times scholarship contest and got my scholarships to Yale School. The fourth year I had saved up enough money so that I could go to LA High School, which was a little farther away than Yale School, and I transferred from Yale School to Los Angeles High School.

Q: Was there an advantage in doing that?

Adm. R.: Yes, because I wanted later to go to the University of California and Yale School was not accredited to the University. Los Angeles High School was and I could transfer directly from LA High into the University of California without examination.

Q: Los Angeles was far less of a city than it is now?

Adm. R.: I can remember Los Angeles very well as a youngster when it had 102,000 people. I can remember very well when it was all concentrated down around the Plaza and railroad station, on North Main Street. My father and mother used to take me down and they'd go along the street and knew everybody, enjoyed speaking to them, and it was just like an old country Spanish town.

Q: So you went for your fourth year at Los Angeles High School?

Adm. R.: I graduated from Los Angeles High School in the summer of 1912. At that time I didn't have enough money to go to the University, which was at Berkeley. That was the only college then.

Q: It had no branches?

Adm. R.: It had no branches at that time so I stayed out for a year and a half and worked in Los Angeles with a clothing company, installment clothing company, collecting installments. At the end of a year and a half I had enough money to start up there, and with a little help from an uncle of mine, I entered the University in January 1914.

Q: Did you have any specific ambitions at that point? What kind of a career did you plan?

Adm. R.: Very definite. An uncle of mine had a big farm. In the 1880s he had come out from New York and taken up some 600 acres west of Hollywood. Mr. Sinclair, of Sinclair Oil, bought it from him later on which was an interesting thing because about 1914 or 1915 he sold the 600 acres for $100,000 and thought he got a terrific price. Now, lots are selling for $100,000 or more.

Anyway, I'd spent a great deal of my youth on that farm. The fact is in my first grade of grammar school I started in the country school, the Coldwater School, right where the Berverley Hills Hotel is now. I loved that part of the country. I loved farm life, and I went up to the University with the idea of going into the College of Agriculture and spent my freshman year there but I wasn't very good in chemistry and I failed in chemistry and had to go to summer school to make that up. There were other technical courses that I wasn't too good in, so I decided to change and I went from Agriculture into the College of Letters and Science, and that's where I graduated from with a Bachelor of Science.

The almost four years that I stayed at the University I had worked all summers at Catalina Island and made most of my money diving for coins when the old steamer <u>Avalon</u> would come in and people would stand there on the decks and toss coins over. There were three or four of us in row boats and we would dive for them.

Q: That was actually your job?

Adm. R.: That was my part-time job. My real job over there was running the water station. At that time, Catalina had no fresh water. The only wells over there were - had sulphur or some metal in them, and they had to carry all the fresh water by ship over to Catalina. From the ship it was pumped into big stand tanks. We had five-gallon glass jugs, and my job was to keep the jugs clean and keep them filled up. They had two delivery trucks that delivered these jugs round to people at 20 cents a jug. That was my primary work, and I worked three summers at that.

One reason, I might say, that I never went into the Army was the fact that at the end of my sophomore year - and, by the way, I had to take military for two years because California was a land grant school and we were required to take two years military. At the end of that time I liked the military pretty well and I decided that I would try to go on, take the third and fourth year in order to obtain a commission as 2nd Lieutenant. To do that you had to take an examination - a practical examination in drilling a squad was part of it, and I went out on old Cal Field - that's California Field, the football field, where they were having the try-outs - and the squad that I was in was composed mostly of juniors and seniors who had failed in military and were having make-ups and they couldn't care less whether anybody ever made a commission or not. Old Major Nance was in charge and he gave me my own squad to drill. If I gave them "squads right," they'd do squads left, "forward march" and they did a beautiful to the rear march. Finally Major Nance came over and he said, "Who in the hell is in charge of this squad?" I said, "I am, Sir." He said, "What's your name?" "Royar," said I. He said, "Royar, let me tell you this. You'll never make an Army officer."

That's actually true. Major Nance and I got to be good friends later on and we often laughed about that. But that sort of soured me on the Army.

Well, I took an active part in the school activities, went out for football, but unfortunately Andy Smith was around there bout that time and he brought up a big group of men from San Diego. I only weighed 175 and I didn't last very long.

In the meantime, I belonged to a house club, which was a local fraternity called the Achaean Club.

Q: Greek oriented, wasn't it?

Adm. R.: That's right. That club now is part of Lambda Chi Alpha. Anyway, I belonged to that club and I earned part of my way through School and I managed the club and did a little work around there so as to relieve me of my board and room charges.

I think it was in April 1917, anyway it was just before we got into the war, a good many of us decided that we'd better hook up with somebody and get going while we had a chance to without being drafted.

I applied to the Marine Corps. They turned me down because of 18/20ths in one eye and because of the fact that Major Nance told me I'd mever make an Army officer I bypassed the Army. A friend of mine came around one day and he said, "I hear they're giving examinations for the Pay Corps in the Navy at Mare Island. Let's go up and take a shot at it." Well, I said, "I've only got 18/20ths in my eye and they turned me down in the Marine Corps, but I'll go up with you."

We went up to Mare Island figuring it would be a day's examination. We got up there and found it was ten days.

Q: Ten days?

Adm. R.: Ten days, and we had no money, either one of us. But we signed up, and they gave me my physical and said, "You've only got 18/20ths in one eye, but I think in the Pay Corps we can get a waiver," which they did. I saw this friend of mine Walton J. Dismukes, he's dead and gone now, but Walt and I went down to the YMCA

Royar #1 - 8

and we talked the YMCA into giving us a room and letting us have meals until the examination was over on the promise that we would go to work in the Navy Yard and pay our bill.

Q: That was quite an arrangement!

Adm. R.: That's right. We took the exam –

Q: Why was it so long?

Adm. R.: That was their formal examination at that time for a civilian to obtain a commission. They gave me an exam on everything that I'd had in college, practically, mathematics, history, everything. It was a complete examination.

Q: You hadn't anticipated this?

Adm. R.: Hadn't anticipated it at all.

Q: So you couldn't bone up?

Adm.: We did. We went to the Examining Board and they told us what the first day's exams were going to be – the subjects – and Walt and I went down to the Library and boned on that till the Library closed. Then we took the next day's exam, went to the Library, and boned again for the next day and so on till the exam was over.

There was one funny experience that we had. One of the questions was, "Give your impressions or your reasons why the United States and Germany would get into war." Well, I had just had a course at the University of California under David P. Barrows, who was later a major general, reserve, in the Army. Dean Barrows was probably at that time one of the best authorities on international politics we had, and he gave us what I thought was a very good course on both sides, the United States side and the German side. I thought this is just down my alley, so I gave a long dissertation and tried to give both sides.

Anyway, if I can digress a minute. Later on when I reported in to the Bureau of Supplies and Accounts as an ensign, I was called in and Rear Admiral Sam McGowan, the Paymaster General, who was quite a character, was sitting at his desk. He had in his office only his desk and his chair. He later told me he had no other chairs because people might sit down and take too much of his time. Anyway, I stood there and he finally looked up and said, "Huh, who are you?"

I said, "Ensign Royar."

"Oh, you're the fellow who wrote about the German side in your examination?"

I said, "Yes. I thought I gave a pretty good story on both sides."

"Let me tell you," he said, "you've been under Secret Service observation ever since we read that thing."

"Why?" I asked.

"Well," he said, "your grandparents on your father's side both came from Germany."

I said, "Yes, my grandfather came to get out of the German Army and he immediately got into the Union Army in the Civil War."

"Well," he said, "that doesn't make any difference. You've

got German grandparents."

"Yes, Sir."

He said, "They were going to throw you out. I told them I thought probably you'd make a pretty good officer. But I just want to let you know that you were under thorough observation and the Secret Service went into your record. I don't want you to let me down."

Returning to my story, as soon as the exam was over we both went to work as laborers in the Navy Yard.

Q: In order to pay your board bill!

Adm. R.: In order to pay our board bill. Walt got a good job. He was a time-keeper, but for some reason in the gang that I was assigned to, the foreman didn't like me and he put me to work chipping rust on one of the new destroyers they had on the ways - chipping rust so that they could red lead it and paint it. It was the dirtiest, hottest job I ever had. He said, "Well, these college boys come up here to work and I'm going to make them work. They are soft, don't know how to work."

He didn't know that I had to work to eat! So I stuck with the job.

Q: You didn't have an obligation to go back to the University?

Adm. R.: I forgot the University. I didn't take my final exams or anything.

Royar #1 - 11

Q: Oh, you didn't?

Adm. R.: No, I was supposed to graduate in the December 1917, but the University later on gave me my degree with the class of 1918. They considered that my war work took up that last semester. So I never took my final exams for the first half of my senior year, and I didn't take any course at all the last half. They did, however, give me my degree.

We worked in the Navy Yard until somebody brought us a clipping from a Vallejo paper giving a list of people who had passed the examinations and our names were there.

Q: Meanwhile, you'd been investigated so you were accepted?

Adm. R.: I was accepted. We took this in to the Supply Officer there at Mare Island, who was Captain Morsell, and he said, "I advise you both to quit and go home."

We had paid our bills by that time and were free and had enough money to get home, down to Los Angeles. Walt lived down in Santa Anna, near Los Angeles, so we went to our homes, and, sure enough, in two or three days a telegram came saying that our commissions were on the way and to wait for them and immediately upon receipt to be sworn in, and to report then to the Bureau of Supplies and Accounts in Washington, D.C.

We were sworn in in Los Angeles, at the Recruiting Station, and we figured we'd better get into uniform, so we went down to "Desmond's" a clothing store - I'll never forget it - and they sold us our first uniforms.

Q: You had enough money to pay for them?

Adm. R.: I had borrowed some money that time. I borrowed enough money to get my uniform and to pay my way across the continent.

Q: This was not paid by the Navy?

Adm. R.: They wouldn't pay me till after I'd completed the travel, so I had to have some advance money to get across. I came to Washington and, on my way, I did find out, as I said before, that I had been under surveillance by the Secret Service. I stopped on my way, in Missouri, to see my grandmother, my German grandmother, and later when I reported to Adm. McGowan he mentioned the fact that I had stopped there. He said they knew why!

Well, we came back to Washington and reported in to the Bureau of Supplies and Accounts in the old State, War and Navy Building in Washington.

The State, War and Navy Building had the State Department, War Department, and the Navy Department –

Q: All under that mansard roof!

Adm. R.: All under one roof, if you can imagine that! The first thing that they picked up on me, as I walked in, was "Where did you get that cap?"

I said, "I bought it in Los Angeles. It was sold to me by a reputable company and they said this was the kind of cap I was supposed

Royar #1 - 13

to have."

They said, "You've got a warrant officer's cap on. You're supposed to have a commissioned officer's cap!" And the first thing I was told to do was to go out and get into uniform, which I did.

We started in immediately. We were ordered to the old Business High school in Washington. They'd established a pay school there. There were 125 of us, all from distinguished military colleges. Some who came in graduated after four years of Military - ROTC. They came in without examination. Those of us who came in with less than four years had to take the examination, as I mentioned before. Altogether, there were 125 of us, and there were some wonderful people in that group.

We started at Business High school but that wasn't satisfactory so they moved us over to Catholic University. We were given barracks over there, when before we were living out in town. I was living in a rooming house. I remember what trouble we had finding a place to live. Walt and I went around, and the first thing that a landlady would say was "Where are your references?" Well, we had no references. Out in California, nobody thought about references at all. They took a look at you, and if they liked you, all right. But here we were supposed to put up references. We finally got into a little rooming house where they didn't require references.

Anyway, we went over to Catholic University and settled in the barracks there - the universities dormitories. That was quite a fine organization. I'll never forget that a lot of the boys had never had much Navy discipline and one of the young faculty officers - I won't mention his name — was supposed to be the disciplinary officer and he was spit and polish. A lot of these boys were good athletes. Some of them — like Bull Durham, who had been —

Q: Bull Durham?

Adm. R.: Yes. He was a supply officer, but he had been quarter back on the Washington State University that beat Brown in the Rose Bowl Game, in the first of the new series of Rose Bowl Games in 1916. Well, Bull was mad at the spit and polish. The disciplinary officer had been quite an athlete down at the Academy and he said he thought it would be a good idea if they had a football game between the faculty officers and the students. This was in the fall, in September. Bull jumped at that. He was going to organize a student team and play for one man. Fortunately one of the other faculty officers found out about the plan and the game was canceled!

Q: Bad for morale!

Adm. R.: Bad for morale.

Q: What did that course comprise?

Adm. R.: That gave us a taste of what the Pay Corps was supposed to do. We had some disbursing, storekeeping, they told us how to run the general mess, as much as you can out of a book. Most of us had no knowledge of the Navy at all, that is, the inner workings of the Navy. We didn't know what we were getting into. It was called the Pay Corps instead of Supply Corps at that time, and we had no knowledge of what the duties of the Pay Corps were whatsoever. So the Faculty tired to indoctrinate us. They made it very evident that you had to have a strict accounting for everything and that if anything was unaccounted for you were liable to go up to Portsmouth Naval Prison - which caused me concern a little later on. I'll tell you about that.

We worked like the devil in that school because we knew it was the only chance to get information that would be helpful to us when we went out to independent duty.

Q: What was you average age at that point?

Adm. R.: About twenty-two or twenty-three.

Q: You were all in the same bracket?

Adm. R.: All in the same bracket, Ensigns. Now, do you want me to continue on?

Q: Yes.

Adm. R.: We had our graduation exercises from the pay school, and I was ordered to the USS Columbia - a coal burner, there's a picture of her over there, that four-stacker. I was just simply ordered to her and had no idea what my job would be. The fact is Leigh Palmer signed my orders: "You are hereby detached from duty at the Navy Pay Officers' School, Washington, D.C., and such other duties as may have been assigned to you. You will proceed immediately to the port in which the Columbia may be in and report to the commanding officer for duty on board that vessel."

Royar #1 - 16

Q: You were then at his disposal?

Adm. R.: I was at his disposal, yes. I received those orders on 14 October and found out that the Columbia was in Norfolk. So I went down to Norfolk and reported aboard a few days later. The captain was F. Brooks Upham. Captain Upham said, "Welcome aboard, Pay."

I said, "Yes, Sir. Who am I assistant to?"

He said, "You're not assistant. You're it."

"Thank you, Captain," I said, "but I didn't expect that."

"Yes. You go down and see Ransdell, Lieutenant Commander Ransdell. He's anxious to get away. He'll turn over to you."

So, he turned over to me. I counted the money. Believe me, I counted every cent.

Q: You were careful that it was all in order when you took it over?

Adm. R.: All in order.

Q: That's one thing you learned at the Pay School?

Adm. R.: Yes, Commander Ransdell said, "I want to get this over with because you're sailing in a day or so, and I want to get off the ship before you sail."

Well, we took the inventory of the clothing and the inventory of the ship's store, and I was sure that everything was there. Then the captain called me in and he said:

"Pay, I want to get your requisitions out. We're going up to New York to coal and to provision, and then we're going on a convoy.

This is all secret. You're not to repeat that to anybody, no one at all."

I said, "Yes, Sir," and we pulled up anchor in a couple of days and went up to New York.

I had my requisitions all in and we started to get stuff aboard. Everybody coaled ship, the yeoman, everybody. It was the dirtiest job I've ever seen, but we got coaled and then we started to provision. Remembering what they'd told me at the Pay School, I was right at the gangway counting everything as it came aboard. One thing I counted in particular was the sides of beef. Of course, in those days, the cold storage was rather small. The ships didn't go on very long voyages. That is, they weren't away from port very long. But on this convoy it took about ten days to go over and we never stopped.

Q: It was a transatlantic thing?

Adm. R.: Transatlantic, and without stopping on the other side we turned around and came back. So the round trip took between two and three weeks. I had to crowd everything I could into the cold storage. I counted my sides of beef, went down to the Pay Office to check over, and I was short a side of beef. My God, I could see shadows of Portsmouth right then and there. I was scared. So I got out the book, and the book said to check over again and be sure that you're right, and then report it to the captain.

So I went down and broke out every side of beef in the cold storage and, sure enough, we were short one side of beef. I went up to report to the skipper and he said:

"We'll search the ship."

They searched the ship, but no quarter of beef and I thought, well, this is a nice way to start off. We went to sea. We took this convoy up through the northern passage in the North Atlantic and it was cold, wet. I'll never forget it. They gave me the duty as junior officer of the deck. You can see in the picture up on that forward mast, about where those crosstrees are, was the watch station about the size and shape of a 50-gallon oil drum. You could stand in it and stand your watch. That was my watch station. You'd go up that mast on a Jacob's ladder, crawl over on one side while the other man was crawling out the other side.

Q: Left you pretty vulnerable to the winds, didn't it?

Adm. R.: Well, I'd never had any experience with that, and the first time I went up it was a windy day and that little Columbia would roll 60° to 70°. She was round-bottomed and didn't have any chocks on her to stop the roll. She would roll one side and roll the other, and here I was slapping against the mast. The whole crew went out to see the paymaster fall down!

Q: Could you chain yourself to the mast?

Adm. R.: No. I went up there rung by rung on that Jacob's ladder and I squeezed water out of that metal container, I think, getting in. When I got in, the other fellow got out. That was my watch.

One night I was up there and the skipper said - we had a voice tube up there for communication.

"You'd better come down. I'm afraid you might roll off that mast top."

I said, "Captain, I'm not coming down. I'm staying right here." I wouldn't go down for anything, and I did a double watch until it had calmed down a little, then I went down. I didn't make any bones about it, I was scared.

Anyway, we were out in the North Atlantic and one time as I came off the midwatch, I met a big water tender by the name of Doty, who was walking the deck and getting some fresh air, and he said, "Sir, have you ever been down in the engine room while we're under way?"

I said, "No, I haven't. I'd like to see it."

"Before you turn in," he said, "come on down."

So we went down to the engine room, and the old reciprocating engines were turning over. It was all new to me and I thought it was quite a sight.

"Now," he said, "We're going to the fireroom."

So we crawled through the little passageway into the fireroom where they were shoveling coal, and I was astounded to see two or three of the snipes - I shouldn't say "snipes," but that was their nickname - firemen with their shiny coal shovels over the open fire with steaks on top of them!

I said, "Where in the hell did you get those steaks?" Looking kind of sheepish one man said, "Remember the quarter of beef you lost?"

And I said, "Yes, but that's ten days ago. How in the devil did you keep it?"

"Oh," he said, "there's nothing to that. We just burried it in coal against the skin of the ship. That icy North Sea is just like a refrigerator."

I said, "You're going to get a little bit less meat now for a while till I make up for that steak." They said:

"You'd better try a piece of this," and I did. It was perfect! It had aged and was just right.

Q: And plenty dirty!

Adm. R.: No. They had it all wrapped in burlap. It was perfectly all right. But I learned something about cold storage.

We had a very interesting cruise. I never forgot that one morning on one of our trips, we always looked over the convoy to see that they were all in place, and there was this I think it was Norwegian ship - it was a foreign-flag ship anyway that was in the convoy - was laying back almost hull down and the old man, Captain F. B. Upham, was mad as the devil. We'd had some reports of submarines around and he suspected that this ship might have been contacting the submarines to refuel them. He didn't know. I'll never forget that we slowed down to let the ship catch up with us and the old man took the Columbia over next to her and he climbed up the yard arm and with a megaphone said, "I want to talk to the skipper."

"Ja," came back, and he said:

"Now listen to me. You fall out of position once more and I'll blow you to hell out of the water."

That was the last trouble we had. He never got out of position again.

Q: How many ships would you shepherd in a convoy?

Adm.: Between twenty and thirty.

Q: With a speed of what?

Adm. R.: Ten knots.

Q: That was a fast convoy, wasn't it?

Adm. R.: Not very fast.

Q: And how many escorts were there?

Adm. R.: Just the Columbia.

Q: Just one escort?

Adm. R.: Yes, we'd circle and we never lost a ship the whole time. But the skipper was quite a character, too. I guess when I was in the Columbia we made three or four convoy trips. We always had a lay-over in New York for repairs in between trips.

Q: What did you bring back with you?

Adm. R.: Nothing.

Q: You just came solo?

Adm. R.: Solo. In those days we only had spark sets – radio and they'd only carry about sixty miles. And coming back invariably – Captain Upham had two of the trips and Captain Harry Brinser had the last two – it was on the two trips that I went out with Captain Upham, he got orders to return to Philadelphia. He had no more use for Philadelphia than the man in the moon. He was a New Yorker. So, instead of going to Philadelphia, we breezed right in to New York, and he got a dispatch from the Navy Department, "You're supposed to be in Philadelphia."

"I didn't get any dispatch, I have no record of any dispatch and I just came into the nearest port."

They let him get away with it.

Q: He was a determined man!

Adm. R.: He was a charmer.

Q: He finally got to be a admiral of the fleet, didn't he?

Adm. R.: That's right, and wasn't he CNO at one time or assistant? He was an excellent officer. He ran a good ship. He was relieved by Captain Harry Brinser. Brinser was another fine officer, too, and he made admiral.

But the ship was wet. She would roll over and roll the gun sponsons under. We had to have those closed up so that we only had the 5- inch forward and aft machine guns topside. She was a good ship.

Q: What was your destination usually on these convoys?

Adm. R.: We would meet a destroyer squadron about 200 miles out from France. The convoy's destination was France. We'd meet the destroyers and they'd take over the convoy, and they would encircle the convoy, figuring, I think, that the last 200 miles were the most dangerous.

Q: How great was the German submarine menace?

Adm. R.: We had no trouble. We did pick up some survivors from a torpedoed ship from another convoy on one trip, but we lost very few ships on the convoy system - very few - that is between New York and France. Our system was pretty good. Nobody knew when we were going out. They kept things pretty quiet and they had comparatively little trouble.

Q: Did you do any zigzagging of your course:

Adm. R.: Oh, yes, zigzagged and changed course. That's one reason it took us so long to get over. We were changing course here and there and zigzagging. But we had, as I say, comparatively little trouble. The destroyers did a nice job. There were several destroyers to take the convoy and they would keep circling them all the time. They lost some, but not too many.

Q: It's rather remarkable that you could carry sufficient fuel for such a long journey?

Adm. R.: Well, when we started we not only had our bunkers full but we had sacks of coal all over the topside. We had to do that and that made it pretty dirty. They had coal sacks on the main deck, on the decks outside and then as they worked it down they dumped it in bunkers. We did all right.

Is there any other question you can think of?

Q: No. These convoys were largely supplies for the armies?

Adm. R.: That's right. They were all military supplies of various kinds.

Q: No transports?

Adm. R.: No, sometimes we'd get a transport that would go out with us for a day or two but, because of their good speed, they'd turn them loose as a rule and they would zigzag and go across on their own. Then they'd pick up the destroyers to take them into port.

Q: They were largely ocean liners?

Adm. R.: That's right, ocean liners.

The living conditions aboard ship were pretty rough because we were in the North Sea most of the time and the excessive rolling and pitching. The fact is that most of the officers, and I did too, slung hammocks in our staterooms. We never tried to sleep in our bunks. You'd roll right out of your bunk. A lot of us, if we didn't have room in the stateroom, slung our hammocks in the wardroom.

Q: So you just swung with the ship?

Adm. R.: Swung with the ship, the same as the crew. The crews in those days, of course, had no bunks at all. They all had hammocks.

Q: What was the complement of the Columbia?

Adm. R.: As I recall it, it was about 250 men.

Q: You say you lost one man?

Adm. R.: We lost one man before they sealed up those gun sponsons on the side. We had a lot of trouble with this youngster. I remember him very well. He couldn't keep himself clean. He was in my division, too. An old Chief came to me one day and said:

"Sir, we don't like this man. He's dirty, and it's no use to report him to the captain. Let us take care of him."

I said, "O.K., Chief. That's fine with me."

So, lo and behold, what did they do? They got him out on the quarter deck, stripped him down, and gave him a sand and canvas, just like the sand and canvas that they gave the deck. They rubbed that sand on him and took the canvas to him. He yelled and hollered, but we never had any more trouble with him. I felt sorry for this kid. I had a lot of talks with him. He came from a broken home, and I tried to help him along. His gun duty was on one of the 5-inch that went out of the side there and he was cleaning it up one morning when the ship took a terrific roll, water came in and washed him out. I can still see that kid yelling and waving his hand, but we never stopped for him.

Q: Didn't stop?

Adm. R.: No, not with a convoy. We'd had information that there was a German submarine around there and they wouldn't stop, and it was a rough stormy day.

Q: As you neared the French coast, was there any danger at all from German planes?

Adm. R.: Not in World War I.

Q: They had planes?

Adm. R.: They had planes, but they weren't bothering the ships, not as far as we know.

Q: This tour of duty lasted for the duration of the war, did it?

Adm. R.: We were at sea when the armistice was signed and we got back into port around the middle of November, 1918. When we arrived in New York I realized that the war was over. The fact is on the night after the armistice we lit up the ship bright as could be, and came in to New York with all lights burning - no more darken ship.

I spoke about being in the University of California in the College of Letters and Science. I had had a great deal of interest in foreign trade and I had a tentative agreement with an oil company to go to China.

Q: You were leaving the service?

Adm. R.: No, that was before I got into the service; when I graduated I would go with this oil company.

Well, we got in to New York and found that the Columbia was going to be flagship of the Caribbean and I wasn't particularly interested in that duty. The New Orleans was in New York, scheduled to go to the Asiatic and, thinking back on foreign trade, I thought I'd like to have a cruise out in the Asiatic before I got out of the service. The fact is, when I came in the service I had no idea of ever making it a career. I was going to help the boys win the war and get out and go into foreign trade, and I felt here's a good chance to see something of the Asiatic Station before I got out.

So we were in New York and the Paymaster in the New Orleans was Lieutenant Ralph Bristol. He'd come into the Navy in the same class with me, and Ralph was anxious to get away. He didn't want to go on to the Asiatic. He was married and had a family and wanted to get out. So we came down to Washington and talked to the Detail Officer, and the Detail Officer said, "All right, if Bristol wants to get away, you can go and I'll get somebody to relieve you." They sent a lieutenant by the name of Soars to relieve me and I went over and relieved Bristol, and the skipper there was Captain E. B. Larimer. I don't know whether you remember Larimer or not. He was later Chief of BuOrd. The medical officer was Lieutenant Commander Ross T. McIntire, later Surgeon General of the Navy and physician to President Roosevelt.

Q: Oh.

Adm. R.: So I went over and relieved Bristol, and on the 9th of January 1919 we started for the Asiatic via the Panama Canal. We went down through Panama and up to San Diego, then to Honolulu. We had another ship with us, the Albany, a sister ship of the New Orleans.

Q: You were both cruisers?

Adm. R.: Both cruisers and went together. Then we went to Yokohama from Honolulu. At Yokohama we split up. The <u>Albany</u> went up to Vladivostok as station ship, and we made a southern cruise from Yokohama down to Armoy, Fuchow, Swatow, Hong Kong, Sandakan in Borneo, Singapore, Saigon, Iloilo, and back to Manila.

Then, from Manila, we went back up into China, Shanghai, and then went up to Vladivostok and relieved the <u>Albany</u> as station ship.

Q: This tour that you made was simply to show the flag?

Adm. R.: Just to show the flag. We were the first ships to show the flag after World War I in Asiatic waters.

We had a very fine cruise, a very interesting cruise, too. I think it was when we went down to Amoy, and the club there was an English club and they invited us over for cocktails and said, please bring ice, we haven't had ice for years! So we took the ice over for the cocktails. We went in to Fuchow and had a very interesting time there. The Chinese commandant of the Army had barracks a few miles above Fuchow, and he invited the skipper and myself out for lunch. So we went up there and I remember Captain Larimer was talking to him through an interpreter and he said:

"How many men do you have?"

He said, "How many men? Do you mean how many people do I actually have here? Or how many people have I got on the pay roll?" He made no bones about it. He collected from the government for the people who were on the pay roll.

The skipper said, "I mean the people that you've got here."
He told him and he also told him how many he had on the pay roll, but

Royar #1 - 29

I've forgotten what it was but there was quite a difference.

Q: There was some discrepancy?

Adm. R.: Yes, a considerable discrepancy!

We had a very interesting time, then we went to Vladivostok, Siberia.

Q: Why were we maintaining a station ship there?

Adm. R.: The reason was that Major General Graves had an expeditionary army up there. In fact, it's been called The Lost Army by some people because very few people knew about it. They had this army up there —

Q: This was an American general?

Adm. R.: An American general, Graves. His son was a major at that time and he lives over in Washington now and is a very good friend of mine.

Q: What was General Graves' first name?

Adm. R.: I'd have to look that up. His full name was Major General William S. Graves, U.S. Army.

Well, we went to Vladivostok and the night we got in — I'm telling my life story now — the Albany was in there and they gave us a dance on their quarterdeck. So Ross McIntire and I went over, among others, and the first person I met over there was the young lady who was to become my wife. She was an Army nurse at the time, and we danced all evening and got pretty well acquainted. That was the first time I met her. Her name was Mabel Lillian McVey. She was from Ontario, Canada, trained in Ottawa and came to the United States as an RN where she joined the U.S. Army.

Q: You had started to tell me about the purpose of General Graves' presence.

Adm. R.: Yes. The Russians at that time had a big German prison camp in Vladivostok, and the Army under General Graves, who was the supreme commander in the place, had a detachment from I think every Allied army that we'd been with in World War I.

A: A sort of a League of Nations army!

Adm. R.: Yes, and he was in command of it. He had several companies of infantry. I've forgotten just how many, but they had this big evacuation hospital - "Evacuation Hospital #17" - there to take care of them. At that time also, the Transportation Corps of the Army had taken over the Trans Siberian Railroad, and were running it. And, much to the astonishment of the Russian people, they were always on time. They had a good schedule. The Russians couldn't understand it. But more or less it was to protect that and keep communications for our allies across Russia.

Q: The Russian government was in a state of turmoil.

Adm. R.: That's right. They were in a state of turmoil. Our side, the eastern part of Siberia, was fairly stable when we first went

Royar #1 - 31

out there. There were no bolsheviks to amount to anything around at all, as I recall. Our Army and the Japanese were there - Americans, Japanese, French, Italians, Spanish, practically a detachment from all, and had kept things in order. General Graves ran a good show out there. That deteriorated later on and they did have some trouble.

We went in to Vladivostok with the ships stern to the sea wall dock. We reached Vladivostok on 17 July to relieve the Albany. His Majesty's Japanese ship Mikasa was there, HMS Carlyle, British, the cruiser Hai Chu, Chinese. They were all in a row right alongside with us. They were station ships for their nations.

As I say, we got there on the 17th of July, and they'd been having some trouble with bolsheviks up above making hand grenades and using them against our troops and against the white Russians too, the loyal Russian.

Anyway, on 29 July Captain Lee of the U.S. Army came aboard and said that he was ordered to find out about these Russians in the vicinity of Tyutuke Bay, just north of Vladivostok. He got a small transport and he also put part of the 31st Infantry aboard the New Orleans. The Czarist Russians supplied a couple of companies in a small transport, and late on the evening of the 29th we started up for this base and got up there the next morning. The Russian transport arrived several hours after we did.

Well, I got permission to go ashore. We sent a detachment from the New Orleans ashore - the 31st Infantry - and the Russians. The bay was at the end of a small valley which had a narrow-gauge railway going up it. The Russians came ashore and they put a hand car on this narrow gauge with a small - I would say about one-inch gun. They all started out. They were pushing the car and they would fire on one side and fire on the other just indiscriminately. The 31st Infantry couldn't understand that and asked them why they were doing it. Well, they said, just to scare the people out.

We went up there - whether they scared them or not I don't know - but I'll never forget we got up, oh, I guess about three or four miles and somebody started shooting out of the hills. That was the first time I'd been on the ground and had people shooting at me. I went flat. I'll never forget this big Army sergeant said, "Sir, never worry about bullets when you can hear them." That taught me a lesson too.

We went up there and they scouted around and never did find anybody. They had those few shots fired and they had two Russian officers and two Russian privates wounded, but none of our people were hurt at all.

Q: An early example of guerrilla warfare!

Adm. R.: Guerrilla warfare, right. Dr. McIntire and I were on the expedition. I remember we talked to a lot of people in a little town we went through - I don't know the name of the town, but they were very much in need of soap. Fortunately, I'd brought trading stuff along and traded some soap, some sugar, and stuff for meat. So we had our camp fires had a meat meal. It was really guerrilla warfare.

Royar #1 - 33

We got back to Vladivostok on the 3rd of August. I don't think we did too much good, but at least we didn't have much trouble after that. It apparently scared them off.

Q: Is that an example of the use of a station ship?

Adm. R.: That would be one use, yes. Of course, we were in support of the Army there, too. For instance, when the Army knew that later there would be a big fight in the area, the Army didn't know what would happen, so they brought about a million dollars in gold to put in the New Orleans for safe keeping, which we locked up just in case they had trouble. We supported the Army and worked very closely.

Q: Was the ship also a communications center?

Adm. R.: It was a communications center, yes, although the main communications center - the Navy had a radio station on Russian Island, which was just a few miles out of Vladivostok. They had a station set up there and, of course, we supported that station, too - our ship did. It was a naval station. Later they had the YMCA in town - they had a big place.

I remember Captain Larimer called me in shortly after we got up there and he said:

"We ought to have a club in here."

I said, "What do you mean?"

"Well," he said, "you can go into town but the vodka's bad.

It's not much good. How about fixing up a club?"

I said, "All right, I'll see what we can do," and I went to my friends in the Transportation Corps and got them to put a wagon-lit car down near the ship, to switch it down there. You know what a wagon-lit is?

Q: Yes.

Adm. R.: Well, we put it down and stretched some wires across from the New Orleans for electric lights. The captain said:

"This is fine, but how about the liquor?"

I said, "We can't buy any in Vladivostok. There's none for sale. The Russians have put a quietus on selling liquor, but I'll see what I can do."

I sent down to Shanghai, to Sacony and Speed, and put in an order for Scotch, Bourbon, and everything that you can think of. They sent it up by commercial ship, and I got notice from the Russian customs that they had it, so I went up to get it and they said, "You will please get the captain to sign with the official United States seal that this is for use aboard the American ship, the Amerikanski Parahote."

Q: Aboard the ship!

Adm. R.: Aboard the ship. I thought, gee, we can't do that. We'll have to see what we can do. So I went back and I had a good friend of mine there by the name of R. Donohoe, who was an Englishman. Don had been a rug buyer in Siberia and all around there for years and he was waiting to get home. He spoke Russian perfectly, and Don said, "Maybe we can do something about this. You come up to my apartment."

I went up there and he got out his Russian typewriter, got some long official paper, and I don't know what he wrote, he wrote it in Russian. "Now," he said, "we've got to get this thing signed."

I said, "All right," and signed it right there. I had some little red tape we used to use in the Navy to tie things up with, he had some sealing wax, and I took a half-dollar, put that down and made a seal with the half-dollar, and signed it "W. T. Door (Water Tight Door), Commanding." Took it up to the Russian customs office and everything went through and we had our liquor. The skipper never knew anything about it.

Those are the things that you run up against.

Q: These were the Czarist Russians still in authority?

Adm. R.: That's right.

In the meantime, after that landing party, we went to Kobe to get coal and supplies. We went down on the 5th of September and returned on October 3rd 1919. In the meantime there were a number of Czechs who had come across Siberia under the command of General Gaida, and General Gaida came down to see us quite a bit. He wanted to set up a republic there and he wanted to set it up about like the United States. He wanted a copy of the Constitution of the United States so that he could write a consitution like ours. Do you know we had the devil of a time trying to raise a copy of the

Constitution on the ship, but we finally found one and gave it to him.

Q: They had escaped from central Europe?

Adm. R.: The Czechs had come across, yes. They were our allies at that time and they were on the side of the White Russians. Gaida wanted to set up a new republic and he said, "I want to get a navy." He went to the skipper, and the skipper said, "What do you need?"

He said, "I want some uniforms."

The skipper said to me, "What can you do about uniforms?" I said, "Captain, you know we're not supposed to sell anthing, even clothing." At that time the men drew the clothing and it was charged off on the pay roll. There were no cash sales for clothing at all. That came in much later. Unless you had somebody sign for it, why, you weren't supposed to do it.

"But," I said, "if you'll sign the fact that under the circumstances necessity requires a cash sale, I'll sell it to them."

He said, "Well, take off all the distinguishing marks." And we sold them about 40 or 50 American uniforms. We took off the distinguishing marks. He had a couple of little tugs there that he manned and called it the Czech Navy. We started that. I got some quizzes later on from the Navy Department about what authority I had to sell clothing to foreigners. I just put a copy of the skipper's letter to me and that cleared it up. I had no more trouble.

Q: What was the outcome of General Gaida's efforts?

Adm. R.: He was about to set up his state but before he was fully organized—he had enough men and was supposed to have more men coming — he really got it. The Red Russians came in and attacked and they had one of the bloodiest fights I've ever seen. It was around the railway station at Vladivostok, which was only a quarter of a mile up the hill. We watched the fighting from the New Orleans. It was bad. We lost one man from the New Orleans. He was hit by a stray bullet. They fought there around that railway station for a couple of days and captured Gaida and broke up his idea of setting up a new republic.

Q: He was going to carve this out of Russian territory?

Adm. R.: Yes. I think what he was going to do was do it in conjunction with the White Russians, with the Czarist Russians. But the fight was all confined to him and the Red Russians. The Americans didn't get into it at all. The Army put a guard right around the area. They wouldn't let the fighting come down into town at all. We finally, under threats, got the Japanese ship to turn a searchlight on the station at night while they were fighting there, so as to light it up and at least give Gaida a chance to get away. The Red Russian troops were under General Rosanoff. We only had one man killed. T. W. Rowland, a sail-maker, first class.

The next day, after fighting stopped, we went up there and found they never bothered to take the bodies away. They left them lying all over the place. By that time it was getting pretty cold and the bodies all froze and they just came in with these old Russian hay racks and wrapped them up, carried them off, and burned them up. It was the most cold-blooded thing you ever saw. No burial, nothing, just hauled them out and burned them.

After that fight was over Rosanoff's troops got out and we had Vladivostok under our control again. They didn't bother us at all.

Q: Where had they come from?

Adm. R.: They had drifted across Siberia.

Q: On the Trans-Siberian Railway?

Adm. R.: Some of them had and some of them had marched across, like the Czechs did. The Czechs marched across. The Rosanoff troops, as I say, were a little too much for Gaida, but he had the right idea. He was going to set up a republic and I think he would have had the people of Vladivostok with him.

We were there until December 20th, 1919, then went on south. The Albany came back and relieved us.

Q: So we continued to maintain a station ship?

Adm. R.: Yes.

Q: How long did this go on? I mean, how long did we do this?

Adm. R.: Our last - we left Vladivostok for the last time in 1920 and they still had a station ship after we left there. I think they had a station ship there until 1922 or 1923.

Q: Under what kind of authority would we do this, as a nation?

Adm. R.: Well, Russia when we went in there, of course, was an ally and we went in, ostensibly to settle that eastern part and also to take charge of that big prison camp there - they had this big German prison camp. It was a tremendous thing. I think the Russians gave consent, as far as I know. I don't know what the agreement was on that Trans Siberian, but that seemed to be one of our chief jobs, to keep that Trans-Siberian open. I rode into the interior once or twice on it and it was very good.

As I was saying, a lady has written a book. She hasn't had it published yet. Mrs. Royar and I contributed some to it. If she ever gets that done, she's got the whole story.

We stayed in Vladivostok till the 20th of December 1919, then went on to Shanghai, where we spent Christmas, then to Olongapo. I met Mrs. Royar down in Manila and we were married there on 28 January 1920.

Q: The romance had flourished.

Adm. R.: Yes. We had a lot of fun out of that romance. I used to borrow the captain's gig to go down to Ulysses Bay to the hospital to visit her. I remember one night, coming back - the gig crew used to like to go down because the gig was a coal burner and I always saw that they had some steaks that they could broil over the coals under the boiler. Coming back one night from Ulysses Bay a ship came alongside - fairly large - and fired a shot across our bow. I didn't know who the hell that was, so I said, go on over. We

Royar #1 - 40

went alongside and I said "Americanski perahote (American ship)." There was no answer and I yelled it again "Amerikanski Perahote" and off of the bridge in good old Brooklyn came, "All right, get the hell out of here!"

Apparently it was a Russian ship with some fellow on there who'd been over in the States! And my crew gave me the ha-ha and we got the hell out of there all right!

We went down to Olongapo and stayed there -

Q: You say that's where you were married?

Adm. R.: Where we were married? We were married in Manila on 28 January 1920 and went down to Olongapo, to the Navy Yard where the ship had an overhaul. We went back up to Vladivostok on 20 May of 1920 and Mrs. Royar went up, too. The South Dakota was up there -

Q: She wasn't able to travel on the ship, though?

Adm. R.: No. She went up on a transport.

The South Dakota was up there at that time and we relieved her. She'd relieved the Albany. We stayed up there from 20 May till 20 November. We didn't have too much trouble. It was rather quiet. We even rented a dacha up on the hill just above the ship. There was trouble at night sometimes, a little shooting, but it didn't bother us very much. We kept a gun up in the house but we never had to use it.

Mrs. Royar left before the ship and we (New Orleans) left Vladivostok on the 27th of September and went to Shanghai via

Japanese and Chinese ports and arrived at Shanghai on the 20th of November. In the meantime, our oldest daughter, Mary Anne, was born in the Army Hospital in Manila, and Mrs. Royar came on up to Shanghai with the baby. That was the first time I'd seen her. We spent Christmas of 1920 - Mrs. Royar got up just in time for Christmas, and stayed there.

On the 18th of January 1921 we had to go back to Vladivostok. The Albany was station ship up there and their chief engineer, Lieutenant W. H. Langdon, was in town one night and he went by the Japanese headquarters, just a couple or three blocks from where the Albany was secured, and the Japanese sentry claims he told him to stop. Why Langdon should I don't know because he was on the opposite side of the street from the headquarters, anyway he didn't and the sentry shot him and killed him. So we had to take the admiral up to hold an inquiry into the death of Langdon. We took him up there and were up there for a couple of days, got up to Vladivostok 22 January and left the 23rd, and got back to Shanghai on the 27th.

It was quite an interesting thing. They had this inquiry and, of course, the Japanese claimed that they were not involved and were not going to do anything about it. I don't know what the final outcome was. There was a strong feeling between the Japanese and the Americans even at that time - that is, there were two kinds of Japanese, the military and the home people, the agrarians in Japan. The people of Japan were just wonderful to us as could be. But up there in Vladivostok, if they were in bigger numbers and you were walking down the sidewalk, they'd push you off the sidewalk.

Q: That was the Japanese Army men?

Adm. R.: Army. They were arrogant, and there was always the feeling that we were going to have trouble with these boys some day.

Q: Did the same thing hold true with the Japanese naval people?

Adm. R.: No, we didn't see much of the Navy people, but they never bothered us. It was the Army that gave us all the trouble. The Japanese Navy ashore never bothered us.

Q: What seemed to be at the root of their anti-Americanism?

Adm. R.: They were that way with everybody, not only with the Americans. They were just arrogant people. They were tops and they wanted to show everybody they were tops. I don't think it was particularly anti-American, I think it was just the way they felt. I know we all felt there was going to be trouble pretty soon. But down in Japan everything was wonderful, as far as we were concerned.

Q: Did you, during your frequent stays at Vladivostok, pick up any knowledge of the Russian language?

Adm. R.: That's a funny thing. When we went in to Vladivostok there were three or four of us who wanted to learn Russian, and we picked up a few words, enough to get around. We got a tutor and started studying Russian. But the Russians wouldn't speak to us in Russian, they wanted English. Before we could learn enough Russian to do anything, they were all speaking English. We just gave up. That was our experience with Russian.

Interview No. 2 with Vice Admiral Murrey L. Royar, U.S. Navy (Retired)

Place: His residence in Vinson Hall, McLean, Virginia

Date: Monday morning, 24th July 1972

Subject: Biography

By: John T. Mason, Jr.

Q: Admiral, it's mighty good to see you this morning. Last time, when we broke off, you were still in Vladivostok in the year 1921. Do you want to resume your interesting story at this point?

Adm. R.: Thank you very much. It's very interesting to talk about those days in Vladivostok where I spent a total of about nine months, as has been told to you. The experience there with the Russians was very interesting all the way through. There were the two types, the partisans and the Russian peasants. It was certainly a divided country and we were there at a most interesting time.

While I was in the New Orleans in October 1920 I had asked for duty at Olongapo or Cavite and had also asked for duty at the University of California or some other university to further my accounting work which I had taken in college.

After we had returned to Shanghai in 1921 - January 1921 - I received orders detaching me from the New Orleans. The orders were for me to report to the Commandant of the Sixteenth Naval District for assignment, and also included a one-year extension in the Asiatic,

Royar #2 - 45

which I had asked for.

I was detached from the New Orleans on the 6th of February 1921. Mrs. Royar and I and our young daughter went to Manila by commercial transportation. We went down on a United States liner. It was a pleasant trip down and no details were bad at all. We left Shanghai on the 7th of February and arrived in Manila on the 11th. I reported the same day to the Commandant at the United States Naval Station, Cavite and Olongapo, for duty as accounting officer at the United States Naval Station, Cavite.

Q: It was your desire to spend another year out there?

Adm. R.: Yes. We both liked it out there and I wanted to get some shore duty in before I came back to the United States. You see, I'd been at sea for nearly four years and had no experience whatsoever - which reminds me of an incident that made me think I should have shore duty.

In the New Orleans at Vladivostok a dispatch came from the Commander-in-Chief of the Asiatic Fleet saying that a transport would be coming up from Cavite, leaving in two days, and that if we needed any supplies we should requisition them immediately. I immediately sent a radiogram down to Cavite with a list of material that I needed on the ship. Well, this transport came up and there wasn't a thing aboard. The skipper was very unhappy, and we sent a dispatch down to the supply officer at Cavite. The officer at Cavite said, well, he received the telegram but it wasn't in proper form and he could not send the material up unless it was in proper requisitions.

The captain got a little unhappy about that and he sent a dispatch to the Commander-in-Chief - it was Admiral Albert Gleaves then - and reported the whole thing. A dispatch went back, copy to us - a copy of the dispatch that he sent to the supply officer at Cavite, saying that he wanted it understood that the Supply Department at Cavite was being run for the benefit of the United States Asiatic Fleet and not for the benefit of the supply officer at Cavite, and hereafter any dispatch for requisitions would be recognized.

That set me to thinking that maybe I'd better learn something about the shore duty, and that was one of the reasons that I asked to stay out there.

When I got to Cavite and reported in I was ordered as accounting officer and also, as secondary duty assistant to the supply officer, who had been changed in the meantime.

Mrs. Royar and myself and the youngster went over to Cavite and we rented a house. There were no quarters available, but just outside of the Cavite Naval Station we rented a small house. It was pretty much of a native Nipa shack, but it was comfortable. We had three or four rooms in it, and we got settled.

The duty, I found, was very good except that although I was designated as accounting officer as my major duty the supply officer, who was then Commander Walter B. Izard, known as "Snake" Izard by his friends, thought that I should spend more time with him than I should on my accounting job, and I had really a pretty hard time of it for a while, until they got it settled and the Commandant told the supply

Royar #2 - 47

officer that my paramount duty was accounting and my secondary duty was assistant to the supply officer.

Q: How big was the accounting job?

Adm. R.: It was a fairly good-sized job. I had about fifteen or twenty employees, and, of course, the Naval Station had 1,200 or 1,500 employees. It was a fairly good job. But we got along all right.

Q: When you took over a job like that on shore as accounting officer, did you have to have a full accounting of what was there in the way of supplies, etc., the way you would on ship board?

Adm. R.: No. The supply officer had physical charge of all the material, and my job as accounting officer was to keep the records of total values of the various material accounts, receipts and transfers, the pay roll records, both civilian and military - I didn't pay the people, but I kept the pay roll records, which were turned over to a disbursing officer for payment. I was responsible for that. So it was a fairly busy job but I did learn a great deal during the time I was there.

As I said, we had this little house just outside the naval yard. Of course, things were rather cheap there. We were able to afford a cook and a lavandera, (a washerwoman) and a maid, which was the height of luxury for us - something that we enjoyed in the Asiatic. We had the same thing up in Shanghai.

I'll never forget one afternoon. We were having Captain and Mrs. Crose - Captain Crose was the Commandant of the Yard - down for dinner. I went home at four o'clock and my wife was very upset. She said that the cook hadn't showed up, and what could we do? Here, we were having the Commandant in for dinner, and no cook. Well, I got hold of the chief of police in Cavite, who was an old friend of mine - I'd made friends with him, and he said:

"What is it that you want? Do you want this man back at your house, or do you want him put in jail? Which ever you want is all right."

I said, "I want him back at the house."

"All right," he said, "I'll see what I can do."

About fifteen minutes later, down the street came this cook of ours, his shirttail out behind, on the fast run. When he got there, I said:

"Where in the world have you been?"

"Oh," he said, "there was a cock fight up here. One of my friend's cocks was fighting and I must see it."

I said: "Well, what made you come back in such a hurry?"

"The chief of police told me to get back or I'd go to jail."

So, we had the dinner party all right. There were a lot of little incidents like that that were very funny.

I stayed there at Cavite about a year.

Q: How close a liaison was maintained with the Bureau of Supplies and Accounts in Washington?

Adm. R.: Only by mail. It was not very close. For example, when I was still in the New Orleans we went in to Fuchow to buy some supplies and my Chinese money was low. I didn't have very much. I bought the supplies for several hundred dollars and I didn't have enough money to pay. Well, the book said that you had to draw a bill of exchange. I went ashore with a bill of exchange. There were two banks there but neither of them wanted it. They said they would buy a Treasury check, however, but not a bill of exchange. So I found out how much my bill was altogether, and I went to the two banks and got a bid from each one of them as to how much they would give me per dollar, and drew a United States check for the exact amount that they would give me in Chinese dollars that I owed so that I could pay the bill, which I did. So I sold that check, which was against regulations, no authority for it, and while I was down at Cavite later on I got a letter back from the Bureau saying that would be disallowed, because I had no authority to sell a Treasury check.

All I could do was write back, through the commanding officer of the New Orleans, saying that that was the only alternative I had for buying the supplies that were needed. That went back and that's the last I heard ot it.

There was no close liaison there at all. You were on your own and had to do exactly what you thought was the right thing to do and then back it up. It was the same thing as I told you before about selling the uniforms to the Czechs for starting a navy. I had no authority for that at all, but it was expedient to do it. We did it and got away with it.

Q: If they had continued to refuse to accept this transaction, then what happens?

Adm. R.: That would have been charged against my account.

Q: Against you personally?

Adm. R.: That's right. You see, I was under bond. At that time all supply officers were under $25,000 bond, and if I couldn't have paid it my bondsman would have had to pay it. But we had to do those things and we had to use some judgment in what we did. Fortunately, everything that I did was approved. Some of the boys were not so lucky, but I was able to establish a need and a reason and was accepted, although it was not according to regulations.

You're on your own. In all these places things came up and it wasn't as if you could get on the phone, call the Bureau, and say this is what's up, what do you want me to do. You did it and had to hope that you'd get away with it.

Q: It was absolutely necessary to have a man in the field who could make his own decisions?

Adm. R.: You had to do it, and it was good training, because if you couldn't make a decision you were just out of luck. You were no good to the ship.

On another occasion, when I was in the New Orleans we went into a Navy Yard for repairs.

Q: In the Philippines again?

Adm. R.: No. This was in Shanghai. We went into a Chinese yard for repairs, and some of the repairs had to be in dry dock and some had to be just alongside the dock. We got bids from two yards in Shanghai. One yard bid low for the docking, the other yard bid low for the repairs alongside the dock. Well, I averaged them out and found out which one had the combined low bid. The captain didn't like that and he said, "No, I want to go into the dry dock for some repairs, and I want to move over to the other yard for the other repairs."

I said, "Captain, you can't do it because those jobs are so interlinked that you could never get your job done satisfactorily."

He said, "I'm going to order you to do it."

"Captain," I said, "if you order me to do it, I'll do it, but if there's any come-back it will be your pay, not my pay that's checked on."

"Oh," he said, "all right. Go ahead and do as you please."

Things like that came up where you had to take positive action, even though the skipper might not like it. I was working for him and I didn't want to see him get hurt.

Another time, down in Singapore, we had to coal ship and I went ashore and got bids from two or three people, let the lowest bid. They came out and coaled ship and I went back to my stateroom and there was an envelope on my bunk with two hundred dollars in it – Singapore dollars – and no address or anything. I knew pretty well what had happened, so I took it to the captain first and said:

"This is what I found on my bunk."

"Well," he said, "that's your cumshaw. On board commercial ships that's the usual thing." He was an old Asiatic sailor. He said, "The chief engineer always got his cumshaw. They're giving you your cumshaw. You had better get an adjustment."

I said, "Well, I'm not taking the cumshaw. I'm taking this ashore."

I took it ashore and asked the company to reduce the bill two hundred Singapore dollars. The Singapore coal company was mad as could be! This was all wrong. "Of course, you're entitled to it. We always give that to every commercial ship, every ship that comes in here." But I got them to reduce the bill by two hundred dollars and returned the money.

You run up against all sorts of things like that. It was a very, very interesting cruise.

Q: A conflict of cultures, really!

Adm. R.: That's right. It was a different culture altogether.

I'll never forget another time, in Shanghai, when I bought some material, some provisions, and my custom after I'd bought them from the different merchants was to go ashore to buy enough Shanghai dollars to pay and then pay the compradors. I went around paying, and the last man - I was a little longer in there, and I saw my chief commissary steward outside. I went out and he went in. He didn't see me. I slipped out, but I went back to the comprador and asked him:

"What did my chief come in for?"

"Oh," he said, "he came in for his cumshaw."

Here, this chief had been following me around as I paid my bills to collect his cumshaw, although he had absolutely nothing to do with the purchases. I got rid of him in a hurry! It was that type of thing.

The Chinese compradors figured that the chief commissary steward, because he ran the mess, was entitled to a little bit of cumshaw.

Q: So that was always figured into the total bill!

Adm. R.: That was figured into the total bill. I learned about that and we never had any more trouble. But you had to learn the hard way.

Q: Then, would you maintain with a new contractor that there was to be no cumshaw?

Adm. R.: No cumshaw at all.

Q: It should be a bare-bones bill.

Adm. R.: A bare-bones bill, that's right. There was quite a story on that.

Getting back to Cavite, there was one time that I got a little bit scared. The captain came in one day and showed me a letter from the Bureau of Navigation, and he said, "You're accused of not paying your bills."

I said, "What do you mean I'm not paying my bills?"

Q: Personal bills, you mean?

Adm. R.: Personal bills.

He said, "Well, here's a letter from the Bureau of Navigation that says that you did not pay your annual dues to the Army and Navy Club in Washington."

I said, "I did pay them. I was in the New Orleans at the time and they sent me a bill and I didn't get it until about - it was due on the last of January and I didn't get the bill till April on account of the way the mail was following the ship. But I sent the payment in. I've got the receipt for the money order that I sent." And I showed it to him.

"Well, that's right," he said, "but this is on your record."

In a couple of days I got a letter from the Army and Navy Club saying that I'd been kicked out of the club for non-payment of dues and returning my money order. I protested about the way they kicked me out of the club. But that stuck. Later on I was first Treasurer and then President of the Army and Navy Country Club, and saw for sure that everybody had a chance to pay his bills before there was any action taken. But I was, I was kicked out of the club for that reason. They finally let me come back in but I had to pay another initial fee.

Those things belong just to show you what can happen. The Treasurer of the Army and Navy Club should never have done that. There were a lot of people on the Asiatic and there was no air mail or anything like that in those days. They had no means of knowing whether a person actually got his mail until they got a reply.

Well, we stayed there at Cavite and I had my mother and sister come out from Los Angeles to visit us. I got them transportation.

There's very little I can say about the duty there because it was very quiet. We supplied the transports that came in to Manila, destroyers and other ships. Destroyers came over to Cavite whenever a destroyer squadron came in. It was pretty routine all the way through.

During that time I went down to Olongapo once or twice to look over their accounting. I was supposed to also supervise theirs, too. Olongapo and Cavite worked together at the time.

In April 1921 I took an examination for permanent rank of lieutenant, jg, and lieutenant, both at the same time. I don't know why they bothered giving them to be because they didn't amount to very much. They went through a routine outline. Then I found out that I'd been commissioned a permanent JG on the 9th of June 1920 and on the 1st of July 1920 I'd been commissioned as a lieutenant, as a regular.

We stayed on in Cavite until the 15th of November 1921. On November 15 I received orders to the Panther. The USS Panther was a repair ship that had been out in the Asiatic and she was to return to New York and be put out of commission.

Q: So this was actually transportation back?

Adm. R.: That was the reason. That saved the transportation.

I got those orders on the 15th of November. I was detached from the Navy Yard on the 16th, and on the 18th of November 1921, I relieved Lieutenant E. L. Bailey as supply officer. A couple of days later I was on my way. I left my wife and baby and my mother and my sister in Cavite, and they were to come back by transport. I tried to get orders so that I could come back with them, but they said no, it was up to me to bring the Panther back.

I didn't know what my duty was going to be. I was tentatively told when I got back to the United States I'd probably go to San Diego, but that wasn't the case. The Panther wandered back through Guam, Honolulu, San Diego. When I got to San Diego they told me that I was to go on to New York and put the ship out of commission.

We had a nice cruise back on the Panther. It was an easy ride and, knowing that I had tp put the ship out of commission, I started a thorough inventory of all of the stores aboard the Panther. This was something that hadn't been done in years. In fact, with the exception of the clothing, provisions and the ship's store, which of course, had to be inventoried regularly, I could find no record of any inventory for any general stores.

Q: This was a good leisurely job, wasn't it?

Adm. R.: It was a good leisurely job. We started and completed it before we got to New York. But I started to say the books and the stock didn't agree. There were a lot of surveys that had to be made, stuff was missing, which was only natural in view of the fact that for years no inventory had been made and the books had never been balanced at all.

Q: So what happens then in the Bureau, when this is the case?

Adm. R.: We had a Survey Board and we surveyed the material and the captain okayed the survey, and that was it. But we did get our books and the stock in agreement before we got back to New York. It gave me something to do on the way back. I had made a note when I took over from Lieutenant Bailey that there were no indications of a recent inventory and that I would only be responsible for what I found on board. It was right after wartime and things were mixed up, so it worked out all right -

Well, we got back to New York and the first thing that I did was - or, when I was in San Diege on the way back I sent a dispatch to my wife that instead of going to San Diego I was going on to New York and she'd better wait in Hollywood with my aunt and uncle there until I found out exactly what I was going to do.

So, when she came in to San Francisco, instead of me meeting here, a cousin of mine went up from Los Angeles and met her, and took her and our oldest daughter - we only had one daughter then - and my mother and sister back to Los Angeles, which was their home. My wife also had on her hands a house boy that we brought over. We thought we were going to live in San Diego and we brought this Filipino house boy back. Well, we found a lot of trouble there, but fortunately an uncle of mine in Los Angeles had been an attorney in the Philippines for a number of years before the war, and he had some American friends in Los Angeles who were ex-residents of the Philippines and one of these agreed to take this house boy over and put up bond for him. He got a wonderful house boy. So that took that off of our shoulders.

My wife stayed in Los Angeles and I went back to New York in the _Panther_, and in March 1922 she came back. I got her transportation by transport around through the Canal. She met me in New York and stayed with a couple of friends of hers, they were nurses with her and had gone to school with her in Canada. They'd also been with her in Pittsburgh before she got into the Army. They had an apartment and she stayed there.

Well, the first thing we did, I got about a month's leave and we went up to Canada to see her folks, Mr. and Mrs. J. F. McVey. They were kind of anxious to see who this new son-in-law was. They'd heard about him but never seen him. We took the train and went in March. It was, of course, winter there. Everything was covered with snow. They met us at the railroad station with a sleigh and horses and drove us out to the farm. We had a very, very nice time up there. My wife, Mabel had a wonderful family. Two of her brothers were there, Bill and Meredith, and we got along fine, so it was a very, very fine experience.

Then we went back to New York. In the meantime, the job of putting the ship out of commission was rather slow. I had one unfortunate experience there that made me feel pretty bad. I had a good pay clerk by the name of Taylor. Taylor was a fine chap except that he liked to hit the bottle once in a while, and over one weekend when

I was away he'd gone out and hit the bottle and gone back to the ship. He had, I think, $1,500 which had been advanced to him, and he took that $1,500 and disappeared. I had to report that, of course, and it made me feel pretty bad. I guess he thought he was doing me a favor because he had paid me I think fifty bucks and I'd given him a pay receipt and he'd very carefully torn that up and thrown it away. But I knew he'd paid me and I saw it was charged on the books in going over his accounts. We set out the amount that he was missing and reported it to the Bureau, and about ten days later I got a phone call from him. He was down and out. He said he wanted to come back, and I said:

"What the hell happened to you?"

"Well,: he said, "you know, I just went out and got drunk. I didn't know what I was doing."

I went down and got him, took him over to the receiving station, and he turned himself in. Of course, he got a general court and went to Portsmouth for about eighteen months, got out, and that's the last I ever heard from him. He plead guilty. He said, "I'm just as guilty as can be." I was very, very sorry about it. He was a wonderful man with a very fine record. Just one of those quirks of human nature.

So I had to settle the accounts. I didn't get another pay clerk. I settled the accounts myself and had to do that to put the _Panther_ out of commission. I was detached and reported aboard the _Altair_ to finish up my work, and then to a receiving ship at New York for final settlement of accounts. The _Panther_ was put out of commission on the 16th of May 1922, and I was detached, as I say, to the receiving ship – to the <u>Altair</u> and then to the receiving ship.

During that time we bought our first automobile, a brand-new Model T Ford. I had never driven a car. We bought it in New York and I learned to drive in New York streets, and the first thing they did was disconnect the horn. My instructor said that anybody who needed a horn to drive should never drive an automobile! So I learned to drive without the benefit of a horn. I didn't have to have a driver's license. They didn't have any in those days. In a few weeks they said I could handle a car all right, and in the latter part of July we loaded our stuff, I had put in for a little leave, and we drove up to Canada. It was a hot drive in the old Model T and going up through Jackman, Maine, she boiled and we had a really bad time. But we spent a week or ten days with the family up there.

When I returned I was detached from the receiving ship on the 14th of September 1922 with orders to go to the Harvard Business School.

Q: This was quite a coup, wasn't it, to go to the Harvard Business School?

Adm. R.: It certainly was. It was something that I'd hardly expected to get. I was detached from the receiving ship on the 11th of September with orders to report in to the Commandant of the First Naval District for duty at Harvard Business School. I got up there on the 15th, reported to the Commandant, and we found a house over in Arlington which we liked very much. We rented it. It was a two-family house, so we rented half of it.

The drive up from New York in the old Model T was rather hot and bad and we got to a hotel there just in time for me to get my clothes changed and get into uniform and get over to the Commandant's to report in. We had about ten days then before school started to buy furniture and get settled in this two-family house. It was quite an experience for me because we had the upper part and another family had the lower part, but we both had separate furnaces in the basement - they were coal furnaces and hot-water heat and, being from California, I'd never had experience with a coal furnace. It was something new to have to keep that going.

Anyway, I reported in and started the Harvard Business School in the last of September 1922. This was the second class that the Navy had sent to the Harvard Business School. The first one had started in 1921 on the two-year course to get a master's degree. In my class there were some old friends of mine - Walter Buck, who was later to be Paymaster General and Vice President of RCA; Howard Shaffer, Walton Dismukes and myself. As I recall, these were the four Navy in this class.

I'd been out of school for a number of years, about five years, and this going back into intensive study was rather difficult. The fact is that first year I pretty near busted out. The trouble was I'd forgotten how to study, and they gave you about ten times as much work to do as you could possibly do, and it was up to you to go through and do what you thought was the most important and would help you most. I tried at first to do everything they told me, do all the reading assignments, to do all the preparation that they told me, and I just found it couldn't be done. So I finally started to choose my own work.

I was taking the accounting and I'd been with a pretty good professor out at the University of California who was well known and had written several books on accounting. At Harvard they also had an outstanding accountant, Professor Hanson, and he kept criticizing the way I did my accounting work. I told him about my experience at California and he said:

"Young man, I want to tell you this. Accounting is not an exact science. Accounting is something that you may do two or three different ways, and yet be reasonably correct. In Harvard, you'll do it the Harvard way and not the California way."

So I immediately changed, and got along well in accounting from then on.

Q: Did the four of you more or less coordinate your efforts and work together?

Adm. R.: We did in many cases, yes, although we could take whatever courses we wanted in the Business School. I went in for accounting and later in foreign trade. Some of the others went in for economics and banking. Some went in for retail work. But the four of us had some courses in common, but not all courses in common. Where we had to make reports we generally coordinated our work.

The Harvard system was very good that way. They did everything on a case system. In accounting, I was given a case, for example, of a big department store where they'd had trouble with their accounting and I had to make decisions on what to do and how to change it to accommodate their business and so on. We'd work through and try to come up with a reasonable decision. They didn't care what the decisions were as long as you could logically defend what you were doing. If you had a logical reason all the way through, that's what they were looking for. In other words, they were trying to make you think logically and develop plans logically. That was the background of the whole thing.

Sometimes you came up with something pretty good. Sometimes it wasn't exactly the same as the instructors wanted. But as long as it had a logical development, that seemed to be the main thing. The fact is that the main thing that I got out of the Harvard Business School was the ability, I think - or it helped my ability - to go into a problem, to find out what the problem really was, and to try to develop a solution logically. That, I think, is one of the most important things that you get out of it.

Q: Well, after all, this is graduate work.

Adm. R.: It's graduate work.

Q: What kind of control or supervision did you have from the Bureau?

Adm. R.: None. Absolutely none. The Bureau turned us over to the

Royar #2 - 64

Business School.

Q: So you didn't have to make any reports?

Adm. R.: No reports whatsoever. The only thing the four of us did was we worked like the devil every day and every night, except Saturday nights. Saturday nights we got together and really let off steam, and then Sunday we started to work again. The one man in the course was Walter Buck. He had the most extraordinary mind of anybody that I have ever seen. He never seemed to work he never seemed to do anything, yet when he finished that school and got his degree with distinction, he had the highest marks of any man who had ever gone to the Harvard Business School. And he never seemed to be doing anything. He had one of those minds that just absorb everything and do it the easy way.

But my first year was really terrific. I worked day and night. The second year I began to get the hang of the thing and I really ended up pretty well. Out of 146, I think it was, I was around 10 or 15 or something like that. But that first year I felt sure they'd flunk me out.

Between the two semesters I had to put in a month's work with a sugar company - a sugar-refining company in Boston.

Q: This was a project?

Adm. R.: This was a summer project that I had to put in, and I worked there for about six weeks. Of course, no pay at all. And then gave a report on what I did and what I found and what my recommendations were in their accounting procedures. Whatever happened to that, I don't know. I turned that in.

Q: You mean a company like that would get free service?

Adm. R.: Free service from a student and whether they took any advantage of it or not I don't know. There were two of us on that and we put in a study and wrote a joint report. It was a very interesting proposition.

We went back to Canada for a week or two, also on leave, and then started in the final year. It was a rough two years but I feel very fortunate that I had the opportunity to take that. It's something I'd hate to try again.

Q: What degree did you get?

Adm. R.: Master of Business Administration, MBA. I've forgotten whether I got a distinction with that or not, but I got a lot better mark than I ever expected to get and got a very fine letter from the Paymaster General.

Living there in Boston was very interesting. I don't know whether you've ever heard of Mayor Curley of Boston?

Q: Oh, indeed yes.

Adm. R.: Well, I got to know Mayor Curley pretty well. We used to go down on some Saturday evenings to the Navy Yard to a dance and the Mayor would be there. I had a great time sitting down with the

Mayor and listening to him talk. I'll never forget he told me his story about how he first got into politics. I suppose you've heard this story but I got it direct from him. He was working in a Civil Service job and one of his friends got sick and he went over and worked in his job while he was away sick, and the friend neglected to report that he was sick. So it went right on and he collected his pay, and they found out about it and Curley was accused of falsifying the records and helping and abetting crime of some sort, and he said, "They put me in jail."

He said, "But that was all right. I had done a favor for a friend. I helped that man and he got to be a fine man. That helped me on my first minor political job. You know, I never had any education. The only education I ever had was from books," and he named a lot of the classics that he had read. He was very fluent with his English, excellent English, excellent talker. His grammatical expressions were perfect. "But," he said, "I got all that on my own. You're here at Harvard - I understand you're at Harvard?"

I said, "Yes, Sir, I'm with the Business School."

"Fine school," he said, "fine school. You're having your diamond jubilee and, you know, as Mayor of Boston, I sent to Mr. Eliot - President Eliot - a letter of congratulation and extended my very best wishes to him and to the school on this diamond jubilee. I got a letter back and it said:

'Dear Mr. Curley,

I want to thank you very much for your very fine letter and for your congratulations. I want you to know that I have always admired you as an Irish Catholic politician.'"

Then Mr. Curley Said, "He could just as well have told me to go straight to hell."! Mr. Curley told me that. I had a dozen conversations with him and he told a lot of stories. I think he was a wonderful man. Of course, he had his faults but he did a lot for Boston. He said, for instance:

"You know, they try to make me out a crook because I have this fine new house out here and they claim that I didn't pay for that house. But I've got receipted bills for everything that went in it." He didn't tell me that he paid for it, but he had receipted bills!

I liked him and I thoroughly enjoyed him. I have a great deal of respect for what he did for the city of Boston. I don't think that he ever got credit for all the good things that he did do. He was quite a character.

In 1924, on the 19th of June, I was detached from the Business School and authorized to report to the Navy Yard, Mare Island, and I had 30 days leave in doing it. Now, you notice that I said I was "authorized to report." The Navy Department had ordered me down to New York. Well, I'd seen enough of New York. I wanted no part of it. They ordered me down to some job over at the clothing depot, I think, and I didn't want New York. I wanted to get back to the West Coast. I'd been tentatively promised once before that I'd go to San Diego. They wouldn't send me to San Diego but the said they had no money to send me over to the West Coast but they would give me orders authorizing me to report, but without any transportation.

I said, "How about my family?"

They said, "Well, we've got money to send your family across, but not you."

So I said, "All right. You authorize me to go and I'll drive across." So I sold the old Model T and bought a second-hand Studebaker, I think it was. A cousin of mine was coming as far east as Kansas City and was going to meet me there.

Well, after I graduated, I got my wife and youngster on the train and they went back to Hollywood to my uncle's place. I started driving. Well, I had more trouble with that old second-hand car than you can shake a stick at. I got to Kansas City and my cousin met me and we limped across and got in to Hollywood I got ten days' more delay. It took me pretty near thirty days to get across. I borrowed some money and got the car fixed up and it broke down again just as I got in to Vallejo.

But we got to Vallejo and stayed at the hotel there a day or two. We rented a house - I'll never forget it, a nice little house on Monterey Street - and I reported in to the Commandant of the Navy Yard, Mare Island on the 28th of July 1924 and the next day reported to the Accounting Department as assistant to the accounting officer.

We had a very pleasant stay at Vallejo. It was a very interesting experience. We enjoyed it.

Q: Your newly acquired education at Harvard, was this useful to you?

Adm. R.: It was very useful there in the Accounting Department. Of course, Navy accounting was altogether different from commercial accounting, but basically I had enough there that it helped me out a great deal. As I say, the main thing that I got out of that Harvard thing was that when the problems came up the first thing was to isolate the problem. We had some problems come up in there that I could help in and I was very glad to do it.

Q: What sort of a problem would you have there?

Adm. R.: We had problems in accounting for material. Some of the accounting procedures were very round about. If you were transferring material from one section of the industrial department to another, there was an awful lot of paper work involved and we were able to cut out some of that paper work. They had two accounting officers there. One was Captain P. J. Willett when I went in, and Captain Wilterdink when I left.

Captain Wilterdink, by the way, was a prisoner of war in World War II.

But they were very sympathetic, and there was a very fine old chief civilian there by the name of Grant McLaughlin. Grant McLaughlin was the chief clerk and an excellent man. He knew Navy accounting from A to Z, and what little I had to contribute was with Grant's help - he was just as anxious to get this extraneous work out, this round about work - and we revised some. I was only there about a year.

In June 1925 I received orders to the Relief, a hospital ship, but those orders were not to take effect until the Relief got back from Australia. It had gone with the fleet on a cruise to Australia, and it didn't get back until October. So I was detached on the 30th of September on thirty days' leave and ordered to report to the Relief in San Pedro in October.

Well, I reported on the 1st of October and relieved Lieutenant William J. Smith as supply officer. The hospital ship was very fine duty. I enjoyed it. She had a line captain.

Q: Her skipper was a line officer and not a medical one?

Adm. R.: That's right. But there was a medical doctor in command of the medical section just as though it was a hospital.

Q: This was a somewhat new policy, wasn't it?

Adm. R.: It was, yes. The medical officer was in entire command of the hospital part of the ship. Captain Wood was the skipper when I reported and he had his staff line officers to run the ship, but he had nothing to do whatsoever with the medical part. Of course, the medical officers were staff officers the same as I was and I enjoyed them very much. The fact is they used to let me go up in the operating room when they had an interesting operation and let me witness it. I thoroughly enjoyed that.

Q: A dubious privilege!

Adm. R.: Well, I enjoyed it. I was curious. I don't know whether I told you back there that my first experience with that was with McIntire in Vladivostok.

Q: Yes.

Adm. R.: Anyway, we were there in San Pedro and, although they'd just gotten back from Australia, we were to make a cruise down to Panama and to the East Coast with the fleet. We had a lot of fun on that. Before we started - I guess it was a month or two after I was aboard - we had an inspection by Admiral Phelps, who was commander of the base force. The Relief was in the base force, as they called it then.

Admiral Phelps came over and he went through my store rooms and, looking at various things, he picked up one of these compasses - you know, the old-fashioned compass that a carpenter uses - and it was all covered with linseed oil. We had covered all our items that were liable to rust with linseed oil, and this linseed oil had caked. Old Admiral Phelps picked it up and looked at it and said:

"Rusty! Zero for this store room."

"Admiral," I said, "that's not rust, that's linseed oil. That's the protective on there."

He said, "Young man, damn it, when I say it's rust, it's rust. Zero for this store room."

So I learned something there. Never, never argue.

Q: You mean accept a bad judgment?

Adm. R.: That's right, sometimes. He gave me that, but later on the staff changed it.

Q: Admiral, your duty as supply officer on the <u>Relief</u> was a little bit different, was it not? A hospital ship?

Adm. R.: No, it was practically the same. We carried general supplies for the operation of the ship. Perhaps the main difference was that when on a cruise, we had to be sure that our special diet materials for foods were there. We got the rundown from the commanding officer of the hospital, of the medical department, as to what we should carry for special diets. For medicines and medical supplies, they ran their own - they had their own supply system.

Q: Oh, I see.

Adm. R.: So we didn't have to bother with that at all. My job was mostly for the operation of the ship.

Q: The medical supplies would be purchased through the Bureau of Medicine and Surgery?

Adm. R.: That's right. They ran their own medical supply system. When we went on this trip to Panama I wanted to carry some ice cream for sale in the ship's store. We couldn't put it in our cold storage because our cold storage was just packed. We took everything we could in anticipation of patients and everything else and there was no place for it. I had a first class storekeeper who ran the ship's stores, the canteen, and he came to me one day and he said:

"Sir, I think I've got it solved, how we can carry this ice cream down."

I said, "Vallee, you're crazy. We can't do it. We haven't got any place to do it, but can you take part of it?"

He said, "You can take all you want."

"Where are you going to carry it?" I asked.

He said, "Come with me," and we went down below and he said, "There," and that was the morgue! We had a big morgue there and it was cold storage, so we filled the morgue with ice cream. We were the only ship in the fleet that had ice cream on the way down for the ships store.

Q: Well, it was logical that you'd have ice cream for your patients! How many patients could a hospital ship like that accommodate?

Adm. R.: They had beds for about forty or fifty.

Q: Were they most often filled?

Adm. R.: On a cruise, lots of times they were pretty well filled. Of course, we had the morgue there in case there were any deaths and the bodies were put in there and brought back.

Q: Did they perform major operations?

Adm. R.: Anything. They had a beautiful big operating room, just as modern as could be. She was a wonderful ship and a wonderful way of taking care of patients.

We went down there, went down to Guantanamo Bay and stayed there a while, and then up to New York, and back to San Pedro. The trip to Guantanamo Bay was very nice, down in Cuba. We enjoyed than. The ship was moderately busy. Health was very good and we had very few - I don't remember whether we had any casualties or not.

But we went back to San Pedro. We only had one cruise down there while I was aboard. That was in 1925. In 1926 I was aboard, and in 1927 I received orders to the Twelfth Naval District as assistant supply officer and as accounting officer for the district.

I was detached on the 10th of October 1927 and given until 1 December to report to the Twelfth Naval District. The reason for that long delay was that we were going to have an addition to the family, and we did on the 14th of October. In San Pedro General Hospital my youngest daughter, Mabel, was born. My wife stayed with relatives in Los Angeles and I stayed around until the 14th of November, and drove up and reported there on the 15th. I didn't report in on the 15th, but I got up there the 15th as it was necessary to find a place to live for my wife and seven-year-old daughter and the daughter about two months old. I found a house over in Berkeley.

We had our household goods shipped up and she drove up. No, she came up on the train about the 20th of November and we stayed at the Durant Hotel until we got the house squared away.

Then I went over and reported on the 1st of December to the

District Supply Officer, Admiral C. J. Peoples, and started in there on duty with him. Adn that was a very interesting cruise there. As I say, I was accounting officer and assistant district supply officer. I was in charge of the office a great deal of the time because Admiral Peoples was also the district general inspector and was on the road a great deal of the time. He enjoyed inspecting and he enjoyed getting out, so I ran the office pretty much while he was away.

Q: And that's a big Naval District?

Adm. R.: That's a big Naval District. Part of the duty was very interesting. We took over, while I was there, part of the Bethlehem Shipbuilding Company, which is now Hunter's Point, and they brought the Lexington and Saratoga around. The only dock that could take them was the old Bethlehem ship dock. As accounting officer and district supply officer, I more or less had to look after that - the arrangements for getting them into that dock. I went out the first time and put the Lexington in first - a very interesting job to see them put her in. She just barely got in. Then she was taken out and the Sara went in.

Other duties I had - we shipped provisions all over the Asiatic and down to Samoa - provisions to ships out in the Asiatic. They went down to Manila and went in cold storage there, then picked up, and very seldom direct to the ships - generally to cold storage in Manila. Then, of course, in Samoa they had their own station and had their own cold storage.

That was a very interesting job because they had a lot of trouble getting particularly fruit and vegetables out in good condition. We went through a lot of experimental packing. We tried it in sawdust, in individual little cartons, various ways and at various temperatures. The steamship lines worked right along with us. They were just as anxious to find out the best way to do it.

Q: Did the canners also? Were they interested?

Adm. R.: No, because canned goods they had no trouble with.

Q: No. But I mean they weren't then beginning to think in terms of freezing?

Adm. R.: No, there was no thought of freezing at that time at all. It was just a constant temperature. And, of course, we had to do a very fine, thorough inspection. We had a man from the Bureau of Agriculture who worked with us, for instance, on lettuce, oranges, apples, and so on. We'd put in our orders and then the day it was to be loaded, we'd go down to the market and inspect what they were going to send us, and inspect it again on the dock because we had a few cases of where they switched shipments on us, even went so far as when you marked a crate as inspected they dumped their contents and put something else in. So after we sent one or two shipments back to the contractor from the dock we got that straightened out.

We came up with some very good packing and we began getting favorable reports from our receiving stations and from the ships to which we were shipping. I think we accomplished quite a bit. It

Royar #2 - 77

was a very interesting job done.

The work, as I say, was practically all about the same, and I enjoyed it very much. In the meantime, as I say, we lived over in Berkeley. I don't know whether you ever knew Admiral Peoples or heard of him or not?

Q: Oh, I've heard about him. I never knew him.

Adm. R.: Well, he was a great man - Admiral Christian Joy Peoples. Christian Joy Peoples, to my mind, was one of the greatest supply officers that I have ever known. He had a wonderful ability to get along with people, he was forceful, he knew how to get things done. To my mind, he did more for the Supply Corps than any other supply officer that I have known. He started in, of course, as an assistant under Admiral McGowan and he had other duties. After this, after he was detached from the Twelfth Naval District, he went back as Chief of the Bureau of Supplies and Accounts. I thoroughly enjoyed working for him. The fact is I had a little trouble in writing letters after he left. Admiral Peoples used long sentences - he'd make a whole long paragraph of one sentence.

He was relieved by another officer, who was a Princeton graduate - and by the way Admiral Peoples never had very much formal education, he got most of it by himself. He was relieved by Rear Admiral David Potter -

Q: You mean at the Twelfth Naval District?

Adm. R.: At the Twelfth Naval District - and Admiral Potter was a

Princeton man, had written a book or two, and had an entirely different style. He believed in short, concise sentences, short paragraphs, and direct speech, you might say – saying what you had to say in as few words as possible.

Well, I had written most of Admiral Peoples' letters and I had to use his style – long sentences, long paragraphs. And when I started in with David Potter, I had to change my style completely. It took me several weeks to work into his style of writing. I remember that very much. Admiral Potter would bring back a letter, "Don't you know how to write a letter? This is not the style that I use." And I'd have to get the thing corrected.

But while there, I knew that the USS Chicago, which was being built at Mare Island, was to be commissioned in 1931 and I wanted very much the job of supply officer in the Chicago. Well, Admiral Peoples wrote a very fine report on my work in the Twelfth Naval District and recommended it before he left. Then David Potter also gave me a very fine letter, and fortunately I was selected as the prospective supply officer of the Chicago.

I was detached in 1930, on 3 December, from the Twelfth Naval District and I went up to Mare Island – No, I was detached on 1 December – and reported up at Mare Island on the 3rd of December. I was then told to report to the prospective commanding officer of the Chicago, who was Captain Manley H. Simons.

Well, the Chicago was being readied, the officers were coming, the crew was being gotten together, and I was given an office ashore to start getting supplies. I had very little to guide me. The Chicago was, I think, the second or third cruiser of this type to be put in commission and they had no experience at all as to what she would need.

Q: The other two were the Augusta and the Houston?

Adm. R.: The Augusta and the Houston. I got their lists that they had taken with some corrections that they had found necessary, and then went to work with my own storekeepers and with the advice of the prospective heads of departments as to what we should take aboard. We made up these lists and started getting the material together in storehouses ashore.

Q: Where was she to be assigned?

Admr. R.: She would go to the Cruiser Force, Pacific. The hitch, of course, was the supply officer ashore wouldn't let me put anything aboard until I could lock up the storerooms because it was still his responsbility, until the ship was in commission. So I had to assemble material in storerooms in the Supply Department ashore, and in lots that I thought would go into certain storerooms aboard ship.

About a week before we finally went into commission I finally got permission to put locks on storerooms aboard the ship and start loading. It was over a lot of opposition, but we got it done. So that we got a lot of our material aboard and locked up before the ship actually went into commission. The touchy part of it was the day she went into commission the captain wanted to start serving meals aboard, and we had to work on that one to get our cold storage locked up, to get the galley squared away, and to get everything just right so that the crew went aboard the morning of the commissioning, the 9th of March, and could go to work on serving the noon meal. But we did it all right.

Q: Was that an unusual procedure?

Adm. R.: It was an unusual procedure in a way. In many cases, the crew would have subsisted ashore for a day or two after the ship had been commissioned. The skipper wanted it done and we got it done all right.

We had the commissioning on the 9th of March and it was a very interesting situation. We got our stuff in there and a few days later on started out on a trial cruise down the bay and around the bay to get a little shaking down. In April we started on the shake-down cruise down to Samoa, which would take us about a month.

We left Mare Island, went down to San Francisco, stayed overnight, then put to sea and went out to Honolulu. In Honolulu we picked up three or four Army officers as passengers. They got permission to make our shake-down cruise with us. We went on down to the South Pacific, went across the equator, and had quite a ceremony there. I'll never forget the three Army officers. They were charged by King Neptune with "being in the Army" and therefore they really got the works! But they were good sports and they took it all right. Some of my crew, enlisted men, really put me through it, too, because that was my first time across the equator. They really poured it on, but it was all right.

We had a very nice cruise down to Tahiti and Samoa. Have you ever been down to Samoa?

Q No, I have not.

Adm. R.: Well, the harbor at Samoa is very narrow. We went in there and there was a very stiff wind off our beam. We were steaming up this very narrow channel, and the officer of the deck and the skipper were up there - he called up the skipper and said:

"Captain, I think we're drifting over towards the beach. I'm scared we're going ashore."

The old man walked over there and he gave him an order about what to do, a few more turns on the propeller, and we moved out. He said:

"Oh, hell, we missed it by a foot!" He was a cool cucumber and a wonderful ship-handler.

We went in to Samoa and we had a very nice stay there, then went on back to Mare Island for post-shake-down repairs.

Q: Did we have a supply depot at that time at Samoa?

Adm. R.: We had a supply department. There were no depots. There was just a small naval station. They had a bank there run by the Navy, just the same as we had a bank at Guam that was run by the Navy. There were only a few officers and men. It was a nice quiet little place. We enjoyed it thoroughly.

Back in the Navy Yard, we stayed there I guess for about six weeks for post-shake-down cruise inspection and repairs. Then we went out to join the fleet. Work with the fleet was very interesting.

These cruisers were good ships. We were the flagship - the Chicago carried the flag. It had a lot of problems, but it was a smart ship. The skipper did one thing that the other ships didn't do. He got them to put a teak deck on the afterdeck of the ship, put some teak ladders up to his cabin and to the admiral's cabin. The skippers of the other cruisers of the same class could never get over how he had something that they didn't have.

Q: They were all flagships, weren't they?

Adm. R.: They were all practically flagships.

Q: While you were in the Chicago you were also interested in athletics?

Adm. R.: Yes, I was interested in athletics, and we had a good basketball team and we had a good baseball team. We unfortunately didn't win any championships, but we did have a lot of competition and this was good for the men.

Q: What sort of peacetime complement would the Chicago have?

Adm. R.: Her peacetime complement was around 300, and we also had on there a small aviation complement. We had a couple of planes.

Q: Were they spotters?

Adm. R.: Well, yes, that's about what they amounted to - scouts. We carried them on the after deck on the catapults, and we had a couple aviators. I was in the Chicago for over three years. We made trips to Guantanamo, New York, worked with the fleet. The trips to

Guantanamo were always very interesting because they meant we'd get ashore for athletics, go on leave up into Cuba, and the crew seemed to like it pretty much.

Q: After the Chicago came some shore duty, didn't it?

Adm. R.: Yes. The Chicago was a happy ship all the way through. The captain and I were very close. For example, we were down going through the Panama Canal, we were on the Pacific side, waiting to go through the canal, and we were going through it that night. The skipper sent down and he said:

"I'd like you to go ashore tonight with me."

I said, "Captain, I'm quite busy with my quarterly returns and don't know whether I can make it or not."

He said, "Well, you're going to make it. Come on," and I said, "All right." So I got into uniform. I went over to the gangway and Commander Riley McConnell, who was exec, called me and he said:

"Now listen. You know that we've got a pilot coming aboard here at eleven o'clock tonight and we're going through the canal. You'd better damned well get the skipper back here on time."

I said, "How can I do that? He's the skipper. I'm only the supply officer."

"I know," he said, "but you get him back anyway."

Well, the skipper had an invitation to a big party. He took me along, and the President of Panama was there and it was a very exclusive party. Along about ten o'clock I went to the Captain and said:

"Captain, it's ten o'clock, I think we'd better go back."

He said, "Ten o'clock? It only takes us ten minutes. We've got an hour yet."

A little later I went down, and he said, "No, it'll only take us ten minutes to get back. I'm not getting back before eleven o'clock."

At ten minutes to eleven I went to him and said, "Captain, we'd better go. Here's your hat. I've got mine and I've got a car waiting for us down at the front door."

"All right," he said, "you're always spoiling a good party."

So we raced down to the ship. They had the lines all singled out. The exec was standing at the gangway, and over we went. The skipper was in civilian clothes. I was in uniform, but he was in civilian clothes. Right by the exec, up to the Bridge and he said, "Take her out."

The exec shook his fist at me and said, "I told you to get him back before this."

I said, "Commander, I couldn't do it. I got him back just as quick as I could."

But the old man went up on the bridge in his civilian clothes and took that ship out and took her right through the canal, and I turned in!

We had a lot of fun on that ship. A fine ship.

In October 1922 the Chicago was in San Pedro and was ordered to San Francisco, California, for Navy Day 1933. On the way up, off Santa Barbara, we ran through a dense fog on the morning of the 24th

Royar #2 - 85

of October. I was in the wardroom at breakfast and suddenly the siren sounded, and two second later there was a heavy bump at the forward end. So much so that it heeled the ship well over and threw the dishes off the table, and shook us up pretty badly.

I rushed out and went up forward and saw a ship backing out from our forward bow. It had hit us on the port side and had gone through the skin of the ship and was stopped by the forward turret. If the turret hand't been there, the bow would have been cut off completely.

Q: Was this a naval ship, or was it a commercial vessel?

Adm. R.: This ship that hit us was the steamship <u>Silver Palm</u>. It was a British commercial ship. It was a British motor ship, not a steam ship, but a commercial carrier. We immediately sent round to survey the damage and find out who was hurt, and found out that two officers were killed. One was my pay clerk, by the name of Troy, who had been down in his quarters and was just leaving to come up to breakfast and he couldn't get out of the way. He was pretty badly crushed. Another was a young officer — I've forgotten his name, but he was in his bunk. He had had a mid watch and was asleep when the thing hit and it folded right around, got him in his bunk, and killed him.

I know those two and I've forgotten whether there were any others, but I think it was just the two officers who were killed. It was the officers' quarters up forward there that were hit. The <u>Silver Palm</u> backed out finally, and we limped on to Mare Island with this broken bow. We went in to San Francisco. We got there late on the 24th and lay at anchor until the next day, when we left for

Mare Island for repairs.

There was quite an ado about the thing. Of course, the Silver Palm's officers said we were at fault. They said that we were not sounding our horn, which we were - not the siren, but the horn. They also said that when they saw us they didn't have time to reverse their motors. It was one of the early diesel-motor ships and it took considerable time to reverse them. So all of us had to go down and testify at the hearing. Fortunately, there was no fault found and our skipper, Captain Herbert E. Kays, was found blameless. In fact, David Sellers, Admiral Sellers, said:

"With reference to the subject collision (that was the Silver Palm) the court of inquiry, the court of inquiry held thereafter, you are being informed by separate correspondence that the court of inquiry has been approved by the Secretary of the Navy, including the opinion of the Bureau of Navigation, that there was no matter of interest therein within the purview of Section 1499 of our statutes relating to the record of any officer in the naval service. Commander-in-Chief considers that no blame whatsoever is attached to any officer attached to the Chicago at the time of the collision."

Q: Was the Silver Palm damaged?

Adm. R.: Some, but not very much. She was damaged below the waterline because we had armor plate along the waterline which was supposed to be protection against torpedoes. She hit that and cut through that, and that damaged her bow to some extent. She went under her own power and was repaird in the Bay area.

Q: Were there any damages as a result?

Adm.R.: They had the court of inquiry, then they had a hearing, and I think the Silver Palm did have to pay some damages. I've forgotten just what came out of it. I don't recall that. The main thing is we were all glad that we were exonerated.

That was about the most serious accident that I've been in, and I tell you I've had a lot of respect for fogs since that time. The fog out there in the channel was terrible. You couldn't see anything. Naturally, we never saw Navy Day in San Francisco that year.

Interview No. 3 with Vice Admiral Murrey L. Royar, U.S. Navy (Retired)

Place: His residence in Vinson Hall, McLean, Virginia

Date: Wednesday morning, 28 February 1973

Subject: Biography

By: John T. Mason, Jr.

Q: Well, it's mighty nice to see you now that spring is coming on, and I'm looking forward today to another chapter in your most interesting story. Last time, you broke off while you were still serving in the USS Chicago. Do you want to continue, Sir?

Adm.R.: I'll be glad to. It's a pleasure to talk over some of the old days.

On the reporting of Lieutenant Commander Independent W. Gorton, SC, USN, I was detached from the Chicago in New York on the 4th of June 1934. I was ordered to the Bureau of Supplies and Accounts, Washington, with a month's delay.

Q: Were you glad to be coming back to Washington?

Adm. R.: Well, this was my first duty in Washington since I was in Pay School in 1917, so it was all new to me. I had a great respect for the Bureau, the people in the Bureau, and I felt it was going to give me a chance to find out what made the wheels go round.

During that month's delay we drove up to the World's Fair in Chicago and went over to Michigan and picked up a new car.

Q: I bet you looked in on Sally Rand, too, didn't you?

Adm. R.: I did! And we came on back via Winchester, Ontario, where my wife had been while I was at sea with the Chicago and my two youngsters were going to school up in Canada. We enjoyed that very much. We picked them up and came down via Connecticut, picked up our dog who'd been farmed out with an officer friend of mine, got in to Washington, and reported in on July 6th, 1934. In the meantime, we had stayed at the Brighton Hotel in Washington and picked up a house in Chevy Chase, Maryland, on Langdrum Lane. A year later, though, we moved into the District on McKinley Street.

I was immediately assigned to the Purchase Division of the Bureau under Captain E. H. Van Patten, Supply Corps, USN, who was the Purchasing Officer. An old friend of mine, who came in the Navy at the same time, Lieutenant Commander Ray C. Saunders, was with me. The two of us had charge of all competitive purchases, that is, preparing the bids, reading the bids, and determining successful bidders. That was quite an eye-opener, because I'd never had anything like that before and it gave me an idea of exactly how the purchasing system worked, and I must say it was very good. There was no finagling at all. The low bidder who was responsive to the bid was the winner. We used to have an awful lot of squawks, however, from some bidders who were disappointed that they had not received the contract.

Q: Bidders were very anxious for business at that point. It was the height of the Depression, wasn't it?

Adm. R.: That's right, and we had plenty of competition and we got good prices.

We also ran into cases where in some of the larger bids a bidder would try to buy the bid. In other words, he would bid an unreasonably low price figuring, perhaps, that later on he could plead that the specification didn't truthfully or completely outline what he was supposed to furnish and that he could put in a claim.

Q: You could anticipate that kind of chicanery, though, couldn't you?

Adm. R.: Oh, yes, we did and in justice to the bidder we would send somebody out to examine his plant, to examine his business, and see whether or not he was actually able to furnish it at the price he bid. We threw out a lot of bad bids that way. It was necessary to do so because otherwise we wouldn't get the material that we wanted and the bidder could well go broke. So it was something that we had to do. Of course, there were a lot of protests.

I'll never forget one time a congressman called up and complained bitterly that his constituent didn't get a certain bid. I happened to know this congressman. He was from California, and I went up to see him and explain the whole thing to him. He said:

"Well, I'm going to call you up again and see if you won't change your mind."

I went back and, sure enough, a little later he called me up and he gave me the devil. He just went off about how everything was wrong and so and so, and so and so. I simply said, "Yes, Sir, yes, Sir, we'll do the best we can" and he finally hung up. A little later he called back and said:

"Don't pay any attention to what I said. My constituent was sitting there and I had to do it."

Q: Hypocritical, wasn't it?

Adm. R.: Well, I remember a few experiences like that, but it wasn't often. Of course, we were subject to some pressure at times.

I stayed in the Purchasing Department for about six or eight months and then they put me in charge of the Clothing Division of the Bureau and that I enjoyed very much.

Q: What did that entail?

Adm. R.: The Clothing Division ran the uniform shop and the naval clothing factory. At that time we had the naval clothing factory in New York, and we also ran a naval uniform shop up there.

Q: The government manufactured these?

Adm. R.: The government manufactured clothing, both officers' uniforms and enlisted men's uniforms. They later discontinued the enlisted men's uniforms, but they ran the uniform shop for a good many years later.

Q: How did that happen to begin as a practice?

Adm. R.: It started because the Navy could not get satisfactory clothing from the contractors. There was too much trouble. The specifications would be given and the clothing business at that time was not of the highest order and the people who got the bids were perfectly able financially and the factories could manufacture, but the stuff came out in bad condition, a lot of it wouldn't pass inspection. There were disputes over that, and it really forced the government into the clothing business.

Q: Hiring tailors.

Adm. R.: Oh, yes, hiring tailors and the whole thing. Later on the clothing business came around and we went back to them. In a good man cases, we bought the fabrics, however. We bought the fabrics because we were sure that they would pass the specifications. We would deliver the fabrics to the manufacturers for the sewing – the cutting and sewing. That came a little later on. It really had to when the war broke out because the clothing factory could never manufacture the –

Q: No. At that period of time, in the early 1930s, how many uniforms would you turn out a year in the clothing factory?

Adm. R.: Not too many. Maybe 100,000 or something like that – or 200,000.

Q: Then they were sold to the men at cost?

Adm. R.: At that time they were not sold - well, they were sold, but not for cash. Now the men buy them for cash. At that time they were charged off against their pay. They went in and got the clothing that they needed and it was charged against their pay. Later on, it was developed that it would be much better to have cash sales, and the cash sales came on three or four years later. Of course, the man who went into the service was given a full bag of clothes when he went in and that was free. If he had to have replacements, he had to pay for them. They were very cheap. Shoes, I think, cost a dollar or a dollar and a half, and the uniforms were very reasonable. I've forgotten just what the prices were.

Q: In the case of officers who wanted to be beautifully fitted and trim, were they permitted to buy elsewhere?

Adm. R.: Oh, yes. They could go to a civilian tailor if they wanted to. But the officers' uniform shop did such a good job that very few of them went to the outside. They were much cheaper there and they were cut to measurement. Later on, the uniform shop started putting out clothing that they could alter to fit a person, but at that time it was mostly tailored to measure.

Q: That later policy is almost universal for all of us now.

Adm. R.: That's right, it is.

I don't know whether you remember Schwartz in Baltimore?

Q: Yes.

Adm. R.: Not at this time, but later on they felt that the uniform shop was giving them too much competition and they got some excellent tailors and they pretty nearly put the uniform shop out of business.

Q: They were pretty enterprising!

Adm. R.: They were very enterprising and very good.

A great deal of my time was spent going up to New York. Captain Simonpietri, Supply Corps, USN, was in command of the naval clothing factory and the uniform shop, and I had to go up there to consult with him a great deal, particularly on the specification, the quality of the material, and each year we'd set the prices for the clothing for the succeeding year. That took up considerable time.

Q: How were those prices determined?

Adm. R.: Just actually on cost. There was no profit figured in at all, and, of course, there was no overhead figured. It was just the cost of the material and the labor, and the men got their clothing, as I say, practically at cost.

I remember that one time we had a material contract going out and there were two companies in Philadelphia, the Delta Finishing Company and the Kent Manufacturing Company, and I had to go down to see them and to inspect their plants. Fortunately, they were both good manufacturers and they were passed, but that was just an example of some of the things we had to do.

Q: Did you use imports at all? I mean broadcloth that came from abroad or anything of that sort?

Adm. R.: No. It was all manufactured in the United States. During this time I was, of course, on the Navy Uniform Board, which met at frequent intervals and decided on specs for both officers' and enlisted men's uniforms. I was very happy to be helpful in getting a last for the Navy shoe. Our shoes hadn't been too good so with the advice of our orthopedic surgeons and advice from the industry we came out with a last that is practically the one we still use.

Q: Not the most attractive shoes in the world!

Adm. R.: No, it's not the most attractive, but very, very comfortable. We bought our own lasts and on the shoe contracts we furnished the lasts to the manufacturers.

Then I was also mixed up with Federal Specifications Executive Committee, the technical committee on wearing apparel, from March 1935 till 1937.

Q: Did that embrace all military services?

Adm. R.: And federal. All federal special clothing, Post Office, and everything.

Q: Oh, I see.

Adm. R.: I was also on the Textiles, Seams, and Stitching Committee in June 1934. I served as chairman of the latter one from 1935 until I was transferred to other duty in 1937.

Q: That put you into immediate contact with the whole industry.

Adm. R.: The whole industry. During my chairmanship I took an active part in the preparation of new federal specifications and the revision of federal specifications. That was a very interesting job because we had everything come up. We had different people from all the other services and federal activities.

What we were trying to do was to modify - make specifications and modify specifications particularly for underwear that everybody could use, that was becoming to everybody and that would cut down on the number of specs floating around and when a contractor got a contract he would know exactly that the federal specifications prevailed. That was one of the objectives, trying to get single specs for the entire federal and military services for the various commonly used articles and garments.

Q: That was really big business!

Adm. R.: That was big business.

Q: Were you tempted at any time - this was still the Depression - to go into the textile business?

Adm. R.: No. The thing was that I was on the administrative end. I wasn't a technical man. If I had had technical training I might have been tempted. But fortunately I had some pretty good advisors with me who were technical people and kept me on the tracks so that I didn't get away from good materials and good procedures, and so on.

Q: The textile industry at that time was going through the wringer, wasn't it?

Adm. R.: That's right. It was going through the wringer.

Q: Wasn't that the beginning of the exodus from New England South?

Adm. R.: They were just beginning. A great many of our contracts, of course, were still in New England, but they had started to move south.

I found particularly my associations with the other services and with the federal people very, very good, and I enjoyed it. As chairman of that committee I had a lot of things to settle and we got along very well.

Q: About how frequently are there changes in naval uniforms?

Adm. R.: Very, very seldom. There might be some slight change, but very seldom any major ones. We didn't have any major ones at all during the time that I was there.

Q: They came later - during World War II - when Admiral King took an interest?

Adm. R.: That's right.

Lyman Briggs, who was chairman of the Federal Specifications

Executive Committee, gave me a very fine note when I left and I was very proud of it. He expressed his appreciation of the contribution I had made.

During that time - just in the latter part of the time - I had a very interesting experience. I was made a member of the Supervisory Naval Examining Board and, as a member, I was sent down to Georgia Tech on May 19 and 20, 1937. My job was to examine about thirty candidates for the Supply Corps, and I ran into a bunch of darned fine young men. They were smart, they were good engineers, they were top students, but they couldn't spell.

Q: That's understandable. I mean the changes had come by that time!

Adm. R.: And I'll never forget, I gave them all an examination and picked out eight or ten excellent young men who went far in the Supply Corps later on. When their written examination papers came back and were given to the main board, they gave me the devil - "Can't you find anybody down there who knows English and knows how to spell?"

Q: Were they NROTC students?

Adm. R.: No, they were just straight students. At that time I think Georgia Tech had an Army ROTC, but there were no Navy ROTCs anywhere and we went around from college to college and picked out young men -

Q: This was a widespread program?

Adm. R.: This was a widespread program.

Q: Why was that?

Adm. R.: Well, we had an idea what was coming up in 1937, and we were getting ready to expand and get good people before the rest of the services picked them up.

Q: That was real foresight!

Adm. R.: We got permission from the CNO to do it, and we got an excellent group of young men who came in in 1937, 1938, and 1939. When 1941 came along we were all set. Of course, we expanded more then, but this was the beginning of it. We were going round to different schools and picking up some excellent young men.

Q: Were the other bureaus doing likewise?

Adm. R.: Yes, the Navy was doing that. The Navy was pretty well into that program.

Q: By that time you had more money to spend.

Adm.R.: That's right. We had the money to spend and we did it.

In October of 1937 I was transferred to the Stock Division and we were then in the process of building up stocks everywhere. We all had the feeling that something was going to break, but we didn't know when. The Navy Department was making plans for the future. We weren't actually buying a lot of material, but we were planning on what we needed and where we were going to get it and how we were going to get it. For six or eight months I worked on that and found it a most fascinating procedure.

Q: This was across-the-board requirements?

Adm. R.: That's right. The requirements for everything but medical supplies and some technical ordnance supplies. We went right to town on it.

Q: This took you into the machine-tool area, did it?

Adm. R.: The machine-tool area to a certain extent. We worked with the other bureaus on that. At that time the Bureau of Supplies and Accounts was buying for everybody, all the bureaus. We had one big purchasing section there in the bureau and we had our field purchasing sections, but we were doing the buying for everyone, except Medicine and Surgery.

Q: They had their own outfit?

Adm. R.: They had their own. Later on, of course, that broke down. I can bring that up a little later.

Q: This involved you with hundreds and hundreds of contracts?

Adm. R.: Prospective contracts. We were lining up our contracts – lining up where we would procure the materials and what material probably would be needed.

Q: You couldn't at that stage, then, determine prices, could you?

Adm. R.: Oh, no. It was just the needs without the price on it.

Q: And the ability of the manufacturer to come through?

Adm. R.: That's right.

I worked on that from the 1st of October 1937 till June 1938, then I was detached from the Bureau of Supplies and Accounts and ordered to the Saratoga, CV-3. I left Washington on the 10th of June and reported to the Saratoga on 30 June in Seattle. We had a nice trip across the continent, drove across with my family.

I forgot to say that just before I left, I got the word that I'd been selected for commander and my wife said:

"My Lord, you've made it. I didn't know whether you'd ever make it, but when you made it I thought you'd reached the top!"

Q: Why did her ceiling remain so low?

Adm. R.: Because I had spent fourteen years as a two-striper, a lieutenant.

Q: But that was fairly common at that point, wasn't it?

Adm. R.: It was, yes. The Navy wasn't moving, but, of course, she thought that after fourteen years as two-striper and then five or six years as a lieutenant commander, if I could make commander, why, that would be it.

We had one of the biggest celebrations at my house that night. We had eight or ten of my compatriots who came in the Navy about the same time and all made it - all selected. Our telephone bills were terrible. We telephoned to Honolulu and everywhere else. That, to me, was the biggest selection that I ever made. In took me into the brass-hat area. We had a wonderful time.

Well, I reported as a lieutenant commander on the Saratoga -

Q: Was this something you welcomed?

Adm. R.: Yes. I always liked sea duty. That, to me, was what I was in the Navy for - to go to sea. I always did like it.

I relieved another chap who came in the same time I did, Lieutenant Commander James Dennis Boyle. Jim Boyle was an excellent officer and he turned over a wonderful department to me. The skipper was quite a famous man, Albert C. Read.

Q: Putty Read?

Adm. R.: Putty Read, and the exec was my old friend Duke Ramsay, another wonderful chap. Putty ran a fine ship. It was a taut ship and everybody was happy. One of the first things he told me when I came on board was, "You're the golf officer," and I said:

"How's that?"

"Well," he said, "you've got two assistants. Admiral Halsey is commander of the Cruiser Division. When he's on here, he likes to play golf and I like to play golf, and it's your job to see that we have a place to play."

Q: Supplies and Accounts!

Adm. R.: That's right! We had a lot of fun. It was down in San Francisco a little later on and I went over and met some friends there and they gave us a card to the Olympic Golf Course - Olympic Club Golf Course, and Admiral Halsey, Putty Read, myself, and I've forgotten who the fourth was, we picked up somebody - went over there and we had a fine time, except that Admiral Halsey didn't have a very good day and I didn't have a very good day. He got so mad he was never going to play golf again! And, off the record, he threw his clubs on the ground and cussed and swore about it, and Putty Read just laughed.

Putty didn't shoot very far, but he was always straight down the center of the course and when he got up close to the green he was deadly, and he pitched right to the pin, and he was beating the devil out of all of us. It was quite an exciting time, but the next morning I was eating breakfast and his orderly came down and he brought me this note. I'd like you to read it.

Q: "The golf beginner swung three times at the ball on the first tee and missed. Undiscouraged, he looked up at the crowd on the clubhouse porch and observed, 'Tough course,'" And then signed "Nothing Personal. A.C.R."

Putty had a good sense of humor. I thought you might enjoy that.

Q: Yes.

Adm. R.: The <u>Saratoga</u> was a good ship. We had a good group on there. She was in the harbor at Long Beach most of the time, training. We'd have our aviators, our squadrons, aboard for a while and then out. We made one trip around to Guantanamo while I was on the ship, but there was nothing particularly spectacular about it.

Q: Your job as supply officer on an aircraft carrier, was it different in any sense from, say, the <u>Chicago</u>?

Adm. R.: No, practically the same. The only difference was that the aviation boys wanted everything yesterday.

Q: They were gung-ho!

Adm. R.: They were gung-ho, and believe me they kept you on your toes. For aviation supplies to keep the planes in the air, you really had to keep going.

I learned a lot on there, too. I learned something about communications. I never forgot that when we had the squadrons on board the cooks got up in the morning and started about four o'clock making hot cakes, and by the time of breakfast at seven o'clock some of them were pretty soggy.

Q: And tough!

Adm. R.: And tough. So I thought, well, why not divide this crew up, this mess up, and give one-seventh of them their hot cakes one day, and do that through the week, so that they'd be good then. I forgot to tell the crew that I was doing this and I did it. Immediately, when one-seventh of the crew got nice, fine hot cakes, the others were all rushing for the bridge to complain about the food. Somebody was getting hot cakes and they weren't, and there was the darnedest mess there for a while. Then I got out a notice and told them what was on, and it was all right. But that was neglect on my part.

We also taught a lot of those boys to eat, too. We had cafeteria style on there when the squadrons were on board, and I'll never forget we had a big ship's cook who was the heavy-weight boxing champion of the Navy. They would take the food from the cafeteria and go to their tables and eat it, and then scrape their plates and put the plates in a pile. Well, he stood while they scraped the plates and he always carried a baseball bat. If a man came up with what he thought was too much food - he was also the ship's first class cook - or had too much left on his plate, up came the bat, "Go back and eat it." And back the guy would go and eat it, and we never had much trouble with him again. So it was only the newcomers generally. He got them all in line.

Q: Enforced feeding!

Adm. R.: He'd say, "Don't take more than you want." He was quite a character.

The ship did a remarkably good job. We got an engineering "E" on her to show how good she was. Everybody got a commendation for it from the skipper. That was for 1939-1940.

Another thing I'll never forget is the first time I went up in a plane off the ship. I didn't mind the take-off so much but coming back - I was in a two-seater and, of course, in the rear seat - and I looked down and saw that flight deck, I thought, "My God, will we ever hit that postage stamp?" It was quite a thrill because it looked awfully small from up there, coming down, and hitting the deck with the hook taking the wires, and stopping. Of course, I did it many times after that and wasn't bothered at all.

Q: The Sara had duty out at Pearl, did she?

Adm. R.: No. In 1948 and 1939 we were right on the Pacific coast. We did a lot of work around Catalina Island and in the area around there, and short cruises. Of course, we went up to Seattle for overhaul from time to time. I'll never forget one time we were up there for overhaul and had a youngster go berserk. He went up the forward mast and threatened to jump. Duke Ramsay was the exec and he went out there and got everybody off the deck, and he stood there and talked to that youngster and talked him down. He was later sent away. He was a psycho. But he got him down, got him under control. It was a remarkable thing the way he handled it. Duke was that way. He was a man anybody would go anywhere for. I've never seen a man so idolized by a crew. He was a remarkable person.

Well, there's not much more that I can tell you about the Sara, except that it was one of the finest jobs that I ever had and one that I enjoyed a great deal. I enjoyed being with the aviators. As I say, they were action men all the way through and she was a beautifully fun ship. The captain was detached in the early part of March 1940 and was relieved by Captain Robert P. Molton. Just before Molton came aboard, we gave Putty Read a big farewell party - stag party - in Long Beach at one of the country clubs. We had every officer on the ship and they thoroughly enjoyed it. To put the final touch to it, Dixie Ketchum and Cat Brown and Artie Doyle went down into Long Beach, to the entertainment part on the beach where you could go down and buy a piece of the evening paper and have anything printed on it you wanted.

They went down, and they must have gotten two dozen copies of the evening paper with headlines saying, "Saratoga Leaves For Alaska Tomorrow." They got those things out, and after the party was over and everybody got home, they went to every officer - they must have gotten fifty or sixty copies - to every officer's home, rang the bell, and left a copy of this thing.

When the people got the first look at it, there was hell to pay! They started calling the ship and calling everybody else. It gave Putty Read quite a kick. They had quite a story on that front page, and it was so well done that nobody - they read the story and started telephoning before they ever realized it was a hoax.

That was the type of stuff we were going through all the time on the ship. We had more fun and it was really a happy ship. I can't ever remember an unpleasant incident.

Well, Captain Read was detached the 15th of March and I was detached on the 31st of March. I was relieved by Commander Percy C. Corning, Supply Corps, and I was ordered to the Navy Yard, Washington, D.C., and given a delay until 15 May, which was about a month and half. I stayed in Long Beach till about the 26th of April, and then we drove across to Washington, arriving on the 9th of May. We stayed at a hotel till we rented a place over on Carolina Place in Alexandria.

I reported to the Yard on the 15th of May 1940 and was ordered to further report to Captain Elijah Henry Cope, Supply Corps, as his assistant. He was a great chap, one of the characters we had in the Navy. He must have weighed around 300 pounds. He was a big man, quite heavy. He'd had quite a life before and he'd come into the Navy as an enlisted man, a ship's cook. Somewhere along the line he'd taken some dental training. I don't know where he got it. Anyway, it was enough to make him want and he got a set of pure gold teeth, uppers and lowers, and what a golden smile that was! He was well known to everybody in the Corps as Lije Cope. A great fellow.

I remember I walked in and reported to him and he said:

"Fine, glad to have you aboard. You're the assistant. You run the show. You make all the decisions. Don't bother me and don't bring anything to me unless you can't solve it."

Q: What would he do?

Adm. R.: He'd play his banjo. He was a great banjo-player. But he was there in the office every day. He read the paper and I'd go in and report to him and tell him what went on and what I had done, and he'd say "All right." He never interfered at all. He let me run the show, which gave me a lot of experience.

Q: Yes, indeed. The Navy Yard was a beehive of activity right then.

Adm. R.: The Navy Yard was a beehive of activity. There was still the gun factory, they were building guns and shipping them out down to the cape to test them, and finishing them off on board ships. They were shipping guns then, now it's missiles.

Q: Was Indian Head in being?

Adm. R.: Yes, that's where they tested them.

We also supplied the Naval Research Lab, down the river over there, and, believe me, it was a terrific job. There's where I first got into the trouble of the Bureau doing all the purchasing. That was in 1940 and everybody knew something was going to happen. Everybody was trying to get squared away, and the Naval Research Lab had a lot of important secret programs and they needed special material.

I put in a requisition to the Bureau, and they'd come up to me a few days after their request, "Where's the material?" "It's gone to the Bureau," and the Bureau was so far behind and so over worked that I told the captain I was going to do the purchasing right there. We were authorized to make purchases I think it was up to $1,000 - maybe $500.

I said, "I'm going to make all the purchases right here, if you'll back me up."

He said, "Sure, go ahead."

So we went right on and I began getting letters from the Bureau to notify them under what authority I was making purchases for more than my allotted amount. I wrote for the captain's signature right back that we needed the material, it was urgent, and we couldn't get it from the Bureau. We couldn't get our requisitions filled from the Bureau.

Q: It would take months from the Bureau!

Adm. R.: Yes. I got no answers to the letters so I went ahead and did it. We bought all kinds of material, regardless of the amount of the contracts. We set up our own contract section and went ahead with purchases. It was the only way we could handle it. In the gun factory there were many, many items that were just so important that they had to have them right away. That was our really big job, purchasing.

Q: Something you developed on your own!

Adm. R.: Something we developed on our own. The other bureaus had started complaining to S. & A. too, that they couldn't get their material, but they had no purchasing divisions. So after we did this, and went on our own, the Bureau sort of got the word and they started installing purchasing divisions in each of the Bureaus and started to decentralize. Then we settled down to a pretty good procurement system. But they were just overloaded. The old system of a single purchasing outfit for major items just wasn't working.

Q: It wouldn't work under wartime conditions?

Adm. R.: No. So we put in a purchasing section which the Bureau of Supplies and accounts controlled under each of the other bureaus and they also established purchasing officers in the field. We did have one purchasing officer in San Francisco, but they put one in Los Angeles and every large activity was given authority to do its own purchasing.

Q: I suppose the GAO was conscious of - or cognizant - of your effort, was it?

Adm. R.: I never heard from GAO. Everything went through. We never got a squawk at all. We just went ahead and did it.

The year and a half that I was there I thoroughly enjoyed it and I picked up a lot of information on purchasing there, too. And then we got some fine young men in there who were coming in the Navy. One who was a very good man, I suppose you might have heard of him, was William H. Bates, the late representative from Massachusetts. Bill came in as an ensign. He was from the Supply Corps School, and I might tell you about how Bill got to be a congressman right here, rather than a little later.

Bill came in and he got his first training right in our section. He was an excellent person, very cooperative, smart as the dickens. He went on and served through the war. After the war he was stationed down in Philadelphia, in the Supply Department. When his father was killed - you might perhaps remember that - in an aeroplane accident - I was in Oakland, and I got a phone call one day from Bill and he said:

"Admiral, they want me to run for Congress for my father's seat. What shall I do about it?"

I said, "Bill, I'm not going to give you any advice, but I'll tell you this. You're the only man who can make the decision. If you are in the Congress and you get on the Armed Services Committee with your background, you'll be of far more use to the Navy and the Country than you would be even as an admiral in the United States Navy. That's my opinion, but it's up to you."

"Well," he said, "but I don't want to leave the Navy. I love it."

"Well," I said, "you think it over. That's the only advice I'll give you."

He called me up again and he said:

"I don't want to resign. I'm afraid I might not be elected."

"I don't know what you can do," I said.

He said, "They want to put my name on the ballot and run me, but I'm in uniform. I can't do a thing."

Q: The Hatch Act!

Admr. R.: I said, "Well, if they put you on the ballot I don't know what you can do about it, Bill. You certainly can't do any electioneering."

They did. The politicians up in the district of Salem, Massachusetts, put his name on the ballot, and Bill never made one speech, he sat there and did his job as a commander in the Supply Corps, and was elected! The day he was elected he resigned and went into the Reserve and took his seat in the Congress.

That's the way it went. And his opponent went right to the Secretary of the Navy and went to the Department of Justice and claimed he had violated the Hatch Act. They could never prove that he had ever in any way taken part in electioneering, campaigning, or done a thing to violate the Hatch Act.

Q: He really didn't have to. His name was established in that district.

Adm. R.: That's right, and his father had a wonderful organization up there. That's the way Bill became a member of Congress. We were always very close friends. I was at his wedding here. Later on, when I was Chief of the Bureau, we used to be very close and I'd give him all the dope that was going on. It was a wonderful relationship. Of course, I felt very badly when he had cancer and died.

Q: Did he get on the Military Affairs Committee?

Adm. R.: Yes. When he died, he was the Senior Republican on it.

Q: The ranking minority.

Adm. R.: Yes, and if the Committee had ever gone Republican, he'd have been chairman.

We had a number of fine young men who came to the Washington Yard to get their early training. I also admired very much the civilian group we had down there. They were old-timers. I never worked with a more dedicated group of service and civilian people. We worked together and lived together, and time meant nothing. When quitting time came, if they had anything to do, there was no overtime but they never worried. There was a job to be done and the job was their life. They never squawked about not getting overtime, it was all volunteer work, but the work had to go. And they loved old Captain Cope. He was a wonderful chap, and they'd have done anything for him. We had a wonderful organization there. That gun factory really developed.

Q: Wasn't the Navy Yard a center for recruiting, too, at that point?

Adm. R.: I don't recall. I never got into the recruiting end of it. I know that we had an awful lot of young officers who were new to the Navy and had just put on their uniforms, and had come down there for training. They got training on the job. The ordnance people had a lot of supply people. Even the medical had some new doctors down there. We had a flood of these people coming and going. As they were needed, they'd be pulled out and sent to sea or sent to other jobs. But I don't recall the recruiting end of it so much. No doubt they did a lot of it.

In the spring of 1941 one of the lucky things that we did personally was that my wife had $500 and we were living over in Carolina Place in Arlington - or in Alexandria, but it's right on the Arlington boundary there. On 26th Place in Arlington she was out going around and she found this lot on 26th Place and talked to a real estate man. He said, "I'll build you a house on there for $12,500. It's a good buy."

She said, "What kind?"

"Well," he said, "I've got some plans here of a beautiful two-story brick house."

And she said, "I've only got $500."

He said, "That's all right. $500 down."

She came home and said, "Do you think we'd better do it?" and I said, "Sure, you're pretty smart. Go ahead and make the deal. I haven't got time to fool around with it now. I'm too busy down at the Yard."

She did. She put $500 down, and she was out there superintending when they built that house for us - a two-story house, four bedrooms upstairs and three rooms down. In the fall of 1941, just before the big blow-up, we moved in. Well, we lived in that house until I was detached from the Washington area in 1946, and we sold it to Curtis LeMay - General Curtis LeMay. We asked $28,000 for it, and he said, "You're robbing me. The Navy always robs the Air Force!"

This was in 1946, and I said:

"No, that's a good fair price."

The reason we sold was - we wanted to hold on to it - but they wouldn't let us charge over $120 a month rent.

Q: There was still a ceiling?

Adm. R.: There was still a ceiling on, and that wouldn't have made the payments on it. At that time we didn't think we could afford to rent it for that and take a chance on its being busted up, so we put it up for sale and Curtis LeMay bought it.

I'll never forget the settlement over in Arlington, and he was still shaking his head. His wife was delighted with it. She thought it was fine and a good deal. This was after the war, or course, 1946, and I said:

"Well, General LeMay, you're just back from the far Pacific. How do you like it?"

He looked at me and said: "You want to know how I like it?"

I said, "Yes."

"Well," he said, "you know, when I was out in the Pacific and I had command out there of the Air Force, when I said anything everybody jumped. I came back here, I'm over at the Pentagon, I give an order, and nobody does a Goddam thing. I want to go back to the Pacific."

That was Curtis LeMay. His wife was a wonderful person. He later sold the place at a very handsome profit.

Q: I'm sure he did!

Adm. R.: Well, that was a little off side there.

One of the things that I liked particularly while at the Yard, too, particularly after we moved into this house, was we had a wonderful drivers' club. The people next door, of course, they went down to the Yard and four or five others, and we settled more business among the four or five us going down and coming home from the Yard - that driver's club – than you could shake a stick at. We all had jobs that interlocked, and we could talk things over and get things settled. It helped out a lot, and that was a very interesting picture, too.

One thing that did happen in the Supply Department down there was that after all this purchasing was going on, the Bureau of Supplies and Accounts sent an inspector down to take a look at it and see just exactly what we were doing. The inspection was in August of 1941, just before I was detached. They came down and they gave us a real going-over, but fortunately we got a good report. It said, "This Supply Department is unusually well organized and staffed. Supervision is particularly effective and efficient. Consequently, the work is up to date. It is rendering excellent service and is worthy of commendation."

So I figured that that worked out all right, as far as our purchasing was concerned.

Q: You won your spurs!

Adm. R.: That's right. That went to Captain Cope and he was very generous in giving everybody full credit for what went on. He was very generous in that.

I was detached from the Yard on the 1st of May 1942 and ordered up to the Bureau of Supplies and Accounts. I reported on 1 June – I might say before I get here – the war was on in 1942, but the night of Pearl Harbor we were sitting in our new house there on 26th Place, South, and were addressing Christmas cards. We had the radio on and the announcement came on of Pearl Harbor, what had happened.

Well, my wife and I were both stunned. We just didn't know what to do, so I said:

"The best thing I can do is get right down to the Yard." I was in civilian clothes and I got into my uniform and drove down to the Yard right away. Captain Cope was in the office. Most of our top civilians came in without being called. Practically all the uniformed staff were in there, and we got together and talked over what we should do. We figured out we'd better carry on just the way we were going. We were up to date, we've got this thing to see through. This was on a Sunday, and we'd go home and be down there an hour earlier the next morning, and we did. That's the way we got the word, and that's what the boys did down there. They put in extra time after the war started. There was no squawking at all. I just have so much respect for those people, both civilian and officers. And it was the same everywhere else, I think, as far as I know, but it was especially fine down there at the Washington Navy Yard.

I was down there until May 31 of 1942, and reported to the Bureau the 1st of June, the next day. On the 30th of June I was promoted to captain, Supply Corps, and put in charge of the Maintenance Division of the Bureau.

The Maintenance Division had charge of the preparation of the budget for the Bureau of Supplies and Accounts and, in addition, had the over-all administration of the Bureau of Supplies and Accounts defense aid and lend-lease functions, and also charge of the plans and operation of all administrative control of civilian personnel in the field.

Q: My, what a tremendous effort! It was just expanding all over the field.

Adm. R.: Expanding all over the field. It was a terrific job. We had new places opening up and it was a case of getting personnel for the key spots, getting civilians to transfer from one key spot to another, from a key spot to fill a new key spot. It was a big job.

Q: In terms of personnel and filling billets, did the Civil Service Commission have to relax some of its stringent rules?

Adm. R.: I don't recall that they did. We worked right with the Civil Service rules and got it worked out. What we would generally do was get a good man from an established activity, who was in a Number Two or Three spot, and put him on top in a new activity, and we had no trouble getting those promotions approved. We did that quite a bit. Of course, there were certain civilians who didn't want to transfer. They had their home near their job and they would rather keep the job they had and keep settled. But we had plenty of adventurers who were willing to try the new ones, and that's the way we handled it.

Q: In terms of your civilian personnel, did you have problems with the draft?

Adm. R.: We did have some trouble with the draft, yes, but not too much. If a man was in a key spot, we would certify that he was absolutely necessary and we could get him out of the draft. The expendable ones we let go.

Q: Most of them wanted to go anyway.

Adm. R.: Oh, yes, they wanted to go. They were perfectly willing.
This lend-lease business was quite a factor.

Q: Tell be about that, because that, historically, is rather important.

Adm. R.: I'll have to go through this to a certain extent because there was so much here. As I said, we had the over-all administration of the Bureau of Supplies and Accounts defense aid and lend-lease functions. That took in all supplies and material. The Bureau of Supplies and Accounts approved all foreign governments' requisitions, including the screening of requisitions for conformance of policy and for availability of funds and material. All these requisitions came in to S & A.

Q: That involved you in priorities, did it?

Adm. R.: That involved us in priorities. We had a set priority schedule and those requisitions had to conform to that schedule.

I might tell you a story here, just before I get into it. We had one foreign country - I won't name it - that came in with a long requisition for material. We determined what the priority was and they didn't like it, they said it had to be higher. Well, we had our ways of finding out whether they needed this material, and we were pretty well convinced that they had pretty good stocks stashed away and didn't need it right away. They would need it later on. So we turned them down. They said they were going to the Chief of Naval Operations. I said, "All right, you can go and if he says you can have it, you can have it."

Well, they went over to the Chief of Naval Operations, ready to plead their case before Admiral Ernest King, CNO. In the meantime, I had briefed him on the matter. Admiral King was inclined to be gruff and to the point. I wondered what his decision would be at the meeting.

The delegation came in to the meeting and sat down in Admiral King's office - sat round in a circle - and I was there too, to speak my piece. He finally strode into the room, sat down at his desk, put his hands on his desk, and said:

"Gentlemen, what in the hell do you want?"

Well, that just broke everybody up! It pulled the rug right from under them, and they didn't have much to say. They gave a pretty weak defense of what they wanted and Admiral King said, "No." I'll never forget that. He was really good. He backed us up. When we made the right decisions we got the backing from our own people.

Q: In terms of their request, as you intimate, sometimes they were simply building up stores, weren't they?

Adm. R.: We had about five or six young men - officers - who could speak foreign languages. Some of them could speak French. We had one Russian student. They were the principal ones. But we had these four or five people who were going all over the world, as far as the Allies were concerned. We had them over in Morocco, where the French were, had them over in England, they traveled in England. This Russian-speaking officer didn't get into Russia but he talked very freely with the Russian Embassy. He could talk the language and pick up an awful lot. So we knew pretty well, if there was any question, what foreign allies had.

There was one case we had of a ship that was coming in to North Africa - I think it was Oran - a French ship, and they would take on a load of stores and go out, be out a little while, and come back completely empty and want another load. Well, after this happened once or twice, the young officer in Oran radioed me and told me about it and I told him to shut them off, that I was going to send someone over to the mainland. So I sent Lieutenant Pierre Guelf, SC, USN, who talked French so well that the French said, "Who is the French fellow in American uniform?" He'd been born in France and both his parents were French.

I sent him over there and we found out that what this ship was doing was going in to Oran to get stores, taking it back to a French port, unloading it and coming back for more, and the French had no more need of the stores than the man in the moon at that time. They had plenty. But somebody in the French Navy thought it would be a good chance to build up extra supplies. So that was stopped.

We had a few instances like that, but normally everything went pretty well. There were very, very few instances of trying to double cross.

Q: The man who was head of the Naval Mission in Moscow told me that he believed firmly that the Russian philosophy was to get as much as possible for the postwar period.

Adm. R.: There's no question about that. I believe it one hundred percent. The Russians were pretty cute in lots of way. They used to send ships in to Seattle to pick up their stores and they'd take theirs home via the Pacific. They would put in their requisitions and we would fill them and ship the material to Seattle. Well, if the ships didn't get in on time we had trainloads of stores outside of Seattle, waiting to unload. Then the Russians would come in late with their ships and complain that they weren't getting the material and they wanted a duplicate. We knew well enough that the material was on a train, waiting for them to take it, and we would tell them, No, take what's on the rails before you order any more.

We had that occur several times.

Q: Did you work directly with, say, somebody like Captain Frankel, who was in Murmansk receiving the lease-lend for the Russians?

Adm. R.: No, we didn't, not directly.

Q: How did you deal with interference from the White House, which came sometimes in terms of Priority?

Adm. R.: We didn't set the priorities in our Division. We took those from CNO, and CNO dealt with the White House on the priority proposition. We didn't set them. They were given to us, and all that we had to do was see that the requisitions conformed to the priority code.

The thing that impressed me about the Russians was the fact that they were dollar-conscious. I don't think that they had any idea that they'd ever pay us for the material, but they were the greatest people to negotiate the price on everything that they took. They would negotiate and try to beat us down on the price that we were charging. With other nations, there was no question at all that the price we set was all right. But not the Russians. They went into the background of the pricing and if it looked out of line to them they'd come to us and we'd have to defend the price. It's the only country with which we had that experience.

Q: Were you directly involved with BuShips where orders were being given for small craft, minesweepers and what have you, and they were being built for the British and the Russians? Did you get involved with that?

Adm. R.: Only to the extent that we would handle the transfer papers. That's all. We didn't do any of the negotiating on those.

I might go back and outline some more that we did.

As I said, the Bureau of Supplies and Accounts approved the foreign governments' requisitions, including the screening of requisitions for conformance to policy. They obtained the necessary approval for the government requisitions from the Munitions Assignment Board, the Office of the Chief of Naval Operations, the Army and Navy Petroleum Board, and the Office of Lend-Lease Administration, and from other agencies involved. The Bureau of Supplies and Accounts would issue authorization for procurement or issue of stores or for the material and grant the funds covering the procurement or issue, grant the authorization where necessary, and other pertinent requirements. And for services, the storage of all Navy defense aid and lend-lease material, except items pertaining to the Bureau of Medicine and Surgery and certain items pertaining to the Bureau of Ordnance.

It secured transportation of blanket foreign-government requisitions, issued shipping instructions, a letter of authorization for procurement or issue. From then on the material was shipped and was consigned within the continental United States. In other words, we ran the travel, or the shipping. The travel of personnel of defense aid governments. We secured the blanket foreign governments' requisitions, handled authorizations for passenger movements, assigned travel charges, operated the housing and training facilities of defense air governments. I've got a very good story on that. We had the subsistence of defense aid governments in USN activities, took care of all that. Administered miscellaneous services, such as repairs to commercial vessels for defense aid governments at USN activities, emergency repairs to aircraft of defense aid governments at USN activities. We coordinated the defense aid lend-lease policies of the Bureau of Supplies and Accounts, received and acted upon directives of the Secretary of the Navy, the Chief of Naval Operations, the Vice

Chief, Munitions Board, Army and Navy Petroleum Board and Office of Navy Material.

We handled liaison functions with other Bureaus and offices of the Naval Department and other government agencies. Represented the Bureau of Supplies and Accounts in liaison with representatives of foreign governments. Represented the Bureau of Supplies and Accounts in liaison with field activities and naval establishments on policy and defense aid matters. Controlled the defense aid appropriations and lend-lease allocations made to the Bureau of Supplies of Accounts.

Submitted reports to all Bureaus monthly of all lend-lease material on hand for more than forty-five days. In other words, if they didn't take it within forty-five days it was reported to the other Bureaus because they might want to withdraw some of it.

Q: And it was re-assigned?

Adm. R.: It was re-assigned. We made them take it and get it in a hurry. We reported everything, of course, to the Office of Budget Reports - the Office of Budget and Reports - and the Vice Chief of Naval Operations. Under the Vice Chief of Naval Operations they had the Russian protocol to establish the Russian requisitions showing funding and value of items contracted for and delivered to the government of Russia. He worked with the Munitions Assignment Board and accounting to the Bureau.

So it was a pretty over-all thing.

Q: How could you set on top of all those activities?

Adm. R.: We just did it. We had a small staff and had officers who were really on the job. That is, the top staff was small. Of course, we had the whole accounting group and the maintenance group which had a couple of hundred people in them. We just kept going.

Q: Obviously, you're a believer in a small staff?

Adm. R.: I am, very much so. It's the way you get things done.

In the Maintenance Division we established the International Aid Division, which was really the core of the whole thing. The International Aid Division was the one that really carried the requisitioning —

Q: The financing?

Adm. R.: And the financing, yes.

I was telling you about the —

Q: Housing.

Adm. R.: Yes, working with the personnel. One of the most interesting things that I had was the establishment of HMS Asbury Park. HMS Asbury Park — excuse me, we took over there the Berkley-Monterey Hotel to establish a British barracks. The men that would come in there were the men who were coming over to the United States to take over the minesweeps and the small boats that we were turning over to the British. Minesweep and —

Q: Landing craft?

Adm. R.: Landing craft and other small craft. They came in there, to Asbury Park, fresh-caught from the British Islands. They were young men, some of them not too bright. All of the good people had been brought out of England and these were - I don't like to put it in here, but you understand what I mean?

Q: Yes. They were getting down to the bottom of the barrel!

Adm. R.: Yes, getting down to the bottom of the barrel.

We established the barracks and the British called it HMS Asbury - His Majesty's Ship Asbury. I put a man representing us down there for liaison, by the name of Lieutenant Commander Harold Baggs. I got him out of the Traymore Hotel in Atlantic City. He was manager of the Traymore Hotel, and I got him in uniform as a lieutenant commander, Supply Corps.

Harold went down there as my representative, representative of the International Aid Division, to work with the British. He had quite a time getting accustomed to it. Of course, he knew food. He'd come up in the hotel from the back of the house and knew everything in that line. He worked with them and he got them started there. He got Captain Bunbury, RN, the Commanding officer, settled down. Harold started out feeding them like it would be in the American Navy. Well, he immediately got a lot of protests, so he had to go ahead and study the British system of feeding, and then put in a fourth meal, tea in the afternoon. The Britishers always favor their tea. So that was one mess we had in the United States where we were feeding a fourth meal.

Q: When these men came over to HMS Asbury, were they fully outfitted with clothes?

Adm. R.: Oh, yes, fully outfitted with clothes.

Q: You didn't have to attend to that?

Adm. R.: No. All that we were interested in was feeding them and housing them.

Q: This was not always true with some of the foreign personnel, was it?

Adm. R.: No, that was not always true, but this was. HMS Asbury commissioned on the 1st of October 1942 and was paid off on completion of their work on the 29th of February 1944. There were some interesting facts here. They had accommodations for 3,800 in double bunks and 375 hotel bedrooms and a cafeteria with seating accommodation for 1,002. Permanent executive officers and ratings was often less than 2 percent of the total number in the barracks - executive staff and officers and ratings. So that every use had to be made of transients.

It was interesting to note that the cafeteria was new to the British and they protested loudly at having to go through a cafeteria line. They had been used to sitting down in a mess and having mess cooks serve them. But we finally prevailed and they got used to it and it worked out all right.

Most of these men usually stayed about three weeks, so there was perpetual instruction and ever-changing of men all the time. At first, we had some trouble with them. These young men came over, and had been used to a light British beer, which is very light - they came over and got out on the town and American spirits would take charge and they'd get a little rowdy once in a while. It was not bad, there was not much damage. Old Captain Bunbury finally put a big sign across the entrance to HMS Asbury: "Beware of American spirits. Some are very bad and some are very bad indeed." That was a big sign stretched across there. But you can see the temper of the whole thing. It was all right.

As I say, we had an ever-changing 900 men who constituted the special parties. These 900 men would more or less come and go in about the same number at a time.

Q: They furnished the complements for all these ships that were going?

Adm. R.: That's right, and they had to be trained in our ways of communication - our radios that were on board there so that the ratings would know how our radios, machines and engines, and so on worked.

Q: And that training was done there, at Asbury Park?

Adm. R.: At Asbury Park - most of it was. Sometimes they were sent out on special parties to nearby naval installations to get fuller training.

As an example of some of the things they had to be taught: some 150 different and usually inexperienced officers had to be taught their duties as an officer of the watch before they commenced this duty. And, strange to say, a considerable measure of success was achieved.

The United States proved over- attractive to a certain type of man – not the United States but its temptations were over-attractive to a certain type of man would appear to be indicated by the fact that a total of fifty years' detention and imprisonment was awarded while the men were there – that is, from mast. Apart from that the customs and traditions of the service were very well maintained. This is a little thing that old Captain Bunbury handed me.

During the commission 400 men passed the higher seamen's ratings, 5,000 were given seamanship instruction, 5,800 did antiaircraft, including firing in most cases, 4,200 passed through the signal school, and 13,000 through the swimming pool, of whom 3,000 learned to swim! Isn't this great? Some 350 officers did a two-week course in navigation and other subjects. HMS Asbury was responsible for the pay and administration of various tenders commissioning around the coast, often at vast distances and the greatest number at any time was 250. The greatest number on the ship's books at any one time was over 16,000. Over 39,000 men passed through the barracks, which involved receiving 48 large drafts. The record was reached on the 13th of August 1943, when 791 joined and 1,128 were discharges, all in four special trains within the course of two hours from the same station. The average sick list was 25 a day. 2,700 teeth were extracted, and 6,400 filled. The captain's office wrote 18,000 letters and in the Union Jack Club there were drunk 375,000 glasses of beer, an average of over 9 glasses per man.

Q: Now, the expenses for the maintenance of HMS Asbury were lease-lend? They were charged to lease-lend?

Adm. R.: That's right. But, of course, as far as drinking the beer was concerned, that was cash. The men payed cash for that.

There's a little poem that one of them wrote, "A Farewell to Asbury."

Q: Admiral, since you're on the subject of these special stations, what about the WAVES - USS Hunter, and places like that? Did you have to supply them?

Adm. R.: We had nothing to do with that.

Q: Nothing to do with the WAVES at all? How were they supplied?

Adm. R.: Through the Bureau of Personnel. No, we had nothing to do with them. They were not under lend-lease.

Q: What about the overseas supply depots like the one in North Africa? This was a special effort of BUSANDA, was it not?

Adm. R.: That's right. We had a supply depot over in Oran.

Royar #3 - 133

Q: That's the one George Bauernschmidt was involved with.

Adm. R.: That's right. Did you get him?

Q: Yes.

Adm. R.: Well, he probably gave you a lot of dope on that.

Q: He gave me a complete report on the whole depot, covering the whole thing. And what about Mechanicsburg?

Adm. R.: I don't think Mechanicsburg was going then, was it?

Q: It was during the war.

Adm. R.: The only thing that we had to do with Mechanicsburg would be withdrawing or putting lend-lease material in there for storage. That's all. We did that in a number of places all over the United States. We had storage spaces set aside for lend-lease.

Q: Then did you have charge of the cataloguing of what was there, or was this somebody else's job?

Adm. R.: No. We had a record of what was there, and also the station had a record of what was there. We had a general record.

Q: You told me off tape that you established a base at Travis Island in New York for the Norwegian Navy.

Adm. R.: The Norwegians wanted to bring some men over and train them to take over ships, similar to what we did for the British at HMS Asbury.

So on the 18th of September 1943 we made arrangements with the New York Yacht Club to take over their establishment. They gave it to the government for a period of time. I don't remember whether there was anything paid for it or what the lease was, and I don't have the record. But I know they did give us their clubhouse and their whole establishment there on Travis Island. We had quite a nice opening there. Princess Martha attended, and the barracks were put in full operation. The problems there were nothing at all. The Norwegians had some good officers in charge and they ran the place in good shape. At first, though, we had trouble with the food again. We finally found a baker in New York who could make the type of bread that they liked in Norway and we bought Norwegian-type bread from him. And we changed the menu around to feed them more fish than normally the Americans would have.

It was a very successful operation all the way through.

Q: This entailed far fewer personnel?

Adm. R.: Oh, yes, there were far fewer personnel. I don't think there were more than 200 or 300. We only gave them a few ships, and it only lasted probably, I think, a year or a year and a half. Comparatively few people went through.

Q: Did you do likewise for the Dutch?

Adm. R.: No. just the Norwegians and the British. Those were part of our lend-lease operations.

Royar #3 - 135

I think the most interesting part, of course, was working with some of the top naval officers of these foreign countries. I didn't see much of the Russians. They did most of their negotiations through civilians. But I did work quite a bit and very closely with Vice Admiral Fenard of the French Navy, and Admiral French of the British Navy, and with the Dutch - I don't recall the name of the admiral there, unfortunately, but the French and the British were the chief people that we were very close to.

Q: This put you in touch with the British purchasing mission here in Washington?

Adm. R.: Yes, but they were of course civilians and there was always friction between the Purchasing Mission and the uniformed personnel. The Purchasing Mission was all civilian. The British Military didn't like the system. They thought our system was much better, far better than theirs, because they said that if they needed anything aboard ship they had to go through this Purchasing Mission and never knew when they would get it or what they would get, and it was upsetting all the way through.

I remember at one time we were talking about taking all the purchasing away from the services and putting it in a fourth service of Supply. The British and the French told us, don't do it, you'll lose everything. It was put off and never came to pass, of course.

The lend-lease in the foreign countries, as I say, we kept under control by having these young officers go traveling around, on the go all the time. They knew pretty well what the score was, kept the supplies moving, I think, in a very economical way.

Q: Did we really think that we were going to be reimbursed for all of these supplies?

Adm. R.: At one time we thought we would, but as the amounts grew so astounding I think people just thought that we probably never would. I don't think any of us ever thought the Russians would pay us. I don't think there was any feeling that the Russians would have any idea of paying us back.

Q: Aren't they proposing to do that now, by 25 cents on the dollar or something?

Adm. R.: Something like that, yes. But at that time, the way they were going, we didn't think they had the money to pay us back in the first place. The thing that always astounded us, though, was how they negotiated down to the penny on everything. They demanded the lowest price just as though they were paying cash over the barrel head. It was a remarkable thing.

I had a very interesting trip in 1943. I was still the head of lend-lease but they attached me to the Naval Inspector General, Admiral Snyder, and I went with him - he didn't go, his assistant, Rear Admiral C. H. Wright, headed the party. We went to Pearl Harbor and were there from June the 19th to July the 30th, a month and a half, on a survey of supplies.

Q: You mean what was there and what was needed?

Adm. R.: Well, the thing was that there'd been a lot of complaints from people in the States saying that Pearl Harbor had requisitioned too much material, and a lot of material that was needed elsewhere was at Pearl Harbor instead of on the States side, and that Admiral Gaffney - John J. Gaffney, who was the commanding officer of the Naval Supply Depot at Pearl Harbor, had robbed everybody and he showed poor judgment in getting more than he really needed.

We spent six weeks on that thing and we came out with a commendation for Admiral Gaffney. He had started well before Pearl Harbor to accumulate material. He believed that there was going to be trouble and it would be in the Pacific, and that Pearl Harbor would need a lot of material for repair work and for replenishing ships. And it happened just exactly as he had figured out. They had Pearl Harbor and they started to bring the ships into the dry docks and he had the material on hand that was needed. It was through his foresight. It was true he had put in for a tremendous amount of material, but it took a tremendous amount of material repairing these ships. They could go right to work on it. And they had to get more, too - more material - but they had enough to immediately start in on repairs, immediately replenishing supplies for the small ships that were in the fleet. It was through his foresight that we got out of that as quickly as we did. His foresight helped out a great deal. I think he was the major factor there.

Q: How did BUSANDA look upon the efforts of men with foresight on individual ships, men who insisted upon having spare parts and so forth?

Adm. R.: Spare parts aboard ship were a different problem. They had allowances on the ships and he went by the allowance list. If the allowance list was not enough, he could always get them enlarged or shortened. But in a place like Pearl Harbor there are no allowance. At that time there were no allowances. You were supposed to have, maybe, a six months' supply, or something like that. In the case of Gaffney, he went ahead and, in terms of normal operations, he probably had several years' supply and that's what bothered people who had gone back and seen where he had drawn it, and they were short, and the word got in to the CNO and the Bureau that Gaffney had an awful lot of stuff piled up on that island out there that he could never use and it could be used in the States.

That's why they sent us out there, and we spent six weeks going through that.

Q: And you came back with praise for him?

Adm. R.: Praise for him because he did have the foresight to do it. Admiral Nimitz was out there and he agreed to it absolutely.

Q: Did you have anything to do with the so-called supply train for the fleet in the Pacific?

Adm. R.: No, that came under Operations.

Q: That, indeed, was a tremendous effort.

Adm. R.: Yes. The only thing that the Bureau had to do with that was to see that there was enough material at the ports for the supply ships to load, but the actual operation came under Operations.

Q: When did you begin to think in terms of a supply depot on Guam?

Adm. R.: Well, on this trip when we went to Pearl Harbor we went on out to Guam and Midway because they were involved, too. You see, Pearl Harbor supplied Guam and Midway.

We went to Midway first and we got there shortly after the Battle of Midway and, of course, everything was upset. Fortunately, they'd sandbagged everything, buried a lot of stuff in the sands, that they could get out, and I'll never forget it. The little hotel there that Pan American had was a submarine barracks, and for the submarine boys that was their liberty. After they'd been on a cruise they'd come in to Midway. The funny thing was when we started out for Midway we got in this plane at Pearl and we got up in the air, and the plane just couldn't get up. A friend of mine, Dan Logan, was with us – Captain Dan Logan – and he said, "My God, this is it. We're going to hit the mountain." And we just barely missed it and turned around and came it. We couldn't figure out what was the matter, and they said, "What in hell have we got on this plane?" We went through it, and it was loaded down with liquor to take to the boys out at Midway!

Q: Almost cost you your life!

Adm. R.: That's right. That would have been a nice news story, wouldn't it?

Q: Well, at that point, Guam was still in the hands of the Japanese, wasn't it?

Adm. R.: Oh, no, that was after the Battle of Midway... Oh, Guam was?

Q: Yes, Guam. Guam wasn't freed for sometime. When it was we built a terrific depot there. When had you anticipated it being freed and anticipated it as a site for -

Adm. R.: Really, that big depot wasn't built till the latter part of the war.

Q: At the time that Nimitz went out to Guam?

Adm. R.: Yes.

Another trip was to Europe. On this trip I went out with the Chief of the Bureau, who was William Brent Young - Admiral Young. The purpose of the trip was to find out what Supplies and Accounts was doing and how it was coming along in the war effort.

We started out on the 1st of November 1943, and we went to Scotland. The travel across the ocean at this time was on HMS _Ajax_, an English cruiser. The _Ajax_ had just finished repairs in Norfolk, Virginia, after being shot up down in South America. I think you probably remember the encounter she had down there. The captain of the ship was a fine chap, Captain J. J. Weld, Royal Navy. We were treated very well aboard ship. We had good quarters, the cruising was easy, although it was wartime. It didn't seem to worry the captain very much and everything seemed relaxed aboard ship.

Q: Did you have a destroyer escort?

Adm. R.: All alone. And it was rather surprising to think that when we went below for dinner in the evening we could sit around and have a cocktail and enjoy ourselves.

Q: It makes a difference, doesn't it?

Adm. R.: It certainly makes a difference.

We got over near Portsmouth - we were going to Portsmouth, England - and I remember the morning just before we got in to Portsmouth, we saw a plane in the air and the captain loaned me - I was on the bridge, and he loaned me a pair of binoculars and I looked up and I could see the German cross on it. I said:

"Captain, hadn't you better go to general quarters? It's a German plane."

"Oh, no," he said, "that won't harm us. No, there's a big convoy about 200 miles from us. If they want to waste any bombs, they'll go to the convoy. They won't bother this sort of ship." He never even went to general quarters, never took any special precautions. The plane didn't bother us and we just went on in to Portsmouth, England.

Q: I guess you can get accustomed to anything!

Adm. R.: You can get accustomed to anything.

From Portsmouth we drove up to London and then on up to Prestwick in Scotland. We had a plane and we went down to Marrakech, Morocco; Oran; Bizerte; and then over to Sicily and Palermo.

That was a very interesting visit in Palermo. We went through the small naval yards here - Italian Navy yard. The Germans, of course, had been driven out at that time and they had gone in there and they had not taken a thing. They left all the storehouses and everything just about intact. Apparently they thought that they would hold it and it was no use taking anything with them, that they'd be back. They didn't. But the most interesting thing, I think, that I experienced there was that evening we had dinner. There were three or four of us in the inspection party and the naval attachés, one of whom was a good friend of mine who is quite a lawyer here in town now, Henry Dudley. He's a member of the firm of Dudley, Easterwood. I'm sure he'd give you a good talk of his experiences over there. He's a fine speaker.

We had this dinner in the little villa that the naval attaché had there. I'll never forget the long table, smilax around it, beautiful. The same servants who had been there with the Italian owner, and one of our guests was General George Patton. That was shortly after he'd had his experience in the hospital when he was accused of slapping a boy, and he was on duty there. Ostensibly, he was in command of a division but there wasn't any division. He was up there doing nothing.

I had the pleasure of sitting that evening with him, just the two of us, and we talked I guess for an hour or so. And I must say that I learned to have a great deal of admiration for the man. He had absolutely no complaint about the way he had been treated, no complaint about the fact that he didn't have any command, and was just as bright and enthusiastic about ending the war as anyone I've seen, and talking about when he was going to move to the front again. He was a very engaging person and I could see why he was a great leader. He was the type of man who may be tough, maybe hard, but the kind of a man that the enlisted men and officers under him would like and follow anywhere. Of course, by reputation he's been very controversial. There are people who like him and those who don't. Well, I'll say for my part he made a very, very fine impression on me. I'm only sorry that I never had the opportunity to serve with him.

After Palermo we went to Algiers, Port Lyautey, and then flew down across the African desert to Dakar. We had very little down there, except that we had a few people stationed there just in case war ever got that far. From Dakar we took a plane over to Natal, Brazil, and then Belem. There was no indication of war in those two South American cities. They were calm and collected and it was very quiet.

Then we flew up the coast and across to Trinidad, San Juan, Guantanamo, and back to Washington. It was a good experience to see those different places and see how they were responding.

Q: Did you find any difficulties in the whole supply system?

Adm. R.: No, no difficulties at all. Of course, North Africa was the place where our supplies were under armed guard all the time. The material would often be unloaded at Port Lyautey and go by rail up to Oran and the cities along the coast up there, and unless they had an armed guard with them half the stuff would be gone before the train arrived at the destination.

Q: Was it just pilfering?

Adm. R.: Pilfering. The pilferage was terrible. Even in Oran the people who had jeeps never left the jeeps parked unless they had them chained to a telephone pole or something. The problem of pilferage there was probably the worst I've ever seen. But we learned our lesson. We lost a lot of stuff at first, but when we finally got the hang of it and had armed guards around, we handled it pretty well. The supply end of it was all right. We found everything in order.

Then, early in 1944 I took over the seven sections of the Accounting Division in addition to the Maintenance Division.

Q: You mean your job wasn't big enough! You had to have —

Adm. R.: I had to have a little bit more. I reorganized that and continued also with the lend-lease work and the Maintenance Division.

In November 1944 I was transferred from that job to the General Inspector of the Supply Corps. I relieved Rear Admiral Pyne at that time.

Q: What Pyne was this?

Adm. R.: F. G. Pyne.

Q: Well, you obviously were in training for this job anyway, were you not?

Adm. R.: I'd been doing a lot of inspecting work, yes, most of it, of course, for the Naval Inspector General. He seemed to like the work that I'd done because he was always asking for me to go back on another job, which would interfere with what I was doing, but at the same time the Bureau would let me go.

Q: This must have been some sort of a certification to your merit as an administrator, that you could pick up and go on these tours?

Adm. R.: Well, I think that I had picked out some of the finest young officers, who were administrators themselves, and I was lucky in picking out the right men. I always believed that if you were going to have a man, you should throw responsibility on him. And these younger officers I gave the responsibility, "you're in charge. If you make a mistake and it's an honest mistake, I'll back you up, but don't make the same mistake twice." I had no hesitation in turning important jobs over to these youngsters and they came winnin g through. One of them in particular in the lend-lease was a lieutenant, junior grade, George F. Baugham. George did a perfectly marvelous job and is now a rear admiral in the Supply Corps Reserve. He's down in Florida and I guess he's administrator of one of the largest businesses down there. I've forgotten what it is. I see him once in a while. He was President of New University in Florida and is now down there and I see him from time to time. He was an excellent man. He studied even while he was working with me. He went nights to American University and got his Ph.D. He did a perfectly marvelous job. He was one of a number I had that I had no hesitation when I went away in turning over the work to them, and they came through.

In April 1945 I was appointed a rear admiral by James Forrestal. In April and May of 1945 I made an inspection trip for the Navy Inspector General with Commodore Thomas E. Van Meter, who was in charge of this. Tom Van Meter is living here in the Hall right now and I bet he could give you a run down on many things because he was with the Inspector General the whole time.

We went over to England. We had our own plane and we started at the Azores and looked at the small Naval Station we had there, and went over to Port Lyautey —

Q: What did we have there? At Ponta Delgada?

Adm. R.: Yes, we had a small Naval Station. And then went over to Naples, Palermo, Oran, and then over to Rome, Toulon, Paris, Cherbourg, Antwerp, Belgium, London, Plymouth, Rosneath, Exeter, Rotterdam, Bremen, back to London, and then up to Prestwick and home. This was a very challenging trip. We were split up considerably because the different sections of the group would take their specialty. I would take the supply end, the aviators would go into the aviation end of it, and so on.

We had to give a report on the situation as it was then, what the probability of future use of the activity would be if it were kept open, what our recommendation was as far as closing and evacuating the material, or should we leave the material there. Would it be cheaper to leave the material there, bring it home, turn it over to somebody else, or what to do with it. It was a very full mission that we had.

One thing I might give you, for example, was at Exeter, England -

Q: That was a big depot, wasn't it?

Adm. R.: That was a big depot. Exeter, as you know, is in Devon and the Supply Officer in command there was a commander by the name of Harry W. Liser. Harry is now out in Oregon doing some writing and working for an association out there. He did a very, very fine job. It was a U.S. naval amphibious base. He relieved a man there. The trouble had been that they had opened this base with a supply officer and immediately he got it started they put a Reserve line officer in there who had never been around a supply base, in command, and there was friction between the two of them naturally. So they took them both out and Liser went in.

Q: That was under Admiral Stark's command, wasn't it?

Adm. R.: Yes. All my orders are splattered with Stark's name. It was a very active little place. I was in there, and they worked with the English. The fact is that it had started up on the 7th of October 1943 and up to the time that I got there, they had done a tremendous lot of work. They had a lot of trouble starting that because there were absolutely no rail facilities in there.

I have a letter here which Harry let me use from George Bishop, who was the Divisional Superintendent of the Southern Railway, Western Division, in England, and it's interesting to hear what he has to say. This was written back in 1946:

"I find from the date of opening, that is, September 7th, 1943, up until today (which is in 1946 shortly after we'd been there and the place was closing) 24,195 rail wagons were discharged, 12,234 loaded away, the total handled 36,429 (those are those small English rail wagons). I have a further record that the highest number cleared on one week was 917 in May 1944, and the highest number dispatched in one week was 398, the week beginning 7 December last (and that was in 1945). I am quoting these, not inconsiderable totals to you for the reason that the whole of this work at the tracks has been performed free of accident to personnel or other damage of a reportable character, which I am sure you will rate as most satisfactory and I would please tender my sincere thanks to you and your staff for the cooperation which permits this statement to be made."

Before leaving the subject, I think you will recall that the proposal to construct the New Court rail sidings (those were the new siding for the extra base) was made by the U.S. Navy about midday on Saturday, 2nd October 1943, and by 5 P.M. on Monday, the 4th, 1,000 feet of siding, complete with main-line connections and signaling apparatus, had been installed in 53 hours, despite the fact that the railway material had to be brought from a distance and on your side a heavy amount of leveling and filling had to be done.

Looking back on the job, surely it merits the comment 'Good going.'"

Well, that was just Exeter. Young Liser said in a letter he wrote to me that he was scared as the devil when I came and inspected him. He was afraid that I would jump him for his unorthodox methods. But here was another one of these chaps that I had recruited. Then anything had to be done it had to be done, regardless of how you got it done, regulations or anything else, and that's just exactly what happened.

Q: He was innovative!

Adm. R.: He was innovative. He'd had a transportation background when he came in, in civilian life, and believe me he ran that supply depot and he ran the transportation in and out of there, and he had a lot of cockeyed ideas but they worked. That's what made the war go in lots of places. That's just an example of it.

Q: Admiral, you indicated just a few moments ago that the orders for your survey group were quite flexible – I mean whether the base should be closed or not, whether the material should stay there or be sent home, things of that sort. What was the overriding policy about sending material back home?

Adm. R.: Whether it would pay to send it back, the condition it was in, whether it was worth the transportation cost to get it back.

For instance, we made some inspections in Guam and Tinian later on where we had a vast amount of material. This was a little after the war. Some of the columnists got hold if it and said that we hadn't intended to bring it back and told about all the great waste of leaving this machinery and material that had been out in the tropics and out in the sun, which they didn't know about, bringing all that back. And when it was rumored that it was going to be thrown in the ocean, which it should have been, they just raised the devil. Later on, when I was in Oakland, I got some of that stuff back from Guam. It was infested with these big tropical snails and we had to use a crowbar to kill them when we got it back. It was in such condition that we just took it out and sold it for junk when we got it back. It didn't even pay the cost of shipping it back.

Q: Wasn t there also the question of bringing things back in great quantities and upsetting the manufacturing schedules?

Adm. R.: That was a great thing, but the trouble is that none of the stuff was in good condition. Most of it was not in such condition that it could be much of a business problem. It wouldn't compete.

We did get some machinery that sold to second-hand dealers and it was rebuilt and I think they made a little bit of money on it.

But when you have war material - and I saw it out in Guam, Tinian, and all over the Orient and here again in Europe - it wasn't like you bring it off the shelf. A lot of it had been stowed in places where it deteriorated to some extent. It had been used, most of it. There was very, very little unused usable material to bring back. Some of it we recommended they sell on the spot. With the condition of the economy in Europe, they could use it without hurting them at all, and they did so, some of them. It was a big problem. You never end a war with everything used up. There's always something left over. But I think we wasted a lot of money bringing back stuff that was just useless.

Q: And we brought it back largely because of the pressures?

Adm. R.: Pressure, that's right. The columnists and there was congressional pressure, too. People in Congress were very honest about it, but they just didn't understand. I know when I got back from this trip I went over to the State Department and gave a lot of their foreign trade people a briefing on the whole thing.

Q: It seems to me that was what was required, some sort of an educational program.

Adm. R.: That's right, but they never got it. I'm the last man in the world to want to lose money because I'm a taxpayer, too, but it just broke my heart to see some of that stuff that they brought back, the condition it was in. They had stuff up in Alaska the same way that they brought back.

On this trip we also went up to Bremen, in Germany. This was just after the armistice, and we were I guess one of the first inspection parties to go in there. That was a very interesting trip. Bremen, as you know, has a shipyard, that's where a lot of the submarines were built. We went down to take a look at the ways there and a lot of the new submarines were still on the way. What they had done - and I suppose it's well known to everybody - they built them in sections, a section maybe large enough so they could transport it by rail. They had several factories outside of Bremen so that they wouldn't be bombed, you see - quite a way away. And each section was absolutely complete, with furniture it it. If it was bunking space, they had the bunks, they had the furniture, they had absolutely everything that belonged in that section. These sections were brought down to Bremen and put on the ways, welded together, and the ship went out.

Q: Reminiscent of modular housing today!

Adm. R.: Yes. It was a remarkable thing. I remember the one that I saw there, all it needed was the tail end of the propellers. Everything else had been welded together.

Q: We hadn't yet adopted that technique, had we?

Adm. R.: Not at all. It was remarkable how they had the factories scattered all around Bremen, outside the probable range of bombing, brought them down, sloshed them together, and sent the ship out.

Q: Did you get to Peenemunde?

Adm. R.: No. I had a little experience coming back. We went back to London from Bremen. It turned out amusing.

We were in this two-propeller plane and it had a red-headed Army pilot. We stopped near Brussels for some gas. We stopped a long way out on the field. We were going to cross the Channel from there back to London. We radioed in to have a gas tank come out. The tank truck came out, put the hose in our tank, and started pumping. One of the mechs went up, dipped it out, tasted it, and said:

"Say, this is water."

Well, the fellow in the tank truck, said, "Oh, nuts, that's gas." A friend of his came up and he said, "I've got some water coming in here." And a fellow below, one of our crew said:

"Oh, you're crazy."

"Well," he said, "come up and taste it."

He said, "You son of a bitch, you're right, it is water."

Q: Cheap fuel!

Adm. R.: So they had to cut that off and sent the tank wagon back with the water, and got another tank wagon out there, and both of them tasted it before they let them start pumping. So we took about half a tank of water back with us to London!

What they'd been doing was get the gas in the tank truck and take it out to town and sell it, then fill it full of water and bring it back. Nobody knew the difference.

Q: Till they tried to start the engines!

Adm. R.: That was one experience I'll never forget. We were a little nervous carrying that tank of water back to London, too. But we got back and came back to the States. It took us quite a while to write that up.

Q: Did you close all of those depots or were some of them -?

Adm. R.: No. Exeter, for example, was closed down a couple of months after we left. We left Oran open for awhile, consolidated everything in Oran. The others were closed down pretty much. We got out just as fast as we could.

Just before I took that trip I went out to Guam. I was put on a committee to reopen the Bank of Guam. Guam had a down there below the -

Q: Recaptured by the U.S. Marine, 20 July 1944.

Adm. R.: It was captured by the Japanese in 1941.

Q: December 10, 1941.

Adm. R.: Recaptured from the Japanese in 1944. There were three of us that were put on that detail for the Bank of Guam and we formulated our plans before we went out. They were approved and then we went out and put them in effect. I was given orders that said in compliance with the request contained in so-and-so, the following officers of the Supply Corps are nominated to serve as an administration board: Captain Murrey L. Royar, Supply Corps senior member, Commander N. E. Disbrow, Supply Corps, USN (Retired) member, and Commander Theodore Nickerson, as the recorder. Then there was Captain Charles P. Franchot, USNR, of the office of the Judge Advocate General who was also a member.

We went out there -

Q: George.

Adm. R.: He was out there already. He joined the group out there.

Nickerson had been a banker, and we formulated a plan for re-opening the bank, and went out for the opening. There was a remarkable thing about that bank. The Japanese when they captured it didn't disturb or wreck it. They carefully boxed up every record, every voucher, everything that belonged to the bank, and stowed them away.

Q: How curious!

Adm. R.: That only thing that we can figure out is that they thought that perhaps after the war ended they would still own Guam, and then they would have everything ready to open up for business again. It was all carefully stowed away and all we had to do was to open it up. There were a few missing records, not very many. Even the notes were there that people on the island owed to the bank. All the records, everything was complete. All we had to, which was a comparatively easy job, was to get our people out who were to take charge of the bank and go over those records and see that they were in order, get them in shape and open up for business.

Q: What a story!

Adm. R.: That's the way it worked. The opening was where I got this check, when they reopened the bank. Of course, now it's the Bank of American out there, but the Navy ran the bank at the time it was captured, as they did down in Samoa. That was a very interesting thing.

Well, let's see. As I said. As I said, I was General Inspector of the Supply Corps and I was also given additional orders as General Inspector for the Atlantic Coast. I don't know why they had to do that, because I had the whole inspection job, but that was the way they had it. I stayed on there until 3 January 1946, when I was detached and went to Norfolk as supply officer in command of the supply depot.

We had quite a time. As I told you before, we sold the house. I never expected to come back to Washington at all. I figured I was through. We got rid of everything and made a clean break.

Interview No. 4 with Vice Admiral Murrey L. Royar, U.S. Navy (Retired)

Place: His residence in Vinson Hall, McLean, Virginia

Date: Wednesday afternoon, 28 March 1973

Subject: Biography

By: John T. Mason, Jr.

Q: Well, Admiral, I see by your notes you're raring to go with Chapter 4.

Last time, you had completed your discussion of the period when you were in Washington tending to lease-lend in the years 1942 to 1945. Do you want to resume at this point, Sir?

Adm. R.: All right.

As I told you, I was General Inspector for the Inspection Service from 1945 on till I was detached from the Bureau on 3 January 1946. At that time, as I say, I was detached from the Bureau and detached as General Inspector of the Supply Corps.

In the meantime we sold our house in Arlington, on 26th Place, South, to General Curtis LeMay of the United States Air Force.

Q: Yes, you told me about that very advantageous arrangement.

Adm. R.: Did I tell you about that.

Q: For him and, in a way, for you too!

Adm. R.: Well, I reported in Norfolk, Virginia, on 4 January 1946 and was assigned quarters in the old Maryland House, which is right next to the Commandant's quarters. The old Maryland House is a very fine old mansion. It had been divided into two parts. The supply officer had one half and the medical officer had the other half. It was the Maryland House at the Jamestown Exposition and was left over from the Exposition. Now it is naval quarters down there.

I reported in on the 4th of January, as I said, and assumed command on 9 January. I relieved Rear Admiral Malcolm G. Slarrow, who went to Washington and took my position as General Inspector.

Q: Musical chairs!

Adm. R.: That's right, just reversing our positions. Admiral Slarrow left an excellent organization, and in January 1946 he had anticipated the reduction that would be needed after the war and he had set up a basic plan that was excellent. All I had to do was to carry on with it.

I think it might be interesting if I gave you some idea of what the Supply Department at Norfolk was like.

Q: Yes, indeed, the scope of the operations.

Adm. R.: In fact, I wrote this.

Q: After the fact, or in preparation for the fact?

Adm. R.: After the fact.

It was then a Naval Supply Depot at Norfolk, located on the naval base, and was originally commissioned on 1 March 1919. The Supply Depot has since expanded tremendously during World War II and, at the time I took over, the Supply Department proper was composed of 52 buildings, 19 of which were used as storehouses. Over 2 million square feet of net storage space was available at the depot. Not included in the figure is the fuel-products storage space, which accommodated some 188 million gallons of petroleum. Two recently remodeled and new constructed piers added over 280,000 square feet of available storage. Admiral Slarrow had been quite instrumental in getting those.

In addition to the storage space at Norfolk, the Supply Depot had over 20 warehouses on a 3,100-acre plot located at Cheatham Annex, which is between Yorktown and Williamsburg, Virginia. The Naval Supply Depot, Norfolk, was the immediate source of supply for all minor activities south of Washington, D.C.

Q: Including Charleston and all the rest?

Adm. R.: At that time. Charleston has since had a Naval Supply Depot established, but at that time we were the main supply for Charleston also. They had a Supply Department down there, but no Supply Depot or Supply Center.

And the principal source of supplies for the forces afloat operating on the East Coast. The stock at that time was approximately $187,000,000, which we thought was an immense amount of money at that time but since it doesn't seem quite so much.

The reduction had started and we anticipated shortly that it would drop to $20,000,000 or $30,000,000.

Q: How was the reduction effected? What did you do with the surplus?

Admr. R.: We got rid of the surplus down there with the War Assets Administration partly. In the first place, we went over everything and found out what we thought would be needed. The surplus that was in good condition, in conjunction with the War Assets Administration, was sold. Some of it we sold at auction right on the base, some we sold on bid, and various other ways.

One interesting thing I had was some sugar that came in. This was after I had taken over - the latter part of 1946 I guess it was. There was about 2 million pounds of sugar came in, and it had been on the beach under tarpaulins around the Philippines, and it was a mess. It was sticky, it was not much good, polluted with oil, and we didn't know what to do with it. So I got in touch with the American Sugar Refinery in Baltimore, and they came down and took a look at it, and said:

"Well, we'll take this and we'll refine it, and instead of trying to work out a contract on how much it would cost, we'll keep a certain percentage of it for our work." I've forgotten what it was, but it was definitely a very small percentage. They gave us a good deal. So I said, "Go ahead and do it."

They took it up, sent the good sugar back, and it was put in stock to use.

In the meantime, Mr. Drew Pearson got hold of that and I had a call from Mr. Drew Pearson personally and he said:

"I understand, Admiral, that your giving away sugar."

I said, "What do you mean by that?"

"Well," he said, "you sent, I'm told, around 2 million pounds up to Baltimore, to the American Refining Company up there. What authority did you have to do that?"

I said: "That's my business. I didn't give it away. That was refined and the majority of it came back."

"Give me the exact figures," he said.

I said, "I will not."

"Well," he said, "I'm going to write you up in my column."

Q: That was his kind of blackmail!

Adm. R.: I said: "Mr. Pearson, if you want to write it up in your column, fine, and if you don't get it right I'm going to sue you to hell."

That was the last I ever heard of it.

Q: A good thing you added that little bit!

Adm. R.: That's right, but he was very insistent that I gave that away. But, supposing I just let that messy stuff lie in my storage center there, you couldn't put it in the storeroom because it was wet.

Q: Sugar rots, doesn't it?

Adm. R.: It gets bad, yes. It gets sour. The thing to do was to act quick, get it done, and get what you could out of it, which I did without going through sources and getting any authority to do it. But it worked out all right. Those are the things you run up against.

Q: I suppose you had a little fleet of lighters, as well, did you?

Adm. R.: Oh, yes. Well, while we were there we dismantled about 384 vessels which had pretty good cargoes and storage materials on them. Altogether, I guess there were about 1,000 ships, craft — a lot of landing craft and so on — that we got rid of there, but there were about 384 large vessels. Those would come to us and we would unload them, leave about five days supply of food on board, then they would go over to the Navy Yard and the Navy Yard would strip them of their guns, their ammunition, and that type of material. A lot of that material that they stripped came back to us after it was pulled off. But the stores that we got, we took them out. They were ships' stores or provisions, and as we called them GSK, general stores — a little of everything.

We had quite an interesting time on that, but fortunately we got pretty good results. As I said, we had about 1,000 vessels of all types and about 384 of the larger ones. The armament equipment and supplies had been removed and stored. They were removed and stored when the ships were stripped by the industrial managers, and this was not only at the Navy Yard in Norfolk, but also at local shipyards, private shipyards. They went in there, too. Some of the facts on that are interesting.

On an average basis, with each 20 ships we'd take an average, and the average ran about 360 tons. Clothing and small stores ran around 3 3/10ths tons, dry provisions 49 tons, tools, paints, and hardware 67 tons, various kinds of cargo that they had on 20 tons. It averaged up around 360. We lost very little of it. The first provisions, if they were not edible, we had a contractor there who ran a pig farm, and we sold them to him. The stuff that was good that came off, we invoiced to the commissary stores or to the messes around there – the provisions.

Q: So everything was sold in some way?

Adm. R.: We figured we got about 99 percent by sale – not the full value, but at least we got something out of 99 percent of the material.

Q: What was the destination of the stripped-down ships?

Adm. R.: They had a berthing area that was established on the James River. All the Hampton Roads and Chesapeake Bay areas were filled. So we had about 35 miles of chain put on the bottom and we'd send vessels up there and they'd hook onto that chain and swing around up in the James River. Most of them were finally sold. There were a few left there in the dead fleet for a while.

Q: Who would buy them?

Adm. R.: We had over 2,000 purchasers come in and look at those ships.

Q: Business concerns?

Adm. R.: Business concerns.

Adm. R.: Yes, they were perfectly good freighters, all freighters. There were no Navy ships. The Navy yards took care of the Navy ships. These were all commercial ships that we'd used in the Navy to carry provisions and carry stores.

Q: On the average, how long would an individual ship remain in the James River before it was sold?

Adm. R.: At that time, the ships were going pretty fast. I can say that we started in this work in early 1946, shortly after I got down there, and by the middle of 1948 they were all cleaned up. So it took about two yars.

I'd say there were about 380 large ships, and altogether we got rid of about 1,000 vessels - a lot of small ones, too, such as Tugs, LCMs, and LCIs.

Q: These are in contrast with the ships that were tied up - I saw them - in the Hudson River, row after row of them, merchant vessels? They were in limbo, so to speak, not sold, but ready to be recommissioned at some time?

Adm. R.: That's right. We had a few that were left up the James River, but we disposed of most of them.

Q: How would you distinguish between what you wanted to sell and what you wanted to keep?

Adm. R.: The Navy had a board of survey go over each vessel and determine whether they wanted to hold it or whether it should be sold. We were not interested in determining what was to be sold.

Q: Did you put the price tag on the ships?

Adm. R.: With the War Assets Administration. Theoretically, we turned them over to the War Assets Administration. We worked right with them. A lot of them were sold on bids.

Q: I asked previously about the lighters. You must have had small ships to use to supply commissioned ships, didn't you?

Adm. R.: No, the commissioned ships came right alongside our piers. No. we were not stuck with lighters in Norfolk, there were plenty of pier spaces.

But we did have a great deal of material and it came in so fast we filled up everything around Norfolk. Then we went up to Cheatham Annex and used a lot of their space. A lot of the material we stowed outside under tarps for quite a while.

Q: I remember being on the mailing list for various catalogues that came to me of naval supplies that were being disposed of. Did you issue special ones out from Norfolk?

Adm. R.: Yes, the War Assets Administration did that. They put out catalogues and advertised the ships, and they did a good job on it.

Q: There were some great bargains listed.

Adm. R.: Yes, lots of good bargains.

Q: How did you determine the shrunken supply that you were going to maintain there? How was this determined? These were early days in the postwar era.

Adm. R.: You mean our – ?

Q: What you were going to maintain as a supply depot?

Adm. R.: The way we figured that out was that we knew pretty well from the budget how many ships would be in commission during the following year. You see, the budget came out in 1946 and the 1947 budget went into effect in June of 1946. We knew even before I got there, when that budget was first submitted to Congress, about how many ships would be in commission and how many would be going out. So we could judge pretty well from that what our stores should be.

But we didn't have to worry much about that at first because we had too much anyway. It was a question of just getting it down. That was the big job – to get rid of it and still not lose anything on it.

Q: You used, a few minutes ago, sugar as an illustration of one of your problems and said that it came from the Philippines. Does this imply that there were supplies shipped from far away like Guam to Norfolk?

Adm. R.: Oh, yes.

Q: What was the general over-all policy in that area?

Adm. R.: Well, of course, what we would like to have seen was to have this material - if it had been me out there in the Philippines I would never have shipped that sugar back because when you figure the cost of loading and the cost of transportation across the Pacific, the unloading at Norfolk, shipping it up to Baltimore to get it refined, and then getting it back, we didn't make any money on it.

I'm speaking very frankly now and if you want to cut it off the record, you can. But it's always been the pressure on the services to salvage everything they can. Congress looks at it. Somebody goes out on a trip and they see stuff on the beach out there that ought to be brought home and used - you ought to get it home. So every ship that came home had a load of junk. I don't say it was all junk, but there was a great deal of junk.

Later on, when I got to Oakland, we got one load of machinery that had been on the beach at Tinian, construction material. That stuff was covered with these great big tropical snails. Have you ever seen them?

Q: No, but I know about them.

Adm. R.: Well, we had a terrific time killing those before we could ever bring that cargo ashore. We didn't have any of those at Norfolk, but we did have a lot of material that had been on the beach and had been weathered, and we had to sell it for junk. It just did not pay to bring it back. It would have been much cheaper and the government would have been a lot better off if we'd just dumped it at sea some place.

Q: A lot of junking was accomplished, wasn' it?

Adm. R.: Quite a bit, and there was a lot of criticism in the Congress about it, too.

Q: George Bauernschmidt told me one time that in the case of certain supplies which had been stored in Guam, that they didn't want to return them, that industry in this country didn't want them back in this country to compete with their current schedules.

Adm. R.: That was really a problem for me at Oakland later on, because they returned from Guam and Tinian and a lot of those islands, construction material that had been on the beach out there, and industry didn't want us to bring it back. The fact is it cost us more to get them back and get them in working shape and selling then than they were worth. At the same time, it was competing with new material.

Q: I should think that would have soothed the ruffled feathers of some of the congressmen?

Adm. R.: Well, they got up and waved their hands and said there was waste because the services were not bringing the material back where it could be used.

Q: What about making some of these supplied available to foreign governments? What was your policy there?

Adm. R.: We did, particularly in Europe. There was a lot of material transferred to foreign governments in Europe, but not so in the Pacific. There was very little. I think we transferred some to the Phillipines, as I recall it, but that's about all. We sold some to the Japanese for salvage - some of the stuff that wasn't any good the Japanese came down and picked it up for salvage, a little of it. The rest of it came back.

Q: I heard of one enterprising group of men who hired a high-ranking retired naval officer, to lend prestige, I suppose, and then proceeded to sell a lot of this stuff to the Chiang kai-Shek government. Many things they couldn't even use. Was there much of that going on?

Adm. R.: If there was, I didn't know about it. I wouldn't be surprised if there was. I was out and conferred with the Chinese later on, but I heard no complaints from them at all. They were very glad to get anything that we'd give them.

Q: Of course, this was before the formation of NATO and I suppose that changed the picture a little bit once it came into being?

Adm. R.: Oh, yes, I imagine it did. We had our first big auction in Norfolk on the 9th of September 1946. That was in conjunction with the War Assets Administration. They set it up and they really conducted the auction. We furnished all the material. We had about $12,000,000 worth of surplus in that first auction, 7,000 items. We had everything from heavy machinery to ashtrays.

Q: What were your terms? Cash?

Adm. R.: Cash, or, if it was too much a deposit and so many days to pay before they took it off. It was a regular auction. Of course, a lot of these companies came in with a bond. So they put up the bond and they were in no danger of losing it that way.

After that we had scheduled auctions right straight through. As soon as we accumulated enough, there'd be another auction. We were overrun with people wanting to buy this stuff. We had no trouble getting rid of it at all. There seemed to be plenty of money.

Q: Was Norfolk unique in this respect, or were the other depots also conducting auctions?

Adm. R.: Doing the same thing. No, Norfolk was not unusual in that at all.

Another thing I helped to do while I was down there was to set up the Armed Forces Staff College. They came down there and wanted to open a staff college and took over some old barracks as the college hall, and the depot got the job of fixing them up and furnishing them. General Emmons - I don't know whether you've ever heard of him?

Q: Oh, yes.

Adm. R.: He was the first commandant - Delos C. Emmons.

Q: I guess Charlie Wellborn succeeded him, didn't he?

Admr. R.: I think so.

But getting rid of that stuff was really something.

The first class at the War College finished in 1947 and that was an interesting thing.

Q: Did you have any particular problems in connection with setting up a school, a college?

Adm. R: No. Of course, we didn't have to get the personnel. All we did was get the furnishings.

A: And you had most of those in stock?

Adm. R: We had most of them in stock. We got practically all of it from excess stock. Some of it had to be refinished a bit, but we had a paint shop and a carpenter's shop, and everything right at the depot where we could repair any of that stuff, and it went down just as good as new. It was a very easy thing to do. I got pretty close to a lot of those people down there and they were fine people.

Q: Tell me about palletizing and how it was employed at your supply depot in Norfolk.

Adm. R.: Palletizing really came into being during the war. There had been some attempts prior to it - to the war - but we were very fortunate in getting some very fine young officers in the Supply Corps from industry. These young officers had been studying palletizing, which I might describe as being - using a pallet that could be lifted by a fork-lift truck, and on that pallet would be packed material, either in boxes or crates, strapped to the pallet as a single unit. As a result, the fork-lift truck could take this palletized material, load a boxcar, load a flat car, put it aboard ship via a gangway into a hold, where the overhead crane could pick it up and drop it in the hold. Of course, at the end of the journey, whether it was a car, truck or ship, it was all ready to be hauled again by a single fork-lift truck.

Q: It was a system of bulk handling?

Adm. R.: Yes, it was a system of bulk handling, and it saved us a lot of manpower, it saved us pilferage, and it saved us time because it was quick.

As I say, I give full credit to the fine development that we had to the young men who came into the service from industry.

Q: This was one of the first general uses of it, wasn't it?

Adm. R.: It had not been used as much or as effectively before, but we really went to town with it during the war and it worked very, very well.

Q: Since you mentioned that bad word "pilfering," tell me about that at a supply depot like this.

Adm. R.: We had pilferage, there's no question about it. In any big operation you're going to have it. There's hardly any way you can stop it, but we kept ours down to a very, very small amount. I've got to give full credit again to the Civil Service people we had in our operation. They were a fine group of people, high type, and they were just as anxious to help out the war effort as anybody in the world, and while you're always going to get somebody in a crowd who doesn't look at the thing that way, there were others who watched and it was surprising how our people caught on to doing it. Of course, going out in automobiles, we'd have searches at unexpected times, and once in a while we'd pick up somebody with something in his car that he shouldn't have and he was fired right off the bat.

But our pilferage was minor. The worst pilferage that you get would be in shipping to a foreign station somewhere where somebody would purposely drop a pallet and break it open, and the contents would disappear. That's common even now, today. It's one of the worst things that the transportation people have to fight. Then, of course, you get in a country like Arabia or North Africa, the pilferage there was terrible, but not by our people. You could ship material in a locked box car and when the train got to its destination the locks would be knocked off and sometimes about half the contents had been dumped out. How they got in or where they got in nobody knew. In many cases we used to put an armed guard aboard the trains just to keep down the pilferage.

That was where we had a lot of trouble, but with our securely packing the material in crates or in boxes and then having them secured to a pallet cut down an awful lot of it.

Q: Was that one of the primary incentives for developing this system?

Adm. R.: Well, it was, of course, ease and quickness of handling was a major thing - speed. It speeded things up terrifically. Instead of having it all manhandled with a big crew of men, why, two or three people could do what many people could do.

Q: Talk about your cooperation with the other component parts of the naval base down there. I mean the repair facility, that sort of thing.

Adm. R.: We were pretty near a little kingdom of our own. The only repair part was at the naval aviation station at Norfolk. They had their own repairs for planes, which we were not interested in, but we furnished material for them, and our relationship there was always good. Of course, the air boys always wanted everything yesterday and we tried to give it to them. They had there for a while the aviation supply depot over in the air station, and then it was moved over and our place became a center on the 1st of January 1948, just about twelve days before I was detached. They only had a small supply department over there. We carried the bulk of the material and just shoved it over to them. We had better control and could cut out a lot of

Royar #4 - 175

administration and it was much better.

Q: Did you have any relationship with Newport News Shipbuilding?

Adm. R.: Very little. The fact is that about the only relationship wehad was when a ship would be over there in dock and we would send supplies over to them. That's about all. But as far as the shipbuilding company went, no.

Q: Then, the sending of supplies was handled by a liaison person?

Adm. R.: That's right. We'd ship it over by barge to the shipbuilding company.

Q: These supplies would be fitings and so forth?

Adm. R.: That's right.

Q: For ships on the ways?

Adm. R.: Ships under repair there, yes.

Q: Was your supply depot a complete unit? Did you have everything there?

Adm. R.: Everything we needed. Well, we had everything that I can think of. The supply depot itself had its own repair shop where we repaired our own mechanical cranes, fork lifts, and so on - we had a repair shop for that because we were the biggest user. The fact is the naval air station sometimes sent a few units over to be repaired but we were a terrific user of heavy-lift equipment. We had about everything that you could think of there.

Q: Since the supply system was decentralized in a sense, why was it necessary, then, to have an outfit like Mechanicsburg in Pennsylvania?

Adm. R.: Well, Mechanicsburg came up later. That was after the war. That came into being while I was chief of the Bureau, or just before. It was the latter part of the war when that came, and they were changing their ideas then. Mechanicsburg was a ship-supply outfit. In other words, it worked practically for the Bureau of Ships — you see we were on the bureau system then -- and they handled material for everything that was under the cognizance of the Bureau of Ships.

We also had an ordnance supply depot. I've forgotten where it was.

Q: Out in the West. Wyoming, wasn't it?

Adm. R.: No. But the ship-supply there at Mechnicsburg handled all ship supplies. It was quite a big naval organization. I remember we used to have little arguments with BuShips sometimes because we didn't have enough of this or enough of that, but we always got along pretty well. We controlled the inventory on their advice, and it still works out pretty well.

Q: You just told me something off tape which was, in a sense, a summary of what went on in Norfolk when you were there.

Adm. R.: During the two years that I was in Norfolk, from 1946 to early 1948, the naval supply depot really reversed its purpose. It was receiving material from all different sources, many places, taking it in and putting it in storage, rather than shipping stuff out. Of course, we did ship material out, but far more came in than ever went out.

Q: And simultaneously, Sir, I suppose your contracts for the purchase of supplies came almost to a halt?

Adm. R.: Very little purchasing. Of course, there were certain new materials that were needed, certain materials that we didn't have in stock, but the purchasing was comparatively small to what it would be in normal times.

Q: Did you have any working relationship with ComTevFor, which was set up down there in Norfolk? This was the thing that Admiral Willis Lee set up first.

Adm. R.: I don't recall it.

Cheatham Annex was established in 1943, as I said, on a 3,100-acre site on the York River, some 30 miles from Norfolk. We had an officer-in-charge down there and had 21 one-story, modern storehouses offering 2 million square feet of net storage space. It helped us out a great deal with the storage problem when we started getting all this material back. Some of those storehouses had been empty, but we soon filled them up again with material coming back until we could dispose of it. We had a big transit shed there with 430,200 square feet and one of the world's largest cold-storage plants.

When I went down there that cold-storage plant had been closed. Immediately after the war, the need of it fell off and we closed it up. However, in 1947 we opened it up again - in November 1947. This was an instance of the way our two services worked together. The Army had been buying a lot of their meat for overseas shipment up in New York and it was costing them quite a bit of money for accumulated storage up there. They came down and wanted to know if we could give them a hand. So, we went up and looked over the storage. In the meantime, our storage down in Norfolk was not too good. It was all right for us, but by 1947 we were needing a little more for overseas shipments.

We got together with the Army and we opened up this big cold-storage plant and, over the protests of some of the Army, they came in. The Quartermaster Corps really wanted to do it because it saved them a lot of money. We had joint storage there. Reefer ships could come right up the York River, right alongside the dock, and load.

Q: That was born of necessity!

Adm. R.: That's right. We were shipping something like 4 million pounds a week out of there. Some of it went to the Army, some of it went to the Navy, went to our ships over in the Mediterranean and so on. We got along fine with them, had no trouble, and it was quite a money-saver for both services.

Q: Since you mention handling food, what is the relationship between a supply depot like that and the commissaries?

Adm. R.: The only relationship was that the commissaries would get their standard items from us. We'd just invoice them for them and they'd pay us for them. Fresh provisions and certain non-standard items they buy on contract, and they make their own contracts.

Q: But if you're buying meat in quantity they get it?

Adm. R.: Oh, yes, they get the meat from us, and get it by the quarter.

Q: This would pertain to all commissaries within a certain radius, would it?

Adm. R.: Sure, wherever they could handle it. Some of the outlying commissaries would come over with their own truck and pick it up. That could be done all right. Small amounts like sliced bacon, packaged bacon, they'd often make their own contracts for things like that.

But we were quite pleased with that work that we did with the Army and the commissaries.

While I was there I got more inspecting work. Captain W. D. Sharp, who was the Fifth Naval District's supply officer, assistant to the Commandant, retired and they gave me that job in addition to what I had. So I had the job of going round and inspecting a lot of the small units in the area.

Q: What did that mean?

Royar #4 - 180

Adm. R.: District supply officer is what it was, and it was his job in the Fifth Naval District to keep an eye on all the supply departments at the amphibious base, the supply department at the air base - air station, the Navy Yard, all the supply departments in the various naval activities in the Fifth Naval District. And at the same time I had to be an advisor on the staff of the commandant. So I had that job and I either went around or sent one of my top officers around to inspect.

Q: Would Guantanamo fall within that naval district?

Adm. R.: No, that was outside.

Q: Was that under San Juan?

Adm. R. I've forgotten what that district number is, but the Fifth Naval was strictly U.S., not overseas.

That was a very interesting job, and we had another interesting thing too, that happened while I was there.

We used to have our disbursing officer work pretty well diversified all over the district. Each supply department did its own disbursing and, as a result, there were two or three dozen accounts in the district going into the Treasury. We experimented. We had Admiral Griffith Warfield, who was the disbursing officer for the depot. We had authority from the Bureau to try it out. He did the disbursing for all of these various areas. In other words, the disbursing officer in each of these various activities was his deputy, but he ran the central accounts and his deputies worked for him. It all funneled right through one office and just one set of returns went in. We found that that saved a lot of time, saved a lot of money, and Walter Buck, who was the chief of the Bureau at that time - Walter A. Buck, Rear Admiral - came down with his people after we'd run this system for seven or eight months. He took a look at it and said, "Fine. This system will go in all over the United States. There'll be one central disbursing office for each district." He put it in effect and it's still in effect. It cut a lot of work, cut a lot of duplication.

We were very proud. Grif Warfield did a beautiful job on it. It was his baby and he did the work. We got the backing of everybody in the district and everybody seemed to like it, so it went through pretty well.

Q: On a base depot like that, what percentage of your employees would be Civil Serivce?

Adm. R.: I just happen to have that, I think. At that time when I went aboard, we had officers and enlisted men on duty, 46 officers and 20 enlisted men; and we had at that time 3,880 civilians. The peak of civilians at Norfolk was about 9,000, when it was at full strength, but they were cutting back when I got there. When I left we were down to about 2,800 or 2,500. During the war they had over 150 officers and many more enlisted men, but when I went in there it was 46 officers and 20 enlisted men and, as I say, 3,880 civilians.

Another interesting thing we had when I was there was that we outfitted a couple of expeditions for the University of California to Egypt.

Q: Into Egypt?

Adm. R.: I was just talking to Dr. Pugh down below here. He was on one of them, or went over for a while.

I got a letter from Admiral Nimitz - he, of course, was living out in Berkeley - and he said he had a young man from the University of California by the name of Wendell Phillips. I don't know whether you're ever heard of him or not?

Q: I've heard of Wendell Phillips, but not that one, I gather.

Adm. R.: The explorer? I wish I had one of his millions of dollars that he made. He didn't have a penny in his pocket when he came to Norfolk. He came to the center and Nimitz wrote to me and asked me to help him. He said that the young man was good. He'd graduated from the University and he had a fine idea and the Admiral had gotten the Navy Department to back him up in some way.

So Wendell came in and he wanted to get a lot of material. Of course, we had a lot of junk there.

Q: What was his idea? What was he going to do?

Adm. R.: He was going into Europe - to Egypt and then over into the Riff Valley and they were going to look for primeval man. They had some indications that they could find some bones, I guess, or remains of primeval man. That was the main thing. The Medical Department was sending along a detachment of doctors to study tropical medicine at the same time.

Well, Wendell came there and he was a go-getter. I know him very well. He was back here to see me only two weeks ago - two months ago. He was trying to get this expedition put together and he finally went down and got the Navy Department to give him a ship to carry his supplies over in. He needed gasoline for some of these trucks and tractors that we'd given him. And he went to Jimmy Doolittle, who was an old classmate of mine in California and I knew him quite well. Jimmy, of course, was head of the Shell Oil Company at that time, and Jimmy got him his gasoline. They put together their supplies at the Naval Supply Center at Oakland. He got everything he wanted and away he sailed.

They got over there and they did a lot of exploring. I don't know the details of it any more. He made friends in Arabia with a sheik who was head of the Arabian government and, incidentally, got some concessions for oil there, while he was over there. He completed his exploration and, in addition, he got another group under a Dr. Van L. Vanderhoot. He was a Stanford man but he went out with the second University of California group. Wendell got that one started and got that through, too. Apparently, from what Pugh was telling me, the medical people got into a row -

Q: The Navy medical people?

Adm. R: Yes - and Lamont Pugh was sent out to pour oil on the troubled waters and get them straightened out. If you ever talk to him, he's got a story about that. He was over there with this group. He knows more about the details of Wendell Phillips' group that I do because he was over there.

Q: Phillips' qualifications were simply that he was a graduate of the University? He was an anthropologist?

Adm. R.: That's right.

Q: And he got the backing of Nimitz?

Adm. R.: And he got the backing of Nomitz, and he did a good job. There's no question about it. He did a beautiful job, not only for the Navy and the government, but for himself.

Q: You say he's now worth many millions? Through oil?

Adm. R.: He got concessions over there from the Arabian outfit. Then he's got more oil down in Sumatra or Java or somewhere. His home office now is in Honolulu. He keeps two offices, one in Honolulu and one in London. He was over to see Lamont Pugh and me just before Christmas some time. He was trying to get something else out of the Navy Department. I don't know whether he ever got it or not.

Q: Did he achieve his initial intention, which was to find prehistoric man?

Adm. R.: Yes, they did, they brought a lot of samples home. What the details were I don't know, but he did do a lot for the Navy and for the government. He made friends with all these Arabians and I don't know, other tribes out there that he got to know, and he got concessions with them. When he got through with this business, then he went into the oil business and that's where he made his money. But he really made it.

Q: They weren't quite as wary in those days as they are now!

Adm. R.: No, and he did a great deal on keeping up good relationships between some of those people out there.

Another expedition was Admiral Byrd's.

Q: Oh, yes, to the Antarctic.

Adm. R.: To the Antarctic. That was in December 1946.

Q: Tell me about that. Was that the first one?

Adm. R.: I don't know whether it was the first one or not. I don't recall.

Q: But you had to outfit the expedition?

Adm. R.: He stopped by and we outfitted the expedition, and it was very interesting.

Q: Well, did you have in stock for him equipment that would stand up in the Antarctic? Or did you have to get special things?

Adm. R.: We got some special. But the funny thing was they had a lot of dogs on there and somebody nabbed three of the pups.

Q: Pilfered the pups!

Adm. R.: Three of the pups, and they had to sail off without them. I don't know how our people found them but our civilians in there were mad as hell because somebody had taken those pups. They thought it was a reflection on the depot, and they found them and had them flown down to Coco Solo and they rejoined the ship down there. Can you imagine that?

That was dog-napping for you!

We did not outfit any foreign ships but we did have a steady stream of foreign officers come through the depot. Apparently the foreign navies had learned something about our system of supply and were very anxious to learn everything they could about it, how we handled it. We had a steady stream of British, Norwegian, Swedish, Japanese, nearly all the nations - even the Japanese after the war.

Q: So soon after the war.

Adm. R.: They came through and we got so many of them that we just set up a special tour for them, and in certain cases, like the Canadian and British officers we'd have them come in and they'd stay for awhile - two or three weeks or something like that. Out in Oakland later on, we had a special billet for foreign officer, the British and the Canadians particularly would come through and they'd stay for maybe six months and, in the case of the Canadians, over a year and serve right in there just as one of our officers.

Q: What were they so anxious to learn about our system?

Adn. R.: How our distribution went, how we handled our stores. The British told me - this was a little before, while I was still in the lend-lease business, they said, "You have the greatest supply system in the world."

I said, "What do you mean? You've got a good one?"

They said, "Ours is no good."

"Why?"

"Well," they said, "our supply system is under the Civil Service. The military personnel have no part in it at all and we have to take what the civilians set-up gives us. We're never satisfied. We can't get the things we actually need. You have your people come from sea, go into a supply depot, and you have your civilians as a permanent staff, and between the two of them you get the right stuff to the right place at the right time. We can't do it."

Q: Was this a correct observation?

Adm. R.: Yes, it was, because I looked into their supply system and I had a great respect for their people, but the people who were doing the supplying had nothing to do with the ships. They knew nothing of how the material would be used at sea, or what would happen to it when it got aboard ship. Do you get my point?

Q: I do, but I should think after a period of serving there they'd learn?

Adm. R.: Well, they didn't seem to. That was where we had the advantage because our people would go to sea and come in and we could keep getting a fresh point of view all the time. And when Mr. Forrestal was talking about a fourth service of supply, which he talked about for a while, my British friends said, "My God, don't let him do it. If you do, you're finished, because we've got it. We've got a Ministry of Supply. It works but it doesn't work well."

All these people, the Canadians particularly, copied us right straight through and they liked it.

Q: So you really had a training school.

Adm. R.: We did. In Oakland we had foreign officers with us all the time.

Q: Was that because Oakland and Norfolk were showcases?

Admr. R.: No, they were just working supply depots. This, of course, was when we were still a supply depot.

Q: What motivated Forrestal to advocate the separate service?

Adm. R.: He liked the British, but he never talked to the British officers. He talked to British civilians. We fought against that and, thank God, we didn't get it. Not that the civilians aren't good.

Lord knows, we could never run these things without the civilians. They were the mainstay, the backbone, of the whole thing. But you've got to keep the customer's viewpoint in there all the time. Things change, little things change. You may get different types of things because of a change of duty or something like that. You've got to use material in the tropics, you've got to use it in the far north, and only the man who's using it really knows what's going to happen to it and whether it's worthwhile or not. And if you get the two put together which, thank God, we did, you're going to have a good supply system.

Our officers and our civilians worked fine. At least with me, there was never the slightest bit of griping. They supplemented each other all the way through and it was a very, very happy relationship, as far as I was concerned. I think it worked out very well.

Q: You were talking, at one point, about the number of civilians employed at Norfolk under your command. I would like to read onto the tape a comment made by somebody who served under you. At the time he made the comment, which was in 1954, he was Vice President of the AFGE, which is the federal employees' organization. Mr. Floyd P. Swiggett said:

> "As an employee of the Bureau of Supplies and Accounts and as the national vice president of the AFGE, I have been able to see Admiral Royar from two distinct viewpoints, and from both he has always been among the best. He has shown a warm, human concern for all employees and their interests.

In meeting on numerous problems with officers and representatives of the AFGE from many parts of the country, he has invariably been courteous, cooperative, and helpful. Not alone from a sense of duty, but because of a sincere desire to do his best for the people of the Navy family who have always meant more to him than merely an official responsibility."

What about your relationships with labor in Norfolk, labor unions.

Adm. R.: Really, I had no trouble at all with labor unions in Norfolk. We n ver had any serious times between us. We got along fine and I think the reason probably is not money but because I had some darned good supervisors. For instance, old Judge E. G. Gresham -

Q: Gresham's Law!

Adm. R.: Uh huh. The Judge was superintendent of transportation in the daytime and at nighttime he was a police judge down in Virginia Beach. He was a typical old Southern gentleman. I remember I went down one time - he invited me down - to listen in and I think that some of the stage people must have gotten a lot of his stuff because I'll never forget one night I was down there and this black man came up. The Judge looked at him and said:

"Boy, what are you up here for?"

He said, "They say I stole some stuff."

He said, "Did you do it?"

"No, Sir," and the judge said:

"Officer, what have you got to say?"

He said, "Well, I caught him coming out of the store with this stuff in his hand."

The judge said, "Boy, how old are you?"

He said, "I's 22, Sir."

He said, "You's going to be 25 when you get out!"

That was typical of the judge. I sat there that night and I laughed till the tears came to my eyes. It was the funniest thing I've ever heard. It was just like a show. But the old judge had that sense of humor, and even though he'd sentence these black boys they loved him, they liked him. They knew he'd give them a square deal.

The judge was one chap and Joe Crosswhite, who was superintendent of labor, was another fine man. He handled all the labor down there. Joe was another fine Southern gentleman, just as dignified and fine as you'll ever see. Nothing was ever allowed to get to the front office. Those two were just typical of the type of wonderful supervisors I had. They never let the boss be bothered with anything below. They were able to settle everything on the lower level and, as a result, we had just a happy family down there. It was a wonderful association. The judge is dead and gone now, and Joe Crosswhite I get a letter from him every Christmas.

Stanley Slack, the chief clerk retired while I was down there and he's dead. And Mr. Stanton, who relieved him, I hear from him.

Royar #4 - 192

We had a wonderful group and, as a result, we had no trouble. We had our own stevedores down there, Civil Service stevedores, so we had nothing to do with the union stevedores. That was another story which I'll tell you about later.

Q: That probably was a blessing, was it not?

Adm. R.: To have those Civil Service?

Q: Yes.

Adm. R.: Oh, boy! It was a wonderful group. I thoroughly enjoyed it. I had a chap by the name of MacKechnie - James MacKechnie - at the field depot over at Craney Island. That was an annex, too. He was a Scotsman and he ran that place, that was his bailiwick, and there'd be no trouble over there. He had a few people living on the island in quarters, civilians, and he ran that place and everything just went beautifully. He was really good.

We had a whole group of them there. Those are only a few of the fine people that I had. I did have this trouble. One of the men living over on MacKechnie's place, Craney Island - that was the fuel depot - claimed that MacKechnie - they had a little counter over there where they sold candy and tobacco and so on, it was an unofficial one that MacKechnie ran and he put the profits into a sort of recreation fund that they had over there. It was unofficial. It was all civilian. This man came over and claimed that MacKechnie had been stealing. Well, I got hold of MacKechnie's books and everything was strictly in order. This fellow then went to the congressman down there. The congressman later became a good friend of mine, but he came storming up and said:

"You've got a crook over there and I want him fired."

"I'm sorry, Mr. Congressman," I said, "if you want him fired you've got to make charges."

"Oh," he said, "I don't have to do that at all. If I want him fired, you fire him."

"No," I said, "I'm not but I'm going to transfer the complainant off of Craney Island. He's a troublemaker over there. I'm going to keep Mr. MacKechnie over there but this man that you're talking about, that made the complaint against Mr. MacKechnie, I am going to transfer off the island over here."

He said, "You can't do that."

I said, "I can. I'm going to do it and I'm going to do it tomorrow."

He stomped out of the office and didn't say a word. In a day or two he called me up and said:

"Admiral, I want you to come down to my office." And I said:

"Well, Mr. Congressman, I'm sorry I'm very busy now and I can't make it."

He said, "You're a stuffed shirt."

I said, "Maybe I am, but really my job is right here and if you want to talk more about Mr. MacKechnie and this other chap, I'll be perfectly willing to do it over the telephone or if you want to come out there it's all right."

He said, "I won't come out." And I said, "Well, I'm sorry."

He said, "I'm going to report you to the Navy Department."

So I said, "Well, that's all right, too. You have that right. Your man has been transferred over here and he doesn't like it but I think that will settle the whole thing. We won't have any more trouble."

In the meantime I got hold of Judge Gresham. The judge was a Byrd man. Old Senator Byrd was running Virginia at that time. I said:

"Judge, there's the situation. This congressman is newly caught, this is his first term, he's wrong and you know he's wrong."

And the judge said, "I know it, and I know MacKechnie and MacKechnie is the most honest man in the world. Admiral, you did just right. I don't think you'll hear from the Congressman any more."

I said, "Why, Judge?"

He said, "Don't ask me any questions." I never heard from him again on that subject. The old judge had enough punch to go round down there in Virginia Beach and write to Byrd and they told the congressman to lay off. That's how Virginia power went.

Q: Oh, yes. Senator Byrd's power was terrific.

Adm. R.: The next time I saw this congressman the commandant had a party. He lived right next door - that was Puggie Ainsworth, Walden L. Ainsworth. I went over to the party and here was the congressman. I went over and shook hands with him and Mabel, my wife, went and shook hands with him. I told him I was glad to see him and asked him if he wouldn't stop at the house and have a drink afterwards. By golly, he came over to our house, we had a drink, and sat down, and we never mentioned a thing. Since then we've been the best of friends.

Q: And it's never come up?

Adm. R.: Never come up. Somebody got to him, and it was through old Judge Gresham. You know, when you have things like that working for you, you can't fail! Isn't that an interesting story?

Q: It is. It's humorous, too, to think about going around behind and applying a little pressure.

Adm. R.: I knew old Judge Gresham. Everybody told me that Judge was a political power in Virginia Beach and Norfolk. There he was superintendent of transportation at the depot! That's how he got his judgeship down there at Virginia Beach. He wasn't a lawyer - no more a lawyer than I am. That was really something. But the old judge was quite a character and that really worked.

The commandant was a very fine chap, and he had a little boat called the *Katinka*. That was his own private boat. It had a diesel in it and it had a sail. One Sunday afternoon in the late fall of 1947 he called up and asked if Mabel and I would like to go with him and his wife and sail up the York River to Cheahtam Annex and back. Well, we said we'd like to go. We had a dinner party that night, but we'd be delighted to go with him.

We went down and got aboard and we sailed up the York River and got up to Cheatham Annex, got out and saw a few people, and then started back and the engine stopped. Puggie said, "We'll just put up the sail and sail down." We put up the sail and went sailing down and the wind went down, so he said, "That's all right." Mabel was getting worried. She said, "We've got this dinner party tonight – "

Q: You mean at your house?

Adm. R.: No, not at our house. We were going out somewhere. He said, "I've got a ship-to-shore phone here."

"I know," I said, "but this is Sunday. There'll be nobody there."

He said, "There'd better be someone there." So he got on the ship-to-shore phone and couldn't raise anybody at headquarters!

Q: Nobody on watch!

Adm. R.: Nobody on watch. They knew the commandant had gone. So we drifted down the river and we got into some fish nets. We couldn't get out of the fish nets. We had some poles and we tried to push her out. It got dark. We had a little lunch that we'd eaten part of, we had that, and by golly he was on the phone trying to raise headquarters and he was trying to start the engine. Nothing would work. So we had to stay on there all night.

About six o'clock in the morning he tried again and got somebody on the phone and there was the most beautiful line of language I've ever heard! Before long they had a boat over there and towed us back! I've laughed more over that. Puggie's dead and gone too, but we had a lot of fun over that. And, boy, there was a quick shift of duty people in his headquarters. Very quick! I don't think anybody neglected duty thereafter. That was great.

I had been making trips around to see different place, but they came down to us and told us in the fall - in October of 1947 - that on 1 January 1948 the depot would be recommissioned as a center - naval supply center - and that I would be the supply officer in command of the center.

Q: What did that entail? What was the change?

Adm. R.: The change was this. It centralized in the depot a lot of the functions that had been distributed around the naval base. The naval aviation depot had been over at the air station. That was brought into the center. The ordnance depot that had been part ours and part under the ordnance officer came in as a division of the depot, the ordnance depot. The administrative functions were all changed, all centralized in the center, for all these various depots and brought in, which meant reduction of force in a lot of cases and simple change in administration. It simplified the whole administration.

Oakland was already a center. They changed that from the Naval Supply Depot to the Naval Supply Center right away - or earlier in the year, rather. So I went out in November to get suggestions. Two days before I got out there my good friend, Rear Admiral John Gaffney, had a heart attack and he was in the hospital. So I was met by Dan Miller - Captain Dan Miller - the executive officer. John Gaffney knew why I was coming out. I had been in correspondence with him and told him I was coming.

Q: You mean to see what they had done?

Adm. R.: To see what they'd done and to look over their organization so that we'd be in better position to handle ours. We'd already set up a provisional organization to be used the 1st of January and I wanted to compare my provisional organization with his out there, and to see if there was anything I'd overlooked.

We spent about a week out there. John was not getting better. He was under intensive care and they let me in to see him once or twice and he very weakly told me he hoped everything would go all right. I was very much distressed, too, because he was a fine officer and a close friend.

I went back to Norfolk and, lo and behold, the day after I got back he died. That was a big shock to me because, as I told you, I'd been out in the Pacific with him when he had the supply depot at Pearl Harbor.

I went to work on the center organization and the first thing I knew the Bureau called me up and said, "You're going out to Oakland."

Q: To fill his place?

Adm. R.: To fill his place. So I went to work down at Norfolk there and we set the center up. On the 1st of January, I assumed command at the first supply officer in command of the Naval Supply Center at Norfolk.

Q: A brief command!

Adm. R.: It was a brief command. Maybe I can read into here a few things:

> "The Naval Supply Center at Norfolk has been selected for the establishment of the first naval supply center on the East Coast. Every naval item from a miniature electronic tube to an entire camp with facilities for 2,000 men will be maintained on hand ready for instant shipment. Rear Admiral Murrey L. Royar has been selected as the first commanding officer. The Naval Supply Center will embrace all personnel facilities and duties presently assigned to the Naval Supply Depot, the Naval Aviation Supply Depot, the East Coast Naval Publications Distribution Center, the accounting and disbursing officers serving the forces afloat and ashore to the Norfolk area. Naval spokesmen advise that the importance of the new activity to the port of Norfolk could not be underestimated. The Center is being established to make possible financial savings." the spokesman continued. "Although the number of civilian

employeed in the Norfolk Center will remain constant. He pointed out that reductions in personnel at the other East Coast activities previously serving Atlantic areas would be made possible by transferring those responsibilities to Norfolk. Efficiency and economy are expected to result from the single administative, planning, procurement, fiscal, medical, and service departments to perform their functions for all activities in the Center. Activities of the Center, nearly all of which were formerly independent, include the General Supply Depot, Aviation Supply Depot, Chatham Annex Depot, Publications Supply Depot, East Coast Small Craft Accounting Office, and Navy accounts disbursing officers. The Center will also include the Bureau of Ships' Supplies Depot, the East Coast Navy Freight Control Center activities are in the planning. The efficiency and loyalty of the civilian employees of the Naval Supply Services, Norfolk, were credited with a part in the decision for placing the Center in this area. They were said to have pioneered in many phases of modern material-handling and inventory control (material-handling was the palletizing). The system of mechanized stock control and accounting are being installed in all major naval supply activities were developed and proven at Norfolk, spokesmen point out."

Q: This is an article from what?

Adm. R.: The Virginian, a Norfolk newspaper, Thursday December 8, 1947.

Q: Tell me about the public relations aspect of the supply center.

Adm. R.: To my mind, the Navy never tried to sell itself. I remember in talking to Admiral King years ago that he said there's no need of public relations, our good deeds will speak for themselves.

Q: That was the prewar attitude, wasn't it?

Adm. R.: Yes, and I had the brash audactiy to tell Admiral King "they may speak for themselves, but who hears them?" He gave me a hard look and said:

"Young man, you'll learn."

Q: Well, you came from the outside.

Adm. R.: That's right. I came from the outside, and whenever I had a chance the first thing I tried to do was to sell the Navy, even way back in the Twelfth Naval District in San Francisco when I was working for Admiral Peoples, I got acquainted with all the newspaper people. Some of them I knew from College days, and whenever we had a story about the Twelfth Naval District I'd give them a call and tell them about it. I didn't worry about the PIO.

Q: You weren't taking any chances, were you?

Adm. R.: Because I had a good boss and I liked to see his picture and a little story about him in the paper. That went in the <u>Chicago</u>, when I was in her as supply officer. The skipper of the <u>Chicago</u> used to give me the job not only as golf officer, as I told you, but if there was anything that he could get in the paper about the ship it was my job to get a reporter for it, which I loved to do.

I followed that through. Of course, in the Bureau I didn't have much of a chance to do it or at the Navy Yard, but when I got to Norfolk the first thing I did was to invite the representatives of the press in, introduced myself, and had a little refreshment for them, told them that I was there, why I was there, what I hoped to do and I hoped to become an integral part of the Norfolk activities and do what I could for Norfolk as well as for the center. And I started off with good relations there.

As a result they would come out. I've got a whole flock of clippings from the Norfolk papers - or did have. Some of them I threw away unfortunately. This book was put out by the advertising people of Norfolk. I got to know them all and when they wanted a story they'd sometimes send a reporter out, but more often they'd call in and ask us to send the story in. I had two or three people who were excellent writers. One of them I mentioned sometimes before, Harry Leiser. Harry was an excellent man. He's written a novel or two since, and he's busy writing a novel now. He's retired. Harry is a good writer, and he'd sit down at a typewriter and knock out a story. I'd dictate a story to my stenographer, of course, they'd edit them when they came in. We always had something in the papers there.

Q: A supply center like that is always good for a story.

Adm. R.: Always good for a story, like that story about the dogs, that was in the station paper but that came out in -

Q: Well, there's a lot of color in such a big outfit as that.

Adm. R.: We really had a good time.

I followed the public relations up out in Oakland. The first thing I did out there was to find out that nobody knew where this naval supply center was located. Mrs. Royar and I went up town to buy some things and we asked to have it sent down to our quarters in the Oakland Supply Center, and they said: "The Naval Supply Center is over in Alameda, isn't it?"

"No," I said, "it's not over in Alameda. It's right here in Oakland."

Q: That was an immediate challenge!

Adm. R.: That was an immediate challenge and the next day I called on the Mayor. Joe Smith was the mayor at the time, and I told him that I wanted him to understand that he had a naval supply center in Oakland and that people didn't know anything about it. Well, Joe got on the phone to some of the newspapers and we started a little campaign about the naval supply center. We had several experiences there which we'll come to a little later on.

In the meantime I got back and I found that I would be leaving around the 18th of January, so I buttoned everything up at the naval supply center in Norfolk. I was very much pleased that I could be the first supply officer in command. I was relieved by Rear Admiral T. Earl Hipp on 12 January, and started out that afternoon to drive across to the West Coast. We had a very nice trip across and we arrived in Oakland, Mrs. Royar and I, on the 3rd of February.

Well, the first thing that I found there was a telegram from the Chief of the Bureau, Rear Admiral E. D. Foster, who said, "Don't unpack until you talk to me."

Interview No. 5 with Vice Admiral Murrey L. Royar, U. S. Navy (Retired)

Place: His residence in McLean, Virginia

Date: 25 April 1973

Subject: Biography

By: John T. Mason, Jr.

Q: Actually, Admiral, last time we broke off almost in the middle of a sentence, so suppose we go back to the beginning of the sentence. You'd arrived in Oakland, California, on the 3rd of February 1948.

Adm. R.: We arrived in the afternoon of February 3rd and, as we went in the gate, I was told that there was an important message waiting for me from Admiral Foster, the Chief of the Bureau.

We went over to our assigned quarters, and I went to the office immediately. The message said, "Do not unpack until you have talked to me." Well, that give me quite a shock because I had looked forward to four years at the Naval Supply Center, Oakland.

Q: In your mind, you were already - ?

Adm. R.: Yes, I was already unpacked. Anyway, I got him just as he was leaving his office in Washington and he said:

"Murf, you're coming back here as my assistant."

I said, "Wait a minute. I just got here and I don't want to go back."

"Well," he said, "I'd like to have you come back as my assistant."

I said, "Dorsey, I can do a lot better job right here in Oakland for the Navy and for everybody else and I'd be more satisfied if you'd let me stay here."

We argued for about ten minutes over long distance and finally he, in disgust, said; "All right, stay there. I'll get somebody else."

So I went home and felt very good about it, and I got ready to take over the next day.

Well, the next day came and I was sworn in and then went over to San Francisco to report to Admiral Beary, Com, Twelve, and Admiral Beary said, "What are you doing here?"

I said, "I came to take over command of the center."

Q: Was this Bernard Beary?

Adm. R.: No. This was D. P. B-e-a-r-y.

Q: Oh, I see.

Adm. R.: He said, "I didn't ask for you. I wanted Dan Miller to stay here." Captain Miller had taken command during the interim between Admiral Gaffney's death and my arrival. We talked a while, and he said:

"Well, I guess there's nothing I can do about it, so go ahead."

With those two things to start with, I didn't think it was a very auspicious beginning, especially as there'd been a lot of talk around that my previous trip out had probably caused Admiral Gaffney's death. That he was upset and he was afraid that I was going to relieve him soon.

Anyway, we finally got started and I made my first tour of the center and spent a week or ten days, I guess, looking things over. The center, of course, is in Oakland, California, right next to the Oakland Army Base. It has about 533 acres, all of which were submerged on the 1st of January 1940 when they started dredging to fill in for it. It was commissioned on the 31st December 1941, shortly after Pearl Harbor. So they did a quick job getting it constructed.

I went up to see the fuel line at Port Richmond, California, which is north of Oakland, on the site of old Winehaven. Winehaven was probably the biggest winery that they had in California before Prohibition and they tried to keep going by selling grape juice after it, but the grape juice didn't go over very well. It was deserted and the Navy took it over. They had about 566 acres up there, and they had four 27,000- barrel avgas tanks underground and twenty 50,000-barrel fuel oil tanks. It, of course, was the place to furnish fuel for all of our Navy ships that came in. They went up there to the pier and loaded or it was barged down below and they took it off the barges.

Q: How did that compare with other supply bases in terms of storage?

Adm. R.: You mean as far as fuel goes?

Q: Yes.

Adm. R.: It was one of the largest, and, of course, we had the advantage of being right next to Standard Oil's big storage base there, too.

Q: So you had an auxiliary.

Adm. R.: We had an auxiliary. We had connecting pipelines between the two and we would get our fuel either by barge or, if Standard happened to have the contract, we'd just run it through the pipeline over there.

I also went up to Stockton, which is about 50 or 60 miles to the east of Oakland, to Stockton Annex. They had about 1,500 acres up there and had a big marginal pier and oceangoing ships could get up there. It was a slow journey because the channel was narrow and they were only allowed to go up at slow speeds, otherwise the wash would go all over everything and do damage to the land and the people on the sides of the channel. It was a good operation up there. That was our backup for Oakland.

When I got there it was, of course, shortly after World War II, three years afterwards, and they were in the process of cutting down. That was the first thing I went into, was to try to consolidate and take care of the work with a reduced personnel. One of the first things that I ran up against there in the fall of 1948 and early 1949 was a strike. Mr. Bridges of the ILWU - Harry Bridges - called a stevedores' strike. We knew it was coming and we were a little bit worried about how it was going to affect us, so before it started we started organizing some stevedore gangs of our own. These men were black, most of them, and were 99 percent veterans which, as you'll see later, was a pretty good thing. We didn't use them until the strike actually came on.

The thing that made it so hard to handle, in a way, is the fact of the way you hire stevedores. There are stevedore companies and you make a contract with a stevedore company. The stevedore company goes to the hiring hall and picks up their gangs there and transports them to the job.

The first thing I did when I got there was argue with Mr. Bridges about that because they had a perfectly good hiring hall in Oakland that they didn't use. All of our stevedores had to come from the San Francicso hiring hall, which meant that we had to pay them from the the time they left the hiring hall till they got into the Center.

Q: Portal to portal!

Adm. R.: Portal to portal, and the thing that irritated me was that 90 percent of their stevedores got in the buses just outside of our gates. They lived on the East Bay anyway, but we still had to pay them from San Francisco.

Q: One of those little featherbedding things!

Adm. R.: One of those featherbedding things. You get the point, don't you?

Q: Oh, yes.

Adm. R.: I might say that I got to know Mr. Bridges quite well.

Q: He was an Englishman, was he not?

Adm. R.: Australian. He'd come over to my office and bring a couple of his rough-looking people with him to discuss things. He was a pretty smooth-talking person. We'd get into some of these arguments and I'd say to Mr. Bridges:

"Now, Mr. Bridges, you and I had better cool down a little bit, so come on in and have a cup of coffee," and I'd take him into my inner office. There we could talk perfectly freely without any witnesses. We got along all right.

Q: Did that change his manner any?

Adm. R.: Oh, yes, sure. He'd talk more freely to me. And I will say for him, although I know he's a Communist and I have no sympathy with the way he thinks along that line - I say he's a Communist -

Q: He so stated, didn't he?

Adm. R.: He so stated, and I have no sympathy there, but I will say that he never lied to me. If he ever made me a promise or said he'd do something, he infallibly kept his word. He was one man in that group there that I had no doubt about at all. If I got a promise, I didn't have to have it in writing. He'd carry it out.

Q: How heavily were you dependent on the employment of stevedores other than government people?

Adm. R.: We had no government stevedores at that time at all. The policy of the government after the war was that we would use commercial stevedores. So we had an annual contract with a stevedoring company and they would furnish us union contractors. When the strike broke, I'll never forget —

Q: What were the issues?

Adm. R.: Wages and vacation pay, hours, such things as that. But there was a long strike, and Mr. Bridges came over when the strike broke and he said:

"Now, we're striking. We have nothing against the government. We like to help them out all we can. But I want you to make a contract with the union of stevedores."

I said, "Mr. Bridges, I can't do that. Your union is not a commercial company, it has no standing as far as commerce goes, and I can't do it. The only thing I can do is to go — if you will not furnish the company that I have a contract with for stevedores — then I've got to go to the government for stevedores, the Civil Service."

Well, he didn't like that and we argued a little bit. In the meantime, a ship came in from the East Coast. This was before our stevedore gangs had come in and he stopped. The ship came in and it was manned by men belonging to the "Sailors Union of the Pacific" whose President was Harry Lundberg. I don't know whether you've heard of him or not.

Q: Indeed, yes.

Adm. R.: Well, it came in there and I worried. In the meantime, the Army had gotten some sort of a haywire contract with the unions. They were right next door to us.

Q: They did what he suggested?

Adm. R.: Yes. I wouldn't do it. I said, "How about unloading this ship for me? I have no stevedores here." And they said, "No, we wouldn't touch that with a ten-foot pole. We'd get in trouble with Mr. Bridges."

I said, "What do you care about Mr. Bridges for?"

"Well, we have orders to use commercial stevedores and we've got them now and we're going to use them."

So I said, "All you're doing is helping the strike out. You're just paying these fellows off so they can strike."

He said, "That's what we were told to do."

Well, this ship came in, so I got Harry Lundberg on the phone and said, "Can you come over? I'd like to see you."

Q: Did you know him?

Adm. R.: Sure, I'd worked with him. He said, "Tsure, tsure," He was an old Norwegian, and he came over. He and all his men wore white hats or white caps. He said:

"What's the matter?"

I said, "Well, you see that ship down there?" He says, "Yeah, my men are on that ship, my sailors of the Pacific."

I said, "I want to get it unloaded."

"Well," he says, "why don't you unload it?"

"I've got no stevedores. I haven't got any trained yet into gangs for Civil Service."

He said, "God damn. Bridges, he won't let you unload it?"

I said, "No." So he says:

"To hell with him. I go down there and tell my men to unload it." And, sure enough, he went down and he had -

Q: The crew!

Adm. R.: He had the crew unload it for us! Bridges was madder than hell about that and he came storming over and he said:

"You can't do that. Lundborg had no business." The story was that Lundborg and Bridges were after the same girl in San Francisco and they hated each other, and I lucky enough to play one against the other!

Q: Without knowing!

Adm. R.: Without knowing. So I got that unloaded

Q: Labor relations!

Adm. R.: And then Bridges came up and he said:

I'm going to have to picket the Army over here." They'd done something he didn't like. "And he said I think I'm going to picket you."

I said, "What for?"

"Well," he said, "you won't use my men."

I said, "Tomorrow, our stevedores are going to start working the ship that comes in here."

He said, "I think I'm going to have to picket you. What are you going to do about it?"

"Mr. Bridges," I said, "I haven't the slightest idea. I'll tell you when you've put the pickets around here. I've got a company of Marines up here in barracks, many of whom served in the South Pacific, but I don't know what I'm going to do. You have a perfect right to picket, but I'll tell you this, it's not going to stop any material going through here."

He said, "Well, I think I might have to picket you."

I said, "That's up to you, Harry. I'm not trying to do anything about it." We never had a picket, not a one!

Q: He slept on that!

Adm. R.: He slept on that one. But the old Captain of the ship that had his crew unloading, belonged to Lundborg's union. He was a character, the captain was. After they'd been in there for a day or so while they were unloading, just before he left he came up to my office. He had carpet slippers on and an old coat, a funny old fellow. He said:

"Will you take that damned telephone off of my ship?"

I said, "Why? I always put a telephone on a ship for the convenience of the captain - all these commercial ships that come in - so that they can use it. That's perfectly all right."

"Oh," he said, "it's not that, but somebody wakes me up in the middle of the night and, God dam it, they're always telling me they're going to get me and beat me up. I'm getting tired of hearing it. They're not going to touch me. They're not going to bother me, but they do wake me out of my sleep and I want my sleep."

Q: That was his only concern?

Adm. R.: That was his only concern.

Q: You said you trained some men for stevedores?

Adm. R.: Yes, we trained the men -

Q: And then they were blanketed under Civil Service?

Adm. R.: They were under Civil Service. We hired them as stevedores. We trained our own gangs, and had our own gangs right down there in the Center.

Q: What was their status vis-a-vis a union?

Adm. R.: They're just like any Civil Service employee, just like a mechanic. They came under the blue-collar per diem people, you see. There was no trouble there at all.

All this time, ComTwelve and the Secretary of the Navy had kept out of it. Bridges had threatened. He said, "I'm going to get you fired out of this job."

I said, "Fine, if you want to fire me, it's all right. Go back and see the Secretary. It doesn't worry me."

I found out later they did go back to the Secretary and Dan Kimball didn't give them much satisfaction. I think it was Dan Kimball at that time. It was the Secretary, anyway.

He kept after me. He tried to get me to fix it up so that he could use his men, and I said, "No, I'm not going to hire your men while you're striking. I'll be favoring you over the contractors. I'm in the middle. I'm not going to favor you and I'm not going to favor the contractors. You work it out and when your strike's settled come back and maybe I'll talk to you."

Q: Actually, in normal times, these men were also hired by the contractors, were they?

Adm. R.: Whose? Bridges'?

Q: Yes.

Adm. R.: His men were always hired by the contractors. His men were the only source the contractors had.

Q: Then, why did he want to undercut the contractors?

Adm. R.: Because of the strike. He was striking against the contractors. That was the thing.

Q: That he'd get more favored terms with the government?

Adm. R.: Right. What would happen was, he was striking against the contractors, and the contractors also furnished stevedores to Matson Line, American Steamship, and all the commercial lines. So what he was virtually doing was striking against the ship-owners, because they couldn't move their ships. You get the point. And if I hired his stevedores, all I would be doing would be paying them daily wages so they wouldn't suffer during the strike, and he would get the credit of helping the government, you see.

Q: You'd be paying what is now unemployment compensation?

Adm. R.: That's right. That's exactly what it was, and I wouldn't do it. He said, "I'm going to see that you do it." He went back and they had quite a session, but I never heard a word from ComTwelve or the Secretary of the Navy or anybody. They left me on my own.

This went on and in 1949, a number of weeks later, the strike finally broke. In the meantime, I'd carried on a study of the costs, and my costs - I've forgotten the figures now - for my Civil Service stevedores were so far under per ton that I didn't want to give them up. I didn't want to go back to Bridges. The minute the strike was over Bridges came back and said:

"You've got to use my stevedores again." And I said:

"I don't think I will, not until I'm told to."

"Well," he said, "you did before the strike. There's no reason why you shouldn't now."

I said, "Listen, I've got seven or eight good gangs of men here, and I can do it cheaper. You won't start this hiring hall over here in Oakland, I don't want to pay that portal to portal pay. This is cheaper."

He said, "Oh, it isn't cheaper. I can prove it. I've got the figures. I'm going to go back to Washington."

Well, in a week or two, a fellow showed up at my office, showed me his credentials, and said:

"I'm from the Department of Labor. I understand that you're using Civil Service stevedores instead of using commercial?"

I said, "Yes."

"Why are you doing this?"

"Well," I said, "I hired them during the strike, they're doing a good job, and I'm saving the government a lot of money."

"Well," he said, "maybe you're saving them a few dollars, but think of all those men that you're putting out of work"

I said, "What would I do with my own stevedores if I fired them?"

He didn't know. So I said:

"You'd better go down and take a look at what these men are doing." He said he'd never seen stevedores before, so I turned him over to my big boss stevedore who was black as the ace of spades and one of the finest men I ever knew. He was a good boss.

He took him down there and took him all around to see all these men and showed him how they were working. The fellow came back and said:

"Admiral, you've got a fine crew down there. The best morale in that crew of any I've seen in a long time."

I said, "That's this boss stevedore I've got, he's the one who's doing it. You don't blame me for not wanting to give them up?"

He said, "No, but I'm going to have to recommend that you go back to commercial stevedores."

I said, "I'm sorry to hear that, but I want you to remember this. Ninety-nine percent of those men are veterans. They belong to the American Legion, the Veterans of Foreign Wars, all these veterans' societies, and the first time the word comes out that I've fired them to let Harry Bridges' men come in here, you're going to have to explain it, not me."

He said, "I never thought about that," he went out, and I never heard anything more about it.

Q: They, too, had a clout politically, did they?

Adm. R.: Sure did. What happened was that we reduced our stevedores so that we had just enough to do the average work. In other words, we had so many ships coming in and we knew how many we could keep actively at work. You see, the stevedore gangs, if there are no ships there's no work for them, and when there was no work, we'd have to turn them onto other jobs, labor jobs, that were not in their category. And, of course, if we'd done that, Mr. Bridges would have been after me and quite properly so.

So what I did was to keep just enough Civil Service to do the average work and if we had any peaks, then I would bring in the commercial stevedores.

Q: What was the wisdom of the federal decision to hire commercial ones, rather than to maintain their own staff?

Adm. R.: At that time there was a lot of unemployment and the policy at that time was to keep the government out of business, and whenever you could farm out things to the civilian economy, you were supposed to do it.

Q: But you're employing men either way.

Adm. R.: You're employing men either way, but there was less sin in employing them from the civilian end than there was from our end - than as a government employee. I had a little argument with the Department on that one, too, and that was the compromise we came to. The Department did want me to cut out the Civil Service, but when I'd given the figures and showed them how I was saving money by using the Civil Service stevedores, then that was a different story. They didn't have much to argue about.

But, in order to keep Bridges quiet, I used the peak people from the commercial stevedores, and that seemed to work out all right.

Q: You say that almost all of your Civil Service stevedores were black men and veterans of war.

Adm. R.: Yes.

Q: Were they part of the contingent of black people who came to the Oakland area during the war? There was a great influx, I understand, from the South.

Adm. R.: That's right. That is why that whole East Bay area is so black at the present time. It all started with the shipyards up at Richmond, California. It started during the war. They opened these shipyards where they were building the merchant ships. They had no labor and the people who ran the shipyards imported blacks from the South. That was where that big bunch of blacks came from. Unfortunately, they didn't bring the best blacks. Most of these people were field hands.

Q: They were rural people?

Adm. R.: They were rural people, not very well educated, and, as a result, at the end of the war when the shipyards closed down a lot of these people were out of jobs. And we at the center were one of the biggest employers of blacks in the whole area. We had a big contingent of blacks, and that was one of our problems, too. Fortunately, I had one of the best industrial relations men that I could get. That was Stub Allison. Stub was an ex-coach of the University of California football team.

Q: What was his real name?

Adm. R.: Leonard B. Allison, known affectionately among the whole Bay area as "Stub."

Well, Stub had the greatest influence over these blacks of anybody I've ever seen. Many of them said:

"Well, anything that Mr. Stub says is all right by me."

But, speaking about the intelligence of them and the education, we did have a lot of trouble with some of the blacks. They just wouldn't work and they were full of sick leave or they'd take leave without pay and you'd have to fire them once in a while. Of course, the minute you fired them the cry was that it was racial. But we had Stub Allison there, and over in Oakland I had a classmate of mine from California by the name of Walter Gordon. Walter is black and he was formerly governor of the Virgin Islands, but at that time he had his law office in Oakland. Stub and I would get these cases where we knew that we were justified in firing, there was nothing racial in it, and we'd get Walter on the phone and say:

"Walter, we've got so-and-so here and we've got to fire him. This is the case," and we'd give him the facts, and Walter would say,

"Forget it. I'll take care of it." He was very high in the NAACP there. We never had any fuss at all. If Walter had any questions at all, we could discuss it with him, and we had no racial troubles whatsoever on this. Only, as I say, some of these people tried to kick up trouble, but with Walter Gordon sitting over in Oakland, there was no trouble at all.

It was a very interesting session there at that time. We were handling a lot of these things that came up. I thoroughly enjoyed it.

Q: Labor relations were a large part of your -

Adm. R.: Oh, labor relations were wonderful. After I got back here and was Chief of the Bureau I got to know Bill Schnitzler over in CIO. He used to be secretary. That was later on, but I got to know him quite well. I was entertained at their house and they'd come to my house. If we had any labor troubles, we'd get Mr. Schnitzler. I've fortunately never had any trouble with any labor people. It was my experience that if you had a good story and you were telling the truth and if you played fair with them, you had nothing to worry about. I had no trouble.

Q: I'm delighted that you showed me those various letters of commendation for the manner in which you handled the labor situation there at the base in Oakland.

Well, Sir, tell me about some of your other problems out in

Oakland.

Adm. R.: In the year of 1949 I had very few problems. We knew that Korea was going to come on and we were readjusting our organization. Although we were reducing all the time, we knew we were going to have a big problem if it ever broke, and we were trying to get adjusted so that we could handle it. Of course, the thing broke in 1950. In June 1950, almost as the President put out his message, we were told to get busy and support the fleet and support everybody. In just a short period of time eleven ships taken out of reserve in the upper Bay up around Stockton - they had them in the river up there -

Q: Were these warships?

Adm. R.: No, these were commercial ships that were going to be operated by the MSTS as transports and also as cargo ships. And, brother, if we didn't have a time. We had to completely outfit those - mattresses, bunks, everything. They'd been stripped clean, you see, before they'd been put up there. And we scoured the whole place. Fortunately, we'd built up a pretty good set of information so that we knew where we could buy, lot buy, and get a lot of this material.

That was really the big problem we had there in 1950. The work of the Center jumped up over 100 percent, and by that time we were getting authority to increase our work force. But I think the preliminary work that we did - and it wasn't at my instigation by far - I fortunately had pulled some of the very, very fine younger officers I had had with me in various places in key spots. These young men helped me reorganize and consolidate.

A naval supply center is made up of several depots - the general supply depot, the ordnance depot, the ships' parts depot, and one or two others. The ordnance depot was a new one. They'd just given that to us in late 1949 and we had gotten our stock for it from Mare Island and some from the East Coast. The idea was that the center would be composed of these several depots, and each depot would more or less run independently. Well, that was good in theory, but the trouble was that, for instance, in GSD, the General Supply Depot, they had four or five different offices scattered around. The ordnance depot had some offices scattered around. Each depot was doing its own packing. A lot of the common services were done under the control of each depot, which we eliminated. We made an administrative department that handled all of the inventory for the whole center and the packing for the whole center, and a freight transshipment branch that did all the shipping for the entire center. We pulled out and consolidated all the common services - services that were common to each depot.

Q: To avoid all this duplication?

Adm. R.: To avoid duplication. And these young men that I had were fine. They did a beautiful job for me, and I gave them free rein to do it.

Q: Didn't they run into trouble' There were a lot of empires there, were there not?

Adm. R.: Oh, sure there were empires, but everybody was so darned busy they didn't have time to interfer. We were on a six-day week at that time.

Q: That was the time to do it!

Adm. R.: That was the time to do it. Nobody had time to fuss around about it. The thing was to get it done.

Some of the preliminary work we had done before the big break, but when the big break came we were on a six-day week, even working overtime on Sundays. It was a terrific job.

Q: Why was this federated system permitted to develop?

Adm. R.: Well, you see the supply center concept was new - when I was at Norfolk I had just converted that activity into a supply center. There were various depots and in a naval supply depot you maybe had only one depot with a few departments. For instance, you'd have the depot there and you'd have one department for ordnance, and one department for general supplies, and so on. But with a center the concept was, as it had been defined, that each of these subjects would have a depot of its own, a federated depot. Each individual depot would be more or less independent under the commanding officer. But we found out that that didn't work well. It worked, but it was cumbersome and was expensive, and it didn't work easily.

So we pulled out a lot of the common services from each depot.

As I said, we started the administration department that controlled the inventories, the machine records, and all those common services. Then we started a study of the shipping functions. Each of these depots would have their own shipping divisions. We pulled all those out and made a transshipment branch, which took all the shipping from each and every depot. That was a case of trying to save labor and cut expense.

Then we had a General Services Department which took care of the labor and the mechanical equipment. Each depot used to have its own and we soon cleared that out and got that squared away. We got it centralized and controlled so that we knew what and where the control was.

Q: It must have been much more satisfying for the CO?

Adm. R.: Oh, sure it was, you knew what was going on. Before, you had a mass of records there, duplicating records, so that you didn't know what was going on.

That was all evolution, and the supply center concept as it is now is an excellent thing. It's efficient and can get things done. During 1950, we took over a lot of extra things. For instance, we established a biological laboratory in the Oakland Center.

Q: Well, you talk about it, will you?

Adm. R.: It was under Naval Research, NRL, and they had a contract with the University of California to make a study of biological warfare, and they didn't know where to put it. So they came down to the Center and asked me if we could find a place for them. Fortunately we had three old buildings that we could let them have and they started up the biological laboratory.

Q: That was in the days when you didn't have a lot of protesters as a result?

Adm. R.: Yes, and you know I learned a lot about biological warfare and what could be done. They worked with rats and they had mice, monkeys, and other animals. And they were studying the winds so that they could throw stuff up in the air and let it float back over the country, or they could spread disease, and that sort of thing that way. It was a very secret operation, and very few people ever knew that we had that on our center. I imagine a lot of our employees if they knew what went on would have felt a little squeamish about it.

Q: The plagues that were being manufactured there!

Adm. R.: It was under my command, but, of course, under the control and direction of Naval Research.

Then we had to take over all the old Army transports - supported them. The Army used to have its own transport system. Now it's merged into MSTS, and it was in 1950 that the Army transports were turned over to MSTS. During all this time we had to go over to Fort Mason and pick up all of the spare parts that they had over there, all their equipment, and bring it over and establish a section where we could service the transports and set up an organization to do it.

And then Yards and Docks had no depot there. Yards and Docks had their spares for automotive and material-handling equipment scattered all over the district. Mare Island had some, Hunter's Point had some, Alameda Air Station had some. Each activity had a little store of these spare parts and material for handling automotive spares. We had to pick all those up. And we established under the General Supply Depot a Yards and Docks section, where we had to handle all those spare parts for the entire district. That gave us a little something to do there.

Then, of course, there came into effect our mutual defense assistance program. That started. We had set up a specific requisition control organization to handle all incoming requisitions from the Pacific. They'd screen them through there and follow them through the center to see that they were filled and got out. So we put this mutual assistance group right in with them.

Q: Will you talk a little about that?

Adm. R.: About what?

Q: This mutual assistance group.

Adm. R.: That was a group that handled all the requests from the Pacific from foreign countries for mutual assistance.

Q: Those who were involved with the United Nations in Korea?

Adm. R.: That's right. The Philippines, South Korea, Japan and a little bit, not much.

Q: Yes, and some of the Latin-American republics - Colombia and others.

Adm. R.: Yes. But we didn't have so much of that. Ours was mainly the Pacific, our allies that we had in the Pacific at that time. Australia got some. They were out there with us.

All of their requests funneled through our Center there and we had this one organization to check them and see if they were ok.

Q: In other words, it was a United Nations force fighting in Korea, but it was all supplied by the United States?

Adm. R.: Most of it by the United States. They had some of their own supplies but what they couldn't get we gave them.

Q: Did you have any problems with some of the things for their ships, which weren't exactly standard?

Adm. R.: We had to do a lot of special procurement for them, although, strange to say, for ships' parts they could go into Japan pretty much and get what they needed for their ships out there - these non-standard parts. Of course, our own standard parts for our ships we handled here.

Then, of course, we had to start up again our clothing-impregnation plant. In conjunction with that we had a contract with San Quentin prison to renovate and repair all of these items of special clothing that you have aboard ship.

Q: You mean fireproof clothing?

Adm. R.: Fireproof clothing and all that sort of thing. We had this contract with them and they did a good job for us over there. They'd clean it up, repair, and send it back in good shape, then we'd impregnate whatever we had to and put it back in stock. That worked out very well. It gave the men up there something to do and it helped us out an awful lot. There was no manufacturing, it was simply repairing and renovating and cleaning and that sort of thing.

Q: This was material left over from World War II?

Adm. R.: Some of it, yes, and material that was sent in there by ships that needed repair and renovating. It'd go through up there in San Quentin, and then we'd re-impregnate it and send it in.

Q: In the field of ordnance, were you getting any new items to replace World War II types?

Adm. R.: Some, yes, although we still had plenty of World War II items at that time.

Q: But some of that was then inadequate, was it not? I was thinking in terms of mines.

Adm. R.: We didn't handle mines. They had a mine depot over on the San Francisco side. We didn't handle mines at all. Most of ours were firearms, all sorts of firearms, small guns. We had a gun repair shop there where we repaired small arms and renovated those right there on the premises. Quite a big operation.

Q: Indeed it was. You must have had to work 24 hours to keep abreast of it or on top of it?

Adm. R.: It was. 1950 and 1951 were practically all six-day weeks. It was really good.

We started a regional disbursing office there like we had at Norfolk, and we put a branch up at Stockton because it was far away. Otherwise, we had a regional disbursing office that did the disbursing for the whole area.

Did I ever tell you about our coffee plant there in Oakland?

Q: No.

Adm. R.: We were talking the other day about the coffee plant in Honolulu. The one in Honolulu that I told you about was designed and started by Lieutenant Commander John Howard Wilkins, of the Wilkins Coffee Company of Washington, and he later was back over here at Oakland running our coffee plant for us.

Wilkins was quite a remarkable young man. Unfortunately, he died in 1967. His wife, Anne Wilkins, is still running the Wilkins Coffee Company plant in Washington. She's very proud of what he did, and we are, too. I tell you he did a great deal for me from the coffee standpoint. He helped us. He was the one who really got us into shipping coffee in five-gallon vacuum tins. Coffee is a peculiar thing. Did I tell you the story about how we finally got to a single brand of coffee?

Q: No.

Adm. R.: That goes back and I was mixed up in that right along. The West Coast coffee all came from Central America. The East Coast coffee came from Brazil, mostly. A man on the East Coast was transferred to the West Coast would get Central American coffee instead of Brazilian aboard ship and to him it's slop, no good, he doesn't like the taste of it. A man from the West Coast goes to the East Coast and gets the Brazilian coffee, and it's just the reverse. It takes him a long time to acquire a taste for the new brew.

Q: You mean to say that the taste buds of the average citizen are that cultivated?

Adm. R.: With sailors it was, believe me. We got more complaints from men going from one coast to the other and having to put up with the coffee that they had. The Army had the same trouble.

Q: They would be more so now, because wherever you go coffee's poor.

Adm. R.: It's about the same. Well, it wasn't then, and there's a funny thing about this coffee business. The Navy got into the coffee-roasting business because the big roasters wouldn't bother with it. I know because I talked with the roaster. The only people who would roast coffee for the Navy in bulk were the small producers and they were terrible. They'd steal, mix up the blends, and everything else. It was terrible.

Q: Why wouldn't the big outfits do it? Was that not in their normal process?

Adm. R.: No, they had enough to do with their own coffee. They didn't want to run the Naval coffee through. It interfered with their runs, and they wouldn't touch it. Hills Coffee in San Francisco, I begged them to take it but they wouldn't touch it. When I was with Admiral Peoples there in the 12th Naval District in 1929 and 1930, he had me working on that. He was a great coffee drinker. We just couldn't get the coffee roasters to do it, so that was the reason that when Oakland opened up they put in a coffee-roasting plant. We had one other plant, which was in Brooklyn. And for a long time roasted all the coffee for the Navy. They even shipped it to the West Coast at times.

The coffee, if you kept it in beans, would hold its flavor prettywell, but they were grinding it and putting it in sacks, oil-lined burlap - I don't know whether it was plastic or some sort of lining - and it soon lost its flavor and took on another. That wasn't satisfactory.

We had Wilkins get on this thing early in the war, when he first came in. Commercially, they'd been vacuum-packed and I guess it was up to about No. 10 tins or something like that. He worked it out and we got it in five-gallon cans, about 20 pounds to the gallon - no 20 pounds to the can, vacuum-packed - ground coffee and it carried fine. But in the meantime, we were working on a blend of Central American and Brazilian, and had one blend for both coasts. And then they raised hell on both coasts, when that went into effect!

Q: Naturally. You had diluted both!

Adm. R.: Sure. But once they got used to it we had no more trouble, because they got the same coffee on either coast.

That roasting plant in Oakland put out around 70,000 pounds a day. It was a beautiful plant. They have since stopped it, and they've got the commercial people doing it. The commercial people found out how big a job it was and they protested that they could do it better, so they let them go back to it. We had three plants in operation there for a while, Brooklyn, Oakland, and Honolulu.

Q: What about the tea supply for the Navy, while we're on the topic of beverages?

Adm. R.: The Navy never drank much tea. We carried a little tea for iced tea, but hot tea, no. We had our trouble with the tea in Asbury Park with the British. They had to have their tea in the afternoon.

But I want to give John Wilkins a good mark on that coffee plant because he did a wonderful job for the Navy. I've talked with his wife here since I saw you and she said that he was very proud of the work he did for the Navy and enjoyed it very, very much. But you've heard of Wilkins Coffee here in Washington.

In May 1950 we had Armed Forces Day out here. We joined with the Army and we put on quite a show. This picture here will give you a little idea of how we organized and had a parade. The Navy Supply Center and the Oakland Army Base adjoined each other and they could go from one to the other. We opened the gates and let them through.

Q: This was in the spring of the year?

Adm. R.: Yes, it was in May 1950, before the Korean incident. We had over 100,000 people in there on that Sunday that we had it.

I didn't tell you, did I, about the time when I first got in to Oakland and talked about public relations?

I went up town to buy some things, my wife and I did, for our quarters and we opened a charge account and they said, "Now where do you live?" We said, "At the Naval Supply Center."

"Oh, yes, that's over in Alameda, isn't it?"

"My Lord, don't you know what you've got in your own city here?"

That made me mad, so I went back and I got my PIO, a good guy by the name of Ed Bear, and said:

"Ed, we've got to teach these people where we live, where our Center is."

Ed got right on it and we got Senator Knowland's paper –

Q: The Oakland Tribune.

Adm. R.: Yes, the Oakland Tribune, and we had an evening paper, too. I've forgotten what it was now. We got all of their staff down there and we took them around the center and got them to run quite a story on the Center and emphasize that it was in Oakland.

Q: Did you have any dealings with Knowland himself?

Adm. R.: Oh, yes. I knew Knowland very well. In fact, we're both members of the same Shrine Temple, the Ahmes Temple.

I used to go over to see Admiral Beary in the early days and we got to be very good friends. He said, "You're doing a good job over there," and I said, "Thank you very much." Then he said:

"I want you to be my PIO for the East Bay. Take all of my responsibilities for the East Bay."

I said, "What do you mean?"

"Well," he said, "I can't get over there very often, and there's lots going on in East Bay. We need somebody who will get around and show the Navy flag."

Q: You mean at all the public events?

Adm. R.: The public events. He said, "I want you to take that over."

"Oh," I said, "no. I'm very happy to do it but I've got a big job on my hands."

He said, "I know you have, but I want you to do that and I also want you to be my representative for the Naval Reserve. Anything that goes on in the Naval Reserve - if you have to establish any units, it's going to be up to you to get them established."

I said, "For line, too?"

"For line and everything."

Q: He must have been in the process of retiring!

Adm. R.: He was. He was a nice chap, though. I like him. Well that gave me quite a good deal to do around there, too.

Q: It involved you in a lot of social life?

Adm. R.: A lot of social life. But, of course, I got very well acquainted with the mayor, Joe Smith at first, and then Cliff Rishell was mayor most of the time I was there. Cliff was always having me out for something up at the City Hall, and he spent a great deal of his time down at the Center. He used to love to come down, go over to the club. We had some slot machines there, and he loved to play the slot machines. Anything the Center wanted around the city we had no trouble at all. We were flying high and had a wonderful time.

My executive officer woke me up one morning and said:

"Admiral, we're in trouble."

I said, "What's the matter?"

"Well," he said, "they had a fire on one of the ships down at the pier, a commercial cargo ship," it didn't amount to very much but he said, "a newspaper reporter from Richmond was down and he insisted on going aboard and I wouldn't let him."

So I said, "Well, what about it?"

He said, "I kicked him out. Didn't want him in the Center."

"Well," I said, "you shouldn't have done that. You should have taken him down to the ship and let him see the darned thing if he wanted to. Not let him go aboard necessarily unless the captain wanted him to go aboard. There's no harm in that."

"I didn't," he said, "I guess I should have, but we were in such a mess getting the fire department down there and putting out the blaze and I got a little rough with him."

The next day this Richmond paper came out with a big story about how their news people were refused entrance into the Center when there was a fire going on -

Q: Curbing the freedom of the press!

Adm. R.: Curbing the freedom of the press. Then the Oakland evening paper - I've forgotten the name of it - came out with a big story on the same thing. The Tribune never bothered me. They did have a little story, but I knew the city editor of the Tribune and I went up to see him and said:

"Now listen, I'm in bad with these people. What can I do about it?"

He said, "Why don't you have the three city editors come down there and talk to your officer?"

I said, "Do you think they'd do it?" He said, "Sure, they would."

So I sent a very nice invitation to luncheon to the three city editors, the Richmond paper and the two Oakland ones. I invited them to come down and said I'd like them to talk to my officers on relations with the press. They came down. We had a nice little lunch over at the club, went over to a little place where we got 40 or 50 of our officers together and each one gave them a little talk and explained to them what the newspapers were after. They admitted that sometimes their reporters got a little obstreperous, please be patient with them. And the kids gave them a good hand when they got through. They all shook hands and the next day they all had a good story about the Center, and we never had any more trouble.

Q: It just takes a little bit of oil, doesn't it?

Adm. R.: Sure does. We had good press relations after that. If any of them found a story that was breaking down there in the Center, they call on the phone and ask if they could send a man down. The standard answer was, "Sure, come on down. I don't know what you will see, but come on down and we will talk to them." We gave them a good reception and never had any trouble at all.

I learned a lot out there. You learn it the hard way, sometimes.

But that public relations business was quite a chore. Everytime they'd have a parade in Oakland I'd have to be in the parade, sit with the mayor or ride with the mayor or some darned thing.

Q: Time-consuming!

Adm. R.: Time-consuming.

Q: And boring, too!

Adm. R.: And boring at times, yes. And you get called on for so darned many speeches. I had some kids who wrote pretty good speeches for me. I'd tell them what I wanted to say and they'd put it in good shape. Fortunately I had two who were very accomplished. Harry Leiser was one of them. It would depend on the type of speech I wanted. He'd give me a good speech and it would come off pretty well. I spent an awful lot of time on that.

Q: What kind of relations did you have with Mare Island?

Adm. R.: Very little. Mare Island was a kingdom of its own. We did furnish them material once in a while, but we got nothing from them. They carried ships' stores. They carried enough stores to take care of ships that were in there and to supply themselves, and that was all. They replenished either from us or from our annex up at Stockton. Stockton would often barge stuff up there.

Another thing that we started there was a cargo-handling school. They had a small one there with about 20 students. We were short of officers who knew anything about loading ships and unloading ships, loading barges and unloading barges, or any work along the shore. And with this Korea coming up, we needed them, so we got the Bureau to get us a commanding officer and we really beefed up the school. We had around 300 students there - officers. Not only Navy but we had the Army in there, one or two Air Force. We had a pretty good reputation. Our friends in commercial shipping gave us a good hand on it. Harry Bridges even sent over pretty good longshoremen to talk to them.

Q: Weren't you in some sense usurping the duties of the commercial people?

Adm. R.: Not in the cargo-handling. These officers, all they would do would be supervise. They didn't do any of the work themselves. These were not stevedores. But in order to handle stevedores, in order to handle the loading and see that a ship was loaded right, the cargo was put in the right places, you're got to know stevedoring from A to Z, you've got to know what it's all about, how they work and how they think, and the process of preparing a load on a ship, a load that will carry and you don't get a lot of heavy stuff on top and light stuff in the bottom of the hold. You've got to find your cargo and check where it is going to go. If the ship's going to make several stops, you've got to know how to load that so that you can take it off as you come to the different stops. There's an awful lot in cargo-handling that can save time and money. Some of the stuff that we sent out at first was very poor because it was poorly loaded and it was over carried. It was way down in the bottom of the hold and when they got there they couldn't have taken it out without unloading half the ship, so they just overcarried it. They got to know all those things.

The Army was very quick to send students - we didn't ask them, they asked if they could send some people over. We had an excellent staff. As I say, the shipping companies - Matson for one, sent over a good man as an instructor - and one or two of the others. I've forgotten which ones sent people over.

Q: Did you have any labor problems during the Korean War?

Adm. R.: No, none at all. It worked quite smoothly. Mr. Bridges and I got along fine and everything worked out.

Q: Of course, at that time it wasn't customary to strike against the government, anyway, was it?

Adm. R.: No. Even during that strike that we had Mr. Bridges told me that he wasn't striking against the government.

Q: We've witnessed a change of attitude!

Adm. R.: He gave us good service during the Korean thing. We, of course, used some of our stevedores and we used his, too.

In August 1950 we loaded and sailed 25 ships out of that harbor of ours - loaded them and sailed them in one month, and that was only one less than we had at the peak of World War II. The biggest month they had in World War II was January 1945 when they sent out 26 ships. So you see we were really moving cargo. It was really going out.

Q: Since you mention World War II and the Pacific coast area, did you have any contact with the most famous citizen of the Bay area at that time - Chester Nimitz?

Adm. R.: Admiral Nimitz was a great friend of ours. We used to see him all the time.

Q: Tell me about him, in retirement then.

Adm. R.: He had a home up on the hill in Berkeley and we were up there quite often, both just visiting and at parties or something like that. He had this beautiful house on a hill where he could look out directly across the Golden Gate. He had a perfect picture of the Golden Gate, and he used to go out there and take his visitors out there and just stand and talk about it. He loved that scene. That was one scene that he just couldn't forget and couldn't get enough of.

His house inside was beautiful, and he had two or three studies that were just lined with pictures and trophies and that sort of thing. He was the most cordial person that I've ever known. The back of the house was toward the Gate and the front of the house faced the street. He'd go out in back and look at the Gate. Then he had a horseshoe place back there and if he could inveigle any of us to play horseshoes, we had to play a game of horsehoes with him.

Q: He was quite a gardener, too, wasn't he?

Adm. R.: The grounds were beautiful. He had a beautiful garden.
He used to like to come down to the center from time to time.

Q: I thought he probably would.

Adm. R.: Yes, and we'd take him around. He was one of the most interesting talkers that I've ever known. He always had a story to fit his little talk, and he had a good sense of humor. Both Mabel and I always like him very, very much, both him and his wife.

Q: Do you, by any chance, remember any of his stories?

Adm. R.: No, I don't, unfortunately. I wish I did. He had plenty of them, but I can't remember any.

We were very proud of our bond sale there at the naval supply center.

Q: Tell me about that.

Adm. R.: In 1950 we had the Minuteman Flag for bond sales. Stockton Annex had 100 percent. For the whole center, I think we were up in the 80s - about 84 percent. So we were very proud of that.

I don't know of anything else particularly. When I was detached that was another fast one too.

Q: That was in 1951, was it not?

Adm. R.: The fall of 1951.

Q: What do you mean it was a fast one?

Adm. R.: Well, on one of my public relations duties I was supposed to go up to Sacramento, to the Sacramento Fair, and make a speech for some darned thing up there. I've forgotten what it was. Some meeting they had. We were going to drive up and were leaving on a Saturday morning. I was to speak that night, and we were going to spend Sunday up there and come back Monday.

Saturday morning, just before we left, I had a call from the office.

The office was just 100 yards away from our house. The Duty Officer said, "We got a call from the Secretary of the Navy and he wants you on the phone right away."

I said: "Can you transfer it?" and he said no, I'd have to come over to the office. So I ran over to the office, and it was Dan Kimball on the phone. He said:

"This Murrey?"

I said, "Yes, Sir, this is Murrey L. Royar."

He said, "I want you back here Monday." I said, "What do you mean?"

He said, "You're going to be Chief of the Bureau of Supplies and Accounts and I've got to have you back here right away."

"Monday," I said, "I can't get back there Monday, Dan, you know that. I've got to turn over and a lot of things."

"How soon can you get back?"

"Well," I said, "I might bet back in a couple of weeks."

"No, you've got to come before that."

"In that case," I said, "I'll leave here about a week from today."

"No, you've got to come before that."

"How about next Friday then?"

You're going to drive aren't you?" and I said yes. He said, "Well, that's all right. You can drive night and day, maybe, and get back here by the following Monday."

I said, "What are you talking about? Is there another war on?"

He said, "No."

"Well," I said, "I'm going to send you my resignation. I'm going to retire. I don't want to come back there. I've bought a house out in Walnut Creek. I've got two or three people who've offered me a job here. I'm not coming back. I'll send you my retirement papers - my request for retirement."

"Ha, ha, ha! Don't you know Korea's on?"

I said, "Yes."

He said, "I won't take your retirement when Korea's on. You've got to come back!"

"Do you mean that," I asked, "that you wouldn't let me retire if I want to retire?"

"No, I've got to have you back here as Chief of the Bureau."

"Well, all right," I said, "I'll come back Friday."

I was pretty well shook up on that, just over the phone. He said, "I'll have your orders there. I'll send them out right away, by telegram."

So I went back to the house and Mabel said, "Who was that?" "Oh," I said, "they want some dope at the Bureau. Come on, let's get going." We got in the car. It was a government car with George Chan, my Chinese chauffeur. I want to tell you about my chauffeur. He was an American-born Chinese by the name of George Chan, and there was the smartest driver I've ever had in my life. He knew every bit of Oakland and San Francisco, everywhere, all around Northern California.

Q: Quite an accomplishment!

Adm. R.: Oh, it sure was. He'd get you there. He knew all the short cuts. But on St. Patrick's Day every year that I was there he'd come with a great big green tie and say, "Mr. O'Chan reporting, Sir!"

So, we got hold of George and we started out, and drove up there. About halfway up I told Mabel, "Well, do you want to really know what the telephone call was about?" She said yes. I said:

"That was Dan Kimball. He says he wants me back in Washington the first of the following week."

She said, "For how long?" I said, "For good."

"What?"

"Yes, he wants me to come back as Chief of the Bureau."

She said, "You turn right around. We'll go home and start packing right now."

I said, "No, we won't either. That's the reason I didn't tell you till we got started."

Q: Going to have this trip?

Adm. R.: I was going to have this trip. We went up there and had a good time. Got home. Our daughter and our son-in-law, who was a captain in the Navy, had come in and we had to tell them that they couldn't stay for two weeks like they were going to, because we'd be gone.

Q: I take it your wife was pleased.

Adm. R.: Oh, she was pleased.

Q: She was thinking in terms of your career?

Adm. R.: That's right.

I got back and I called up Cliff Rishell, the mayor, and said, "Cliff, I'm leaving." He said, "You can't do that." Well, you know, that gang over there in the city on the Thursday night before we left - we left on Friday morning - at the Leamington Hotel they had a party and they had that place overflowing and gave Mabel and me one of the finest going-away parties I've ever seen. It was wonderful.

Then the next day we had the turning-over ceremony. I turned over to my executive officer, who was Bernie Bieri. Cliff was there and all the people were around. Admiral Bert Rogers, the District Commandant, and ComWestern Sea Frontier, and they gave us a nice sendoff. Cliff said, "I'm going to see that you get out of here safely." And he had a squad of four motorcycle police, two in front and two behind, and he said, "You get the hell out of here," and they took me through the streets of Oakland and got me out of the city in no time at all. It was really something. It was the only time I had a motorcycle escort!

Q: But you didn't arrive back in Washington, driving, over the weekend, did you?

Adm. R.: We drove over the weekend and we got back on Tuesday on Wednesday, or something like that.

Interview No. 6 with Vice Admiral Murrey L. Royar, U.S. Navy (Retired)

Place: His residence in McLean, Virginia

Date: Wednesday morning, 6 June 1973

Subject: Biography

By: John T. Mason, Jr.

Q: Well, it's certainly good to see you today, and to anticipate this chapter, which is the crowning glory of your most interesting naval career.

When we left last time you were leaving Oakland to return to Washington, D.C., at the behest of Secretary Dan Kimball, to take up your duties as Chief of BUSANDA and paymaster general of the Navy, and the date you assumed these duties was 10 October 1951.

Adm. R.: That's right. We had a very nice trip across the continent, took it easy, and arrived in Washington on the 1st of October. I reported to the Secretary of the Navy immediately.

Q: You arrived to meet his requirements. He was so insistent!

Adm. R.: That's right. He was very insistent, and we got down on the 1st of October and reported in. He gave me a few duties, incidental, before I was sworn in on the 10th of October by Francis P. Whitehair, who was Assistant Secretary of the Navy.

Q: Incidentally, why the great urgency for getting you there? Did you discover that?

Adm. R.: The reason was that the Office of Chief of Naval Materiel was vacant and he wanted to get Vice Admiral Fox in there as Chief of Naval Materiel. Admiral Fox had been the chief of the bureau and he went over with the addition of one star to vice admiral to be Chief of Naval Materiel. So for a few days there, the Bureau was run by our good friend George Bauernschmidt and George did a fine job during the time that I got settled and was sworn in on the 10th.

This was, of course, a big job. It was something I had to take a look at. Charlie Fox had left a wonderful organization and had done a perfectly splendid job, but things were beginning to get stirred up a bit. We were getting into the Korea situation and nobody knew exactly what was going to happen. They didn't know whether it would blow over, be just a small action, or whether it would blossom out into a gigantic World War No. 3. Everybody was very, very much worried at the time.

Q: You said that Secretary Kimball gave you a few little things to do before you actually took over as chief?

Adm. R.: That was primarily getting myself acquainted with the people around without the mantle of the bureau. I went up on the Hill, introduced myself to the congressmen who were close to the bureau or close to the Navy Department, to other departments of the government around that I would be working with, and it was all on an informal basis, which made it very nice and I made some very fine contacts.

Then, of course, we had to get settled. It was only five years before that we'd left Washington and sold our house, sold everything and got rid of everything, figuring that I'd never be back again.

Q: You were always fighting the idea of Washington!

Adm. R.: That's right! And the thing was that with this Korea situation Washington was crowded, there was no place to rent, and we finally had to buy a little place in Falls Church.

On the 10th, when I took over, I began to look at the problems we had ahead of us, and there were two conflicting problems. One was, what's going to happen? Are we going to spread out and expand in case of another war? Or, are we going to contract and get rid of a lot of the surplus that was left over from World War II? We had a tremendous amount of surplus. The committees in Congress were looking down their nose at all the services because of the great amount of money that was tied up in inventory.

Q: Just as a kind of a footnote, I would ask how did the surpluses existing then compare with what we have now and we've seen listed in the press?

Adm. R.: Oh, far greater.

Q: Far greater then?

Adm. R.: Yes. The surpluses now - there will be surpluses after we get through with this aviation exercise we're going through in Vietnam at the present time. Of course, in the aviation end we're keeping our stocks up very well, but the other stocks are getting pretty well settled down.

Q: I was thinking in terms of metals and such.

Adm. R.: Yes. But in this case we were under pressure to reduce and were also under pressure to be ready in case anything happened. So we started an exercise we called Operation Slim Trim, and that exercise we put into effect in all our bases. In the first place, we were converting to the federal stock numbers in all of our stocks. This had gone along pretty well and we were pretty well along in that conversion, but we had to finish that up and at the same time go over our stocks to eliminate any obvious surplus, to get rid of the obsolete material - we had a lot of obsolete material ins tock -

Q: That was the overriding criterion - to get rid of the obsolete?

Adm. R.: To get rid of the obsolete was the main thing. We knew we could get rid of that without endangering anything. Then we also knew that we did have certain surpluses in items that are seldom used. For instance, anchors, certain parts of ships. We knew that for the foreseeable future we probably wouldn't have any big action and wouldn't need them.

We segregated our inventories into the different types of material. That which was readily used every day, and we called it fractionation - the parts that were used every day, those that were seldom used, and those that were only used for new construction or something very, very seldom used. The part that came under rapid use we put those in depots and centers where they could easily be obtained. Some of the other material that was seldom used we put in inland depots like Clearfield, which was the main one then.

At the same time the Department of Defense was worried about what might happen if Korea broke out.

Q: And we got involved with China?

Adm. R.: With China and also Russia, but primarily China. The thing that we were looking at and made a big study of was the location of future supply depots. We had Clearfield, which was inland from the West Coast, but we felt that in case something should happen we ought to have an inland depot on the East Coast. A lot of us were a little bit skeptical about it but, playing on the safety side, we went to work on it, and I had a very interesting situation there with Mr. Carl Vinson.

We sent out teams, we consulted with the Office of Naval Materiel, the CNO, and everybody else, and we decided that, on the side of safety, we would establish an East Coast inland depot. We had a group studying localities all up and down the East Coast, and they finally came up with a site at Byron, Georgia. It's inland and we could get transportation from there to Savannah, Norfolk, and East Coast ports. It was fairly good, it was central.

Q: And a very convincing voice for that site must have been Carl Vinson himself!

Adm. R.: Well, I'm going to tell you about how Mr. Vinson was.

It was my job to go up and talk to Mr. Vinson. I went up to see him and I told him why we wanted it and wanted to know if he thought I could get approval of the committee.

Q: You'd already selected the Georgia site?

Adm. R.: I had, but I hadn't told him. And he said:

"Now, Admiral, where do you want to put that?" I said:

"Well, Mr. Vinson, we've decided on Byron, Georgia."

"Oh," he said, "Byron, Georgia. That sounds very good. It's not in my district but it's in my State. Are you convinced that that's the best location?"

"Yes, Sir," I said, "we've spent a great deal of time and work in picking this spot, and we think from a utility standpoint it's going to be the ideal spot."

He said: "Are you prepared to come up before my committee and say that?"

I said, "Yes, Sir."

"Well," he said, "I'm going to have a committee meeting here in about two weeks, and I want you to appear. I want you to know that this is going to be a very difficult thing and you've got to be well prepared, and you've got to be able to answer all the questions."

I said, "Yes, Sir, I realize that."

He said: "You've given me a very fine presentation. You have convinced me, but we have other people on the committee who will be a little harder to convince."

Q: Why the difficulty?

Adm. R.: Because it was in Georgia.

Q: Too many things had gone into Georgia!

Adm. R.: That's right. And another thing was that there was a feeling among a lot of people on the Hill at the time that the services were too concerned about what might happen and were going overboard in preparing for what might happen.

Well, I went back and I had dry runs on this thing, and I had people asking me all sorts of questions. I went up fully prepared on the day of the hearing and Mr. Vinson said:

"Well, I see there's a request there for a new supply center in Byron, Georgia." A little hum went up from some of the other members. "Is there anybody here to justify that?"

I stood up and said, "Yes. I am, Sir."

He said, "Will you give your name and rate and present station and come forward. Are you prepared to justify this?"

I said, "Yes, Sir."

"Have you had a good examination of all the coast?" and I said:

We've spent about six months going over all sites and this we find to be the most practical."

He said, "You're convinced of that?" And I said, "Yes, Sir."

He said, "Granted."

Q: He didn't allow anybody else - !

Adm. R.: A Republican got up and said, "Er, ah, er." and that was the hearing! Here, I'd spent all this time getting ready for it and the dry runs and everything else, and that was the complete hearing.

Q: Sounds like it was true to form! With the Slim Trim operation, you must have had available storage space that had been used heretofore. How did you use that, what did you do with that?

Adm. R.: We were reducing spaces. For instance, around Oakland we eliminated a lot of rented storage space. We had a tremendous amount of rented storage space all over the United States, and, of course, that was the first thing to do. Our depots at the time we cut down and regenerated some space that we used for material that other departments of the government needed. GSA, for example, was looking for space and we accommodated them in certain spots. But it took a long time to Slim Trim. You couldn't do that overnight. It took us a year or two to really -

Q: I'm sure it did. You said earlier that you were under some considerable pressure to eliminate some of these things. Where did the pressure originate?

Adm. R.: A good deal of it originated in the committees of Congress. I don't know whether you ever heard of Herbert C. Bonner, I've forgotten what committee he had, but the Bonner Committee was a committee that - as I recall it, it was a subcommittee of the Armed Forces Committee - and the Bonner Committee went all over the United States and visited Army, Navy, and Air Force locations with the idea of trying to force the services to reduce even further and to find out - investigate and find out where all the surpluses were that the papers and the reporters and other people said that we had.

The Bonner Committee, I know, went to Oakland and went to Clearfield. I was with them on one of their trips to Oakland and they were very well satisfied with the way we were doing our business. They went to visit the Army and I don't recall that they had too much criticism of the Army. They did tell us that we were on the right track and to give our people in the field a few pats on the back for the way they were really going to town. Of course, this Byron, Georgia, has since been closed up, but we did open it up -

Q: How long was it used?

Adm. R.: It was used for about ten, fifteen years. Then the Marines took it over from us, and they finally closed it up.

Q: Why the inland bases?

Adm. R.: The theory then was that they'd be less liable to attack from an enemy. They thought that probably the enemy might get into the coastal bases and do a lot of damage, but if we had an inland base they would be less liable to hit it.

Q: They weren't thinking in terms of missiles, then?

Adm. R.: No. This, you see, was 1951 and that's over twenty years ago, and the thinking was not as far advanced as it is today. There were a lot of us that were not too sure, but we thought we ought to play it safe.

Q: Isn't that the task of the military, anyway, to anticipate?

Adm. R.: That's right, and we didn't want to get caught short. Those two operations took up an awful lot of our time. We were very busy with that and I think, as a result, that our support during the Korean crisis was excellent. We never had trouble from the fleet at all. They got what they wanted as far as the Navy was concerned when they needed it.

Q: This applied to mines and things like that, which they used in considerable numbers?

Adm. R.: Everything. I think it was a well worthwhile operation. I enjoyed that operation, enjoyed doing it, and I enjoyed the setup in the Navy Department at that time. You see, it's completedly changed now. At that time we had the Bureau of Ships, the Bureau of Supplies and Accounts, the Bureau of Ordnance, the Bureau of Yards and Docks, the Bureau of Medicine and Surgery, and we had a head of each of those bureaus, we were on top of it, and the way we operated was entirely our responsibility.

The Assistant Secretary of the Navy for Installations was more or less a coordinator. The Office of Naval Materiel was a coordinating office under the Assistant Secretary. In other words, it brought the heads together and saw that they worked together and helped each other out and there was no bickering back and forth. My relations with the other chiefs of bureaus were excellent. I never had any trouble at all. If I have any questions, if I had anything that worried me that I needed, I got on the phone and asked the Assistant Secretary, do you have any objections to this, this is what I intend to do. No. And I said, well, I'm going to talk to the Secretary and I called Charlie Thomas, or whoever was Secretary at the time, and I'd call him up and say: "I've got this problem. This is what I intend to do. Have you any objections?" Sometimes, they had objections and would say, "Yes, I think you'd better do this or that first, or consult somebody else." Nine times out of ten it was, go go ahead and do it. It was very simple. You'd get things done in a hurry.

This present system, I don't know how I could work with it.

Q: When did the Naval Materiel outfit come into being?

Adm. R.: Well, the Chief of Naval Materiel has been in existence for a good many years but, as I might say, it was really the staff of the Assistant Secretary for Installations, and his principal work was, when I took it on later on, helping the Assistant Secretary to coordinate the bureaus. He had a lot of responsibility with no authority - I say "with no authority," the Assistant Secretary had authority, the Chief of Naval Materiel didn't have authority. To my mind, it worked out fine because it was a coordinating body. The chiefs of bureaus were really important people. They had a job to do, they had authority to do it, and they could go direct to the Assistant Secretary of the Secretary and get an answer and get it done.

It was in the late 1950s and 1960s that they changed all that. The Chief of Naval Materiel was elevated to four stars and put on a par with the Chief of Naval Operations. He has the same control over the bureaus that the Chief of Naval Operations has over the military, and, while the Chief of Naval Materiel works with the Assistant Secretary, his primary boss is the Secretary. And they changed the bureaus to Commands, as you well know.

Q: Yes.

Adm. R.: The poor devil who is the head of a Command has to go to the Chief of Naval Materiel, then the Assistant Secretary, and then the Secretary to get things done. It's a long way around. For my part, I think that was the worst move the Navy ever made. I went through with the bureau system in World War I and World War II, we got good service from the bureaus, we got quick service, that is, for a government organization, and I think we had a tremendous operation compared to the Army. Friends of mine in the Army used to come to me and tell me that they thought our bureau system was tops and for God's sake don't let it get away from you.

Q: But you did!

Adm. R.: We did. Why it was done I don't know. I argued against it. I was, of course, retired when it went through but I argued against it. When it went through the chap that was in there, he was for it, he was a line officer. He was for putting that through come hell or high water. I went to the Secretary and argued against it, but it prevailed and they've got it now. The thing also is that it took away a lot of the incentive of staff people like the EDOs, Supply Corps, and so on, who were really the top people in the bureaus. There was even some talk, a year or two ago, of doing away with the bureaus or some of the bureaus. They were going to do away with S and A, and my question then was "what do you do with supply officers?"

"Oh, we'll just put them around like the EDOs."

"Who'll be the head of them?"

"Well, they don't need a head."

"How are you going to have any morale? The reason that the Supply Corps people do a good job now is that they've got a head, they've got a Corps, they're proud of it, and they do a job to support that Corps as well as the Navy. You've got to have morale to do it, or you're just going to kill everything."

That's one thing that I worry about with the EDOs. They do have in BuShips an EDO top and that helps out a great deal, but you've got to have a top somewhere, you've got to have an organization to keep your morale up. For my part I think that was one of the worst things the Navy ever did, was to change from the bureau system.

I don't know whether you want this on here or not?

Q: Yes, indeed. I'm glad to have it, actually.

Going back to the period when you were Chief of the Bureau of Supplies and Accounts and involved in the Korean War, what type of things did you continue to stockpile?

Adm. R.: Stockpile parts for the material that we had over there, that is, in hardware. We kept up our uniform stocks, of course, but in the hardware end of it and general supplies we just stockpiled everything that we had. At Mechanicsburg we stockpiled metals, copper and some lead and other metals that might be in short supply.

Q: Metals that would be hard to obtain from abroad?

Adm. R.: That's right. We carried all that stuff. We didn't let that drop down at all.

I was in there, of course, as chief of bureau from October 10, 1951 until February 1954, which is about three years. Another thing that it was important for me to do was to get into the field. We had crying letters from the people in the field. They didn't know just what was going on, how things were going. We had a lot of young officers who didn't think that they were ever being heard from and didn't know whether anybody knew that they existed.

The first thing I did was to make some trips around the United States to some of the smaller installations, and then I had to go to Europe during the first year I was there on a MAAG proposition, to visit the MAAGs.

I went over to London and to Paris, to Italy, and to Portugal. I made another trip to Portugal, but I made a Portugal trip that time. We went to these MAAGs and, as chief of bureau, I had a full open door from the Secretary of the Navy to go in and see what things were and, at the same time, to look over any excess stocks that our people might have in Europe. The fact is the Department of State asked me to do some work for them, to look at some of their things that they had over there. They had some minor things. I spent several weeks over there in Europe looking at the MAAGs and discussing with the people there how they were getting along, whether the material that we still had over there was being properly used or not. That was one thing that give our people concern, when we turned it over to the foreign government whether it was being used as it should be used.

Q: We had no further control over it?

Adm. R.: We had no further control, and we set up a program to see - it had little plaques from the foreign governments on it - but we set up a control to see where and how that material was being used. As a result of that, we did cut down on some of the amounts of material that were going over.

Q: Did this entail loaning personnel, perhaps, to the foreign governments in order to better understand how they used some of this material?

Adm. R.: It did, in a way. We had a few exchange officers. We did that in two ways. We had exchange officers, then in our supply centers we got officers from other governments who came over and took courses or who worked with us in our supply departments and learned how we took care of things.

Q: I suppose that was the better way, wasn't it?

Adm. R.: That was the better way. They went back very sympathetic and they were glad to see our people when they came in. They wanted to know how we were getting along. Those connections paid off 100 percent.

Q: Did the MAAG requests put a strain on your bureau?

Adm. R.: No, not too much. You mean in material or personnel?

Q: In material.

Adm. R.: They put in their requisitions and they were okayed and we would see that they got the material.

Q: What sort of thing did they requisition?

Adm. R.: Practically everything. We had a big purchasing office in London.

I had a young man by the name of Lieutenant Commander Don Kent – I was just looking over some old letters and Jack Koehler, who was Assistant Secretary at the time, had been over there, and I gave Don Kent authority to do local purchasing in London and to establish branches of the London office wherever he thought it might be necessary in Europe. Well, Don got authority to make purchases in the amount of $50,000 or less without further authority. Anything that was more than that he had to get approval from the Bureau. But he did a perfectly marvelous job in buying stuff there and putting it into the MAAGs as it was needed. Not only for the MAAGs, but he, of course, was buying for people who were over there through our naval personnel. They had the U.S. Naval Purchasing Office, London. That worked out so that minor items that they wanted he could buy right there. If they had any material that had been manufactured in Europe and needed spare parts, he could purchase them right there and saved all the trouble of coming over here and shipping them back. That cut down a lot of time and expense. That was one thing that we worked out.

But the MAAGs really did a good job.

Q: They weren't confined to Europe, were they?

Adm. R.: Oh, no, they were all over, but the European MAAGs were the ones that I went over to talk to. Later, in 1953, I made a trip around the world. I went over to Japan and then down into Taipai, China.

Did I tell you the story about Taipei, China? It was a funny one. I'll clean up the language a little bit.

Q: Why?

Adm. R.: I went out to Japan, we had a supply center out there - a supply depot, rather.

Q: Where? At Yokosuka?

Adm. R.: Yes, Yokosuka. I went through that and helped the boys get squared away, then I took the plane down to Taipei. It was a Northwestern plane, civilian plane. The pilot was a little red-headed fellow. I'll never forget him. He said:

"Admiral, come on up here in the pilot's seat. We're out of the United States, you can come in the cabin. There are no regulations against it here."

So I sat up in the cabin and we went down over Taipei and he said, "I'll take you around the island first. I'm a little ahead of time."

Q: A sightseeing trip!

Adm. R.: So I got a good view of the island and then he said:

"The last time I was in here I brought in a chap who used to be the station agent here. He was the big man in Taipei. We came in and they put out the red carpet. He got off the plane and he started sniffing, and said 'What's that smell?' His successor said 'You know what it is. That stuff that they carry away and they put in the fields for fertilizer - human.'"

Q: Night soil!

Adm. R.: "He says, 'Yes, but what in the hell have they done to it?'"

Q: This trip was ostensibly to inspect the MAAGs, too?

Adm. R.: The MAAGs, yes, and we had this MAAG in Taipei which was very important. The Chinese were quite good people. I went in there and the commanding officer wanted to give me a little dinner that night. Commander Joe Shea was the MAAG officer and he said, "The commanding officer is a general, but he'll appear as an admiral tonight. He changes his uniform to comply with all these visitors."

So, sure enough, he came in the uniform of an admiral, and we had a very nice visit.

The Chinese were using our material in good shape and they did a good job with it.

Then I went on down to Korea - this was in 1953 - and the South Koreans were using our stuff, too. In all of these places I talked to the people and got them to promise to send some of their responsible supply officers over to the States — one or two, Korea, Philippines — the Philippine Navy were tickled to death to send somebody over.

Q: And then we sent them to school?

Adm. R.: We had a course for them right in our supply system. We kept them over here about six or eight months and it gave them a good idea so that when our people went over they knew what our people were talking about, and our people could tell them how to do things and they had enough background.

Q: Who paid their expenses?

Adm. R.: Their own government paid their expenses.

I went down to Saigon and from Saigon I went to Thailand — went to Thailand before Saigon — then I stopped down in Singapore. We had no MAAG there but I wanted to talk to some of the people down there about perhaps getting some supplies. We never worked anything out.

Then I went over to Italy and from Italy on to Portugal, and then back home.

We had a regular system set up. We took these officers from our allies and had them in different classes. We'd take maybe eight or ten at a time and schedule them through. The fact is with Canada we had regular exchange officers. They sent their officer down there to work in our supply depot and we sent a man up to New Brunswick where he worked in theirs. That did a lot. Those exchanges did a lot to keep our people closer, and it enabled our people to get in and know what was going on.

Q: Admiral, what, in a very rough way, is the yearly total of the MAAG program, the cost of it?

Adm. R.: I don't have those figures. It was tremendous, though. I'm sorry I don't have them.

It was an interesting thing on that trip. I not only went to MAAGs, but the ambassadors were all interested in this thing, too, and I had a conference with Spruance in Manila, Ambassador Heath in Saigon, Guggenheim in Lisbon - everywhere that I went I met the ambassadors and got splendid cooperation from them.

Q: Well, part of their duty was to be cognizant about the MAAG operations, wasn't it?

Adm. R.: That's right, and they were, too. They were very much interested in it.

Q: I would think that it might be useful to an ambassador in terms of his own relationship with the government. He had this material support.

Adm. R.: That's right, yes, indeed. It was a tremendous program.

Along with this we had a transportation problem. In S and A, we were the transportation people of the Navy Department.

Q: For the entire Department?

Adm. R.: Yes. That is, I'm talking about not personnel transportation. BuPers had the personnel transportation. We had material transportation. I didn't think, and our people didn't think, that we'd been giving enough attention to it. We'd started this little school in Oakland - transportation school -- but it was more or less an informal affair. We went to work and got a spare ship, the Ross, from the ships that were located in the Bay, anchored in the Bay above Oakland -

Q: What was she, a DD?

Adm. R.: No, that was a commercial cargo ship. We brought it down and put it in Oakland. Of course, we couldn't have steam on it, so we worked a system of using compressed air on the winches, so they could operate the winches. We started a formal school with a nine-month course. We did that under the blessing of DOD. They were a little skeptical at first. We had a chap there by the name of Kenneth Vore, who had been commercially in transportation and he took it over in the Department. He brought in as a consultant a Dr. Edwin A. Nightengale. Nightongale was from the University of Michigan. He headed up the Transportation School in Michigan. Ed was a very fine chap. I went over this whole thing with him and he helped work out our course, what we would teach, and gave us a lot of help on it. He went out to Oakland and got it going, then later went out and evaluated it, and on our first graduation, in June of 1952, he was out there, and he brought back such a fine story about it to the Department of Defnese that we were getting officers from all the services. The school is

Royar # 6 - 272

still running, but only about a third of the class is Navy. The rest are Army and Air Force.

It was a very, very fine course. It gave these people good instruction. We were fortunate, of course, in being near San Francisco and Oakland, where we could get professionals from civilian life to come in and give the people lectures. So they got it from both the service side as well as the commercial side. That turned out very well, and it's helped us out in all the services, I think, a great deal.

There were a lot of things that we had to do. I remember getting a letter from a Captain Patton who wrote to me from - I've forgotten which center it was, but he wrote to me and told me about ships' stores - industrial shop stores, rather, not ships' stores. He thought that the method of operating shop stores in the Navy Yards and our installations was obsolete. We sent some people out to look at it and he was right. It was one of the poorest operations that we had.

Q: Would you tell me about shop stores?

Adm. R.: Shop stores are what you have in a Navy Yard or in a manufacturing outlet in a yard or station. It's the store that carries all the immediate material to go into the operation. It's really a small supply department for the operation. It carries maybe sheet iron, it may be the tools that they use, it may be the greases and oils that they use in the operation. It's a little shop store that gives them all the material they need to carry on their operation.

Royar #6 - 273

These shop stores have their stocks but they did not have any system of inventory or very good control. The control of most of them was pretty near nothing. A man could go in and get whatever he wanted from the shop storekeeper.

Q: Wasteful!

Adm. R.: It was wastful, and through his calling it to our attention we set up a method of control and, instead of letting the operators run it, we ran it from the supply department and charged the operators for whatever they got out of it. As a result, it was surprising the thousands and thousands of dollars that were saved there.

Q: It was really a tightening up, but you still maintained these local stores?

Adm. R.: Oh, yes, we had the shop stores just the same but they were put under much better control.

That was one of many things that we got from our people in the field. We encouraged our people in the field if they saw a bad operaation or something that could be improved to come in and give it to us. We took it under study and, if need be, changed it. Our Supply Corps people were wonderful young officers. They were well trained and observant and they were dedicated in their work. I can't say too much for the way they handled themselves.

Going back to this freight transportation school, James W. Haggard, he was a commander and commanding officer. He'd had some experience in transportation before he came in the Navy, and when he and Ed Nightengale got together and set that place up he really did a good job.

Q: I see your skill at public relations and understanding of human reactions in operation in that first tour you made of all the centers in the United States to talk with the personnel in the little places.

Adm. R.: That was one of the greatest things that could be done.

Q: This was your own doing?

Adm. R.: That's right. I got to the places that nobody went to. I've got files of letters here. I kept a lot of my personal letters. These young officers who said they never expected to see the chief of bureau in their place. But I think it did more to pep those people up because at the same time they weren't afraid to write me a personal letter and tell me this operation, they thought, could be improved. They weren't criticizing. It was a sense of trying to improve the operation, and I always took it that way and I tell you it paid off.

Later on, in 1954, Mrs. Royar and I made a trip over to Europe. I had to go over again to the MAAGs. We planned a big meeting in London. An aunt of mine had died and left me $1,000, and I told Mabel, "I'm going over there and if you want to use that $1,000 to go, it's yours." She said, "But I don't want to fly." and I said:

"Well, you're going to fly or you don't go," so she said "I'll go."

Q: That's blackmail!

Adm. R.: Just about. We went over and Admiral John Cassidy turned over his London suite to us while we were there for three or four days, and she was the biggest help to me that I've ever seen.

While I was working with the men and we were having our conferences, she was organizing the gals, talking to them, finding out how they liked the place, how they liked the duty, what they needed, and so on. Not only in London. We went to Oslo, Copenhagen, Brussels, Paris, and then to Spain and Portugal. Each place that we went, she was with the gals, and I began to understand why I had been getting letters from some of these men asking to be transferred home. Some of the wives didn't like it. They were young wives, they'd never been away from home before, they were living in a foreign country, their youngsters were going to school in a foreign school, and they wanted to get home. My wife did a marvelous job in talking to these young women. She'd get them together and say, "Why, you've got an experience here that you couldn't pay for. Your children are getting an education that you couldn't buy." She had them on the line.

Q: Giving them a different point of view.

Adm. R.: A different point of view, and she did a perfectly marvelous job. That was one of the jobs that she did and I was pretty happy about it.

Q: Your $1,000 paid off!

Adm. R.: It paid off. But that was one of the troubles we were having. We had these fine young officers there but their wives were unhappy. They just couldn't see living in a foreign country and they didn't know what they were getting. You see the problems, and we're getting the same thing today, I think. A lot of wives just don't like the service life, but they have all these opportunities which pays off.

Well, we had a very fine tour and she worked just as hard as I did. It was a wonderful experience for her, too, to go over there and see these people. I know one young man who was going to get out of the Navy because his wife didn't want to live there. And I think as a result of her talking to his wife they stayed, and he'll be up for selection for admiral next spring. He was a fine young man. That I think did a lot of good.

These people over in the foreign countries weren't hearing from the bureau very much. They didn't know particularly what was going on and, as a result of this, we set up a better system of communication. We sent out a monthly letter of some sort to let them know what was going on and how things were going. It brought us all together a little bit more.

We had this meeting in London first. I had all the MAAG people come in. We talked the thing over. Each one had a chance to tell what he was doing, what problems he had, how he'd solved them, and that way it helped out some of the others. Then I sent them on back and I went around and visited each man.

Q: Admiral, would you say that the MAAG program was in any sense a deterrent to these foreign countries in developing their own supplies?

Adm. R.: No, I think it helped them out.

Q: In what way?

Adm. R.: They knew, we told them without any equivocation that this supply business was going to stop, I didn't know when.

Q: It had a terminal date?

Adm. R.: It had a terminal date, and they had better get ready to take care of themselves. Our people went in preaching that sermon. They said we're here to help you, we're going to help you get what you need at the present time, but we don't know when it's going to stop. We'd also like to help you develop a system where you can take care of yourselves. We got a lot of good response from that. I think that helped out a great deal.

Our associations with foreign countries through the MAAGs, as far as I'm concerned, were always very pleasant. We had occasion where the MAAGs thought we didn't give them enough or that we were trying to gig them or something, but we worked those things out. The caliber of these men that we sent over there was tops. Most of them picked up the language right away, or they got a smattering of the language so they could talk it with the people.

Q: Did you have special requirements for such assignments?

Adm. R.: No, except that our personnel people looked the men over pretty well and knew how they could get along. Most of these men asked for the duty. It was when they got over there - their wives got over there - the wives didn't like it so well. The houses weren't as well furnished, the bathrooms sometimes weren't modern like the ones that we have at home, and there were inconveniences. That's where most of the trouble came. But as far as our men went, they were very happy. They were working on a high level and they really had an important job.

Q: That's very consoling.

Adm. R.: I can't say too much for our younger officers. They were given a job, the responsibility was put on them, and I don't recall anybody we had to bring home. I have a tendency to forget the rough spots and only think of the good. There were so many things that had to be done over there and the boys did a perfectly good job.

Q: Tell me about your budgetary problems as chief of the bureau.

Adm. R.: My budgetary problems were very small. I was very fortunate. I had two people in my budget division, Commander Bob Williams - R. A. Williams - who is now teaching school out here. "Budget Bob" I used to call him. And Robert C. Moot, who was recently head of the budget for the Department of Defense. Those two people were two of the best budget people I have ever seen. Two or three times I had to appear before the Bureau of the Budget. We worked our budget out, and the three of us went up as a team. I would give the presentation, then the details I would turn over to Commander Williams and Mr. Moot for questioning and they never let me down. Those men had the details all the way through. The last time I went up, in 1953, was the only time I didn't have a single cut. I got exactly what I'd asked for. Not a penny cut, and the Chairman looked at me and said:

"How in hell did you do it?"

So, budget problems I didn't have. Of course, we had to go through the Navy budget first and we had to justify that before we went on the Hill. I thought we were cut pretty close a number of times, but I never had any serious trouble at all. The way we handled it on the Hill was wonderful. I learned a lot because I had gone up before as a junior officer. I may have told you this before, I don't know, but I'd gone up to support on previous budgets before I was chief. I'd had a chance to watch the operation of the budget.

I'll never forget there was one naval officer — he wasn't in our group — who was defending — and I've forgotten what it was and the amount — but he was very insistent in telling how he needed it and had to have it, this, that, and the other thing, and this congressman had been up there a long, long time. He was a good friend of mine, too, and he probably knew far more about the Navy budget than this officer who was testifying. He started to ask him questions, and this chap started to stutter a little bit, he was a little vague, and he would give answers. I remember one answer he gave about the amount of something, and the congressman said, "You're wrong. The amount is such and such. Look in your records." The fellow looked in the records and blushed.

"Now, Captain," he said, "you go back and study your figures and study your budget. When you know what you want and are ready to testify come back up again."

Well, that taught me a lesson. I listened to that, and, believe me, when they asked me anything and I didn't know it, I'd say:

"I don't know, Sir, but I'll get the answer for you."

Q: That was Congressman Harry Shepherd.

Adm. R.: Yes. Harry Shepherd was a very good friend of mine. He came, of course, from Redlands, California. I'd lived down there a long time and he knew my uncle and some of my people. When I was chief of the bureau he called me up one day and said:

"Admiral, "I'm very much displeased with what you're doing. I have some constituents in my office and they have had a contract with the Navy. It's been months since they heard from them. They haven't been paid and they need their money. What in the hell are you people doing over there. Why don't you take care of your people? Why don't you pay your bills? I'm going to see that something happens." He was hammering on his desk and he just gave me the devil. Then he said, "Now that's all," and he hung up.

About twenty minutes later he called back and he said:

"Murrey, I hated to make that speech but I had those constituents in there and they're very important people and I had to make an impression. Will you look out for it and see what you can do for me?"

I said, "Harry, we'll have that thing settled in thirty days or less."

He said, "Thank you. That's all."

That was Harry Shepherd for you. He was a fine chap. I had very fair treatment all the time on the Hill, before the Appropriations Committee, before the Armed Services Committee. The only one that I got bawled out a little bit by was Mr. Flood. He's still on the committee.

Q: From Pennsylvania?

Adm. R.: Yes, I went up there one day as chief of the bureau to defend the Boston Navy Yard. They were going to close up the paint factory and Mr. Flood didn't think it should be closed. I went up and I told him and said, "Here are the figures. It's costing us money to make this paint up there. We can buy it cheaper on the outside. I hate to see it closed, too. For many years when we couldn't get the right kind of anti-fouling paint and special paints for the Navy that did a good job. But we can get those paints now and get them much cheaper.

"You're telling me," he said, "I know more about paint than you do. You're just a stuffed shirt. You don't know what you're talking about."

"Well," I said, "Mr. Flood, if that's your opinion, that's your opinion. I'm giving you the facts."

He went on and he just gave me the devil. The funny thing was when the committee voted, they voted with me not with Mr. Flood! But Mr. Flood I've known ever since and we've been very good friends. I admire him very much. He's a very fine congressman. He apparently had something on his mind that he had to defend. And that's the thing that you do in working with these committees. You know that these people have to be elected and they've got constituents that they've got to satisfy. As long as you know that, to work with them is very easy. I have yet to see any of them that I didn't like or didn't get to know very well. They've been fine with me.

Of course, I did have a very big aide and a tutor, too, and that was Earl Chesney. I don't know whether you ever heard of Earl Chesney?

Q: I knew him.

Adm. R.: You did? Well, the first thing I did when I got into the Bureau was to recall Earl to active duty. He was a Supply Corps officer. I recalled Earl to active duty as my PIO.

Q: Nobody knew his way around Congress better than Earl.

Adm. R.: No. So I had Earl right there in the bureau with me, and Earl was watching me to see that I didn't make any mistakes, and I learned an awful lot from Earl. He was with me for a couple of years until he finally went over to the White House.

Q: Yes. He was on Eisenhower's staff. So he learned in the old school.

Adm. R.: Yes, and I couldn't have had a better teacher, could I? I was very, very fond of Earl, and his death was a great loss.

Another interesting thing was in February 1954 I went out to witness Operation Castle.

Q: Castle?

Adm. R.: Yes, Operation Castle was at Eniwetok on the 24th of February 1954. It was the firing of one of the biggest bombs. I wanted to see that because I felt that somebody in our Corps ought to know what the results of these bomb explosions were, what happened. It would help us to see it first-hand and help us a little bit more in the planning.

We left Washington, flew out to Honolulu, and then went out to Eniwetok and stayed out there for a day or so prior to the firing. We first went over to Bikini, which was about 140 miles away, where they were having the shot. They took us around and showed us the bomb and exactly what they were leaving on the island. The bomb was on a small island, which was an atoll, Bikini Atoll. Then we went back and on the day of the shot we got into a plane and were about 60 miles away in the air. We waited there and they made us put on very thick, black, dark glasses, and we were there watching it when that shot went off. Even with those thick glasses which you practically couldn't see anything through it was just like daylight. It was the most awful thing that I have ever seen - and I mean awe-ful. That thing just blossomed out, just clear daylight practically. We got a little shock from it in the plane although we were between 50 and 60 miles away. We could see the whole thing, the mushroom, and everything else. We flew around afterwards and let the cloud be blown away. We went right back to the island, but we couldn't land because it was still radioactive, but we went down close enough so that we could see. The little island that this bomb had been on had completely disappeared, just gone. The buildings and things that were on the island were just nothing - trees and everything else. It was completely bare - nothing but the sea.

The destruction that that thing did you just couldn't realize it. I feel very fortunate that I was able to see it, and it gave me an idea that I didn't want to have anything to do with hydrogen bombs again or be anywhere near them when they went off. It gave the people who were on the trip a realization of what could happen if we ever got into a hydrogen-bomb war. The absolute destruction and the absolute disappearance of everything around on that Bikini Atoll. It was hard to believe. Just no sign of anything. That, to me, was an opportunity that I had wanted and that I got and I don't know that I'd want to see another.

Q: How did it help you in your bureau planning?

Adm. R.: Well, in our planning if there was a danger of a hydrogen bomb we would have to have our material, if it was in a susceptible place, underground. It also started us thinking, and the fact is they almost had an experimental trial, of undersea storage, putting things under water. Earl Chesney was working on that.

Q: Kind of a Sealab?

Adm. R.: That's right. Tanks underwater for oil, have specially made containers that would sink to the bottom of the ocean and could elevate as you needed them, with material in them. Then there was the question as to whether it would be worthwhile to go into the mountains to establish a storage space for critical materials in case of a hydrogen attack. It gave us a lot to think about.

What's been going on in the last ten or fifteen years since I've been out I don't know. But they were starting to think along those lines because it did give you an idea of what would happen and how you'd have to have your material scattered out. You couldn't concentrate for fear of having it destroyed.

Q: So it was very useful?

Adm. R.: Oh, very useful. It also got these men to thinking on transfer of material, not so much along hydrogen lines, but the helicopter was coming into vogue at that time and the old system of transferring material at sea and carrying it to sea was, of course, to have a supply ship, and they'd go alongside another ship under way and have lines between them so that they paralleled each other, then use a high line to transfer things across from one to another. That was the standard way that they were using, and they may be using it now, I don't know. I haven't been that close to it.

But the thing that they began thinking about was using helicopters and letting the supply ships stay behind the lines quite a way, and using helicopters to transfer supplies.

Q: And land on the deck?

Adm. R.: Land on the deck, yes. Have each ship have a helicopter landing pad. Most of them have now, anyway. We're away from the big ships now. They have the cruisers and missile ships and later they could be handled that way very easily, but some of the people when I left were beginning to talk about that. Whether they ever did that I don't know.

You can see that my time in the bureau - I will say that I've got files of letters from People needing help, and I never failed to answer the letters and I helped when I could - but as far as the administration of the bureau went, I had a good organization. After George Bauernschmidt I had Walter Honaker, who was a rear admiral, and then after him, about the time I left, I had Bear Arnold.

Q: Bear?

Adm. R.: That was his nickname, his full name is Ralph J. Arnold. Bear Arnold, I might say, succeeded me when I was detached. Those three men were excellent men. George Bauernschmidt wanted to get away. He wanted to get some operating duty. And Walter Honaker wanted to get operating duty after a year or so there and I let him go and brought Bear Arnold in. But I turned over the actual operation of the bureau to those men. They were deputies. I concentrated on policy and general operation and not so much in the detail. I did get into the personnel detail because a lot of my officers wrote to me personally - personal letters - and, where it was necessary, I'd call in Walter Honaker and get the thing squared away and answer them.

But I'm a great believer in giving a man responsibility and seeing that he accepts it, and I must say that it worked out as far as I'm concerned. I never had any trouble with the operation of the bureau and as far as I know the Secretaries were all well pleased with what we did.

Are there any particular questions you want to ask?

Q: You wore another hat simultaneously with that of the chief of the bureau, and that was paymaster general. What did that entail?

Adm. R.: That came from the old days way back, when the paymaster was head of the Supply Corps. It was called the Pay Corps at first, when it was first originated, and that's why the word "paymaster" — the members of the Corps were called paymasters. As that grew and it became a big organization, they were looking for a name for the head of the Corps and they simply decided that Paymaster General would be the head of the Corps. So the paymaster general had two hats. He was paymaster general and head of the corps of specialists and paymasters. For some reason or other, they didn't like the name "paymaster," and they didn't like to be called "pay" for some reason or other. I never resented it. I was a paymaster, and they called me "pay" but it never bothered me in the slightest. I took it as a note of distinction. However, Supply officer seemed to describe the duty better.

Q: That was the acceptable nickname? Pay?

Adm. R.: Pay. Anybody that was in the Pay Corps was Pay, whether he was an admiral or an ensign. They they changed it to Supply Corps, but the term "Paymaster General" for head of the Pay Corps was never changed, and he was the senior man in the Corps. Of course, that doesn't stand now because we have some vice admirals, but they're on duty outside of the Corps. Vice Admiral Wheeler is now Number Two on the staff of the Chief of Naval Materiel. But the paymaster general was the head of the Corps and the top man.

Q: As chief of the bureau, did you have a relationship with Admiral Rickover?

Adm. R.: Oh, yes. Yes, indeed. I had a very close connection with Admiral Rickover. He's a very good friend of mine, and I admire him very much for what he's done. I think he's done a great deal. However, I didn't always agree with him and I must say that I never came out on top with him. The experience that I remember particularly well is the fact that Rick was up at Mechanicsburg when I was Chief, and he didn't like the way Mechanicsburg was being run. He wrote me several letters and gave me several suggestions, some of which I could take, but the others, much to his disgust, I couldn't possibly use.

But the experience I refer to was when he was in the Polaris program, the atomic submarine. He needed good officers and he asked me one day for a list of five or six Supply Corps officers and he would pick one for his operation. And I said:

"Rick, I know my officers better that you do, and I'll give you a good man who'll go to you and do you a good job."

He said, "I'll have no part of it. I pick my own people."

I said, "Rick, you're being foolish. What do you mean you pick you pick the best people?"

"Well," he said, "I can judge men, and I want to take who I want."

I said, "I prefer to send you people."

And I said, "No, I don't want you going through my people all the time and saying 'I'll take this one and that one.'"

He said, "You send me the list." I said, "I'll think about it." I got on the phone to Charlie Thomas and said:

"Charlie, Rick wants me to send over a list of people and he'll pick his own officer. I'm far more capable of picking a good man and I'll get him the best one I can."

Charles said, "Oh, for goodness sake give him what he wants. Let him do it."

I said, "You mean that?" "Yes," he said, "I don't want any fussing. Let him do it."

So I did, I sent him over a list. Two of the men who were on the list came to me and said:

"Admiral, I don't want to go to Rickover. He insulted me. He may be a great man and a fine person but he insulted me in my interview. I don't want to go."

So I said, "Well, it all depends."

Finally, Rick had seen everybody and he said, "I want this man." Fortunately the officer who had come to me wasn't selected. What Rich had done, he'd deliberately insulted a lot of these officers to see how they could take it. He would ask them the darnedest questions and put them through the greatest rigamarole you've ever seen.

Q: Really personal questions?

Adm. R.: Personal questions. But I will say for Rick that the people he did take and who worked with him, you could never find more loyal people in the world. They thought he was just tops and they were absolutely loyal to him all the way through.

Q: The man he selected from your list, was he the man you would have sent him?

Adm. R.: No. He was a good man, but he wasn't the man that I would have sent to him. The man that I would have sent was one that got mad, too. I didn't tell these boys anything. I knew what they were going to go up against. But I would have told him exactly what would happen and how to handle himself and he wouldn't have had any trouble.

Rick did that with these people, but I will say that the officers he had -- and I repeat it -- were the most loyal people you could ever have. He got loyalty from his people. That's one thing he could do.

When Mr. Charles E. Wilson was Secretary of Defense he instituted a very interesting annual meeting. The first one, as I recall it, was on the 23rd of July 1953. It was from the 23rd to the 26th of July 1953 at Quantico. We took over part of the Marine Corps base there, some of the barracks and some of the FBI barracks there, and Mr. Wilson invited the ranking people from the Army, Navy, Air Force, Marine Corps, and a number of the civilian agencies. I remember very well Mr. Dulles was there. In fact, President Eisenhower was down.

The object of this was to get the tops of these various agencies together for two or three days of very informal meetings. We had meetings during the daytime, organized; the afternoons were devoted to either golf or swimming or some sort of sport like that, where the various people could intermingle and talk to each other and get to know each other. President Eisenhower came down one day and spent most of the day there, and had dinner with us in the evening. He was very informal. He moved around among people, talked to everybody, and all in all it was a very satisfactory gathering. I certainly got a great deal out of it because I met a lot of people from the other services and the other agencies who I knew of but didn't know personally.

Q: A cross-fertilization sort of thing.

Adm. R.: Sort of a cross-fertilization. I talked to Mr. Wilson about that personally down there, and he said he wanted to avoid an polarization at all among the people. He believed in this.

Q: This was a part of his administrative acumen, was it?

Adm. R.: That's right, and that was a very wonderful thing.

Q: And you say this was on an annual basis?

Adm. R.: Yes. There was a later one, that was in 1955.

Q: Does this still go on? Did it after Wilson left?

Adm. R.: After Mr. Wilson left it died. That was one thing that he had that I think was a very fine thing that he did.

Q: In 1954 you reached the pinnacle of your particular profession in the Navy, October 2nd 1954, you became Chief of Naval Materiel. Tell me about the circumstances under which this appointment was made.

Adm. R.: At that time the current Chief of Naval Materiel was a line officer, Vice Admiral John Gingrich. John was a very good friend of mine and a very, very fine officer, and during his time as Chief of Naval Materiel, which lasted I think about a year or a year and a half, John came to me for assistance. We'd known each other for years and years. He was not familiar with the supply end of the Navy — when I say "not familiar" I mean with the details — and there were a lot of things that came up, policy matters and so on, so I spent a great deal of time with him, working with him, and he was most appreciative. We worked together very closely. He had a very fine personality and I think he was tops in the office as Chief of Naval Materiel. He had the bureaus working together, he had them enthusiastic, and I think he did a wonderful job.

He came to me one day and he said: "I've been offered a good job on the outside. I think while I'm still able to, I want to get out and take it. If I go to the Navy Department and recommend that you succeed me, would you do it?"

And I said, "Would I do it? I'd be delighted." So he said, "Well, let's you and I go over and see the Secretary of the Navy."

We went over and saw Charlie Thomas. Charlie tried to talk

John out of retiring. He was going with an electronics company in a very high position, and he said, "no," and I couldn't blame him. He said, "I've still got a few years yet and I want to build up a little estate before I have to quit."

So Charlie turned to me and said:

"Well, if John's going and he recommends you, it's all right with me. Fine. I'll get the OK of DOD and we'll put in your nomination." So they did. That was in September.

Q: This had to be approved by the Senate?

Adm. R.: That's right. They put in my nomination and I got orders and took over as of 2 October. However, my commission wasn't confirmed by the Senate till several months later. There was nobody there so I went in on an interim commission and started to work on the 2nd of October. John was detached and went on to New York to his new job.

I found the job very interesting. I'd been so close to it that it wasn't very hard to slide in to the work. I, of course, worked very closely with the Assistant Secretary.

Q: The Assistant Secretary was Franke?

Adm. R.: The Assistant Secretary was Franke later on. Mr. Fogler was in there when I first went in, and he was a very fine person. Bill Franke I liked very much. I can remember one time that I had a question or a proposition and I went into his office, argued very estensively and forcefully, and he finally said no. I said:

"All right, Mr. Franke, no it is, and we'll put your order in all the way and do exactly as you want."

He looked at me and said, "How can you do that?" I said, "What do you mean?"

He said, "Well, you came in here, you don't like this thing." I said, "No, I don't like it. It's wrong, but you're the man who's making the decisions and are responsible for it. When you give the order, we get it and we do it for you."

"But," he said, "you can't if you don't believe in it."

"Oh," I said, "you don't realize for over thirty years I've been in this man's Navy and it's my job when I don't believe in a thing to come in and argue with my boss and tell him what I think, and tell him frankly. But if he doesn't like it, whatever he decides, it's my job to carry out what he wants. That's been my life for over thirty years."

"Remarkable," he said. And I don't think he ever believed me. He just couldn't understand how you could argue against something and then turn right around and get it done. Mr. Franke was a wonderful person. But the time that I was in there nothing particuarly startling happened. It was a year and a half of very interesting work because I worked with the heads of all the bureaus. I had regular meetings with them, conferences, and it was more or less carried on in the Forrestal concept, instead of forcing or having an organization that made the bureaus do something, we did it on the basis of their wanting to work with others - be on their own but still work in consonance with the other people.

We had fine people as heads of bureaus and they all cooperated in excellent style.

Q: The Department of Defense at that time was not nearly as large and extensive as it is now?

Adm. R.: No. The Department of Defense wasn't. It was, of course, still growing. I think Mr. Forrestal had the right concept of the Department of Defense. His idea, of course, was and he told me this several times when I talked with him that he wanted only a small staff over there, a coordinating staff, that's all he needed. He felt that the services were big enough and were able enough to do their own jobs, but there should be some coordination so that there could be transfers of materials and transfers of personnel, if necessary, in between and that they would work together. He realized, as I've always known, when you talk about the interservice bickering and fighting, that that's mostly in Washington. In the field, I've never had an occasion where my opposites in the Army or Air Force ever did any fighting at all. We worked together when we had a problem.

Q: The bickering originates largely in terms of budget matters.

Adm. R.: That's right, and it's right in Washington. That's where most of it comes.

Q: But Forrestal's concept of the Department of Defense began to change rapidly under his successor, didn't it?

Adm. R.: His successors changed it. They wanted more of an operating outfit, and that went on down into the departments, too. For example, in the Navy Department the Bureau of Supplies and Accounts had done all the disbursing and accounting for the entire Navy, and while I was in the ONM, I guess it was, the Navy Department decided to put the accounting and disbursing right under the Secretary, that is under the financial Secretary.

I argued against that because I didn't think the Secretary's office should be an operating office at all. It's administration, and the operations should be in the bureau. So they moved all of the accounting department, man for man, took them across to the Pentagon and put them in the Secretary's office. There was absolutely no change in the operation at all, except that they were operating directly under the Secretary. That's the only operating activity in the Secretary's office today. Why they did it, I don't know. I never got any satisfactory explanation.

But I agree with you that Forrestal's was an administration and not an operating job, and the Operations, DOD, is more and more trying to get into the operations as a whole. They talked about a single service of supply and we fought that one. I helped fight that when I was chief of Naval Materiel. My British friends told me, "For God's sake keep out of that. We have it in England and it's the worst thing ever. You never know what you're going to get. It's run under civilians. They don't know the service, they don't know how the material is used, and they don't know how it's going to be handled, how it's handled in the field, or anything like that at all."

Q: How far along did the idea get?

Adm. R.: To the talking stage. They talked about it a great deal.

Q: Who were the principal advocates?

Adm. R.: The DOD people. In fact, Forrestal even talked about it for a while, and he was talked out of it. Then some of his successors, Johnson, I think, put up a big speel about it, too. But we kept it away and fortunately each service has its own supply system, which they should have to serve their particular needs. The common material that they have GSA is the source now. For instance, the common things like stationery and that sort of thing.

Q: How did that work in terms of MAAG, for instance? The three services were contributing to - ?

Adm. R.: To their opposites. We took care of the navies. The only trouble was with the chief of Naval Materiel at that time. As I say, there was a lot of responsibility but no authority. If I'd had the bad luck to have one of the chiefs of bureau refuse to do something, I would have had no authority to tell him to do it. I would have had to go to the Assistant Secretary and ask him to tell him. On the one occasion when it almost came to that situation I went to the Secretary and told him.

"I'm having a hard time with this particular bureau chief. I think he's wrong. He doesn't want to play on the team. He wants to go off on his own on this thing and I would like to write up an order to him for you to sign, and tell him to comply and go along with the plan that has been made up by the Chief of Naval Materiel and agreed to by everybody but him."

The Assistant Secretary wouldn't do it. He said:

"I don't know. I just don't know whether that's the right thing to do." In this case, he hadn't been there long enough to really know the background.

Q: Was this Franke?

Adm. R.: Yes, this was Franke, and he didn't do it, but fortunately enough it worked out.

After Franke once got his feet on the ground and knew what the score was, there was no trouble at all. He was a fine man to work with, very fair, he knew what he was doing, and he was a grand person.

Fogler before him was another fine man. He'd had a lot of merchandizing experience with Montgomery Ward, as I recall it. He was one of the big officials there. He, too, was a little hesitant about going out and giving orders but after he got his feet on the ground he was good. He would take responsibility.

I think these civilian people who come into jobs like that deserve a great deal of credit because it's a brand-new life for them, they don't know what it's all about, and they have to depend on a lot of the old-timers like myself to help them along. They don't know us.

They don't know whether we're trying to slip something over on them or not, and they just have to take their time and work into it. But I found that when they once got into it and they know what the job's about, in six or eight months, they're wonderful people to work with. You could get a decision, you could get the backing, and it's fine.

Of course, the chief of Naval Materiel, as I told you, after I left they changed it all and went to this system that's now in existence. I think all that they needed to do was to put a little more authority in the chief of Naval Materiel as they had it, and charge him with the coordination of the bureau work, and if he couldn't do it, then the dissident bureau had an appeal to the Secretary, which would settle it. But I think any chief, any officer, with a sense of balance could handle that because the chiefs of bureaus are all mature men. There are no radicals or fanatics among them at all. They're wonderful people.

Q: Well, the process of selection was so very careful, wasn't it?

Adm. R. It was careful and they only put good men in these jobs.

Q: As you indicate in your own case you were something of an understudy for a while?

Adm. R.: That's right. The year and a half that I had there, from 2 October 1954 to 31 January 1956, was a very, very interesting thing.

We, of course, came a great deal in touch with outside industry. I remember Mr. Romney came in when he was with American Motors. He wanted to get a contract for American Motors, and I had to explain to him that we'd be very glad if we needed his material, but he would have to go through exactly the same process as any other motor company would do to sell their products to the services, to the Navy.

We got in the Secretary's office there the tops of industry from all over the United States. When they had their troubles they came right to that office - that is with the Navy. When they had trouble with the Navy they came right to that office for assistance, which we were glad to give them. The worst thing that we had to do was to convince a lot of these people, particularly when they were looking for contracts, that if they didn't win a contract it was because they didn't bid low enough. Then when they bid too low and our people would go out and make an investigation and find that if we let that contract on that low bid price, these people would lose money and possibly be in a bad financial position. But to tell these people that was a tough thing because they'd go to their congressman and say, "we bid low, we deserve the contract, and we ought to have it." Then, to shut them off because they bid too low. We had some pretty big fights sometimes.

Q: Can you give me an illustration of that?

Adm. R.: Well, I don't remember the name, but there was a fellow that came in and he had bid on a contract for some pallets, wooden pallets, and it was quite a big one. He came in, and he was way under anybody else, so far under that we got suspicious and we sent our inspectors out - the inspector of naval material in his district - and they came back with a report that said that he couldn't possibly deliver those pallets at the price he bid because the cost of the material plus his labor costs were more than what he bid for.

This man went to his congressman, and the congressman came in saying you're depriving my constituent here of a legal contract that he's earned and I intend to see that he gets it. I explained to him, showed him the figures and everything, but he wouldn't believe it. This was when I first went in and so I said: "All right, let him go."

About eight months afterwards, the fellow came in looking for relief. He said: I'm broke."

"Well," I said, "I hate to say 'I told you so,' but you remember the meeting, I've got the record of the meeting in my files here. I can't do anything for you."

He said: "I'm working for the government, and the government's going to get it all right, but I'm going broke."

I said, "That's just too bad," and we let him go and he did go broke.

Q: No repercussions from the congressman?

Adm. R.: We had the files where we had the meeting and told him so. After that I never let another one go through. I took the repercussions from that, and that was the only one that taught me a lesson, the only one that I ever knowingly let him buy a bid.

Q: How frequently did that sort of situation develop?

Adm. R.: For big contracts that would develop - oh, I can remember dozens of them. I can't say exactly how many, but I know a great many contracts came about which we had that discussion.

Q: What's involved? The prestige of a government contract?

Adm. R.: Well, here's the thing. On some of these contracts, especially if it's a cost-plus contract - well, not a cost-plus contract, but cost plus fixed fee - you can get away with it by bidding pretty low because you can bid your costs low and then, if your costs are higher than you bid or they're running higher, you can figure you can get a changed contract in there. That is, they'll come in and say, well, your specifications weren't just exactly right, the specifications were changed which forced our costs up beyond what we estimated, therefore we're entitled to a change order in there. Get it?

Q: Yes, I do.

Adm. R.: A lot of people who bought contracts would just deliberately figure on that.

Q: Isn't that a fairly transparent technique, however?

Adm. R.: Sure it is, and a lot of these cost overruns that you have, a lot of these people have bought contracts, deliberately gone in on low prices figuring on change orders to bale them out. That comes in a great deal in shipbuilding and new types of material where there are no specifications, or the specifications are a little vague, they've never made them before and they don't know.

Q: Well, then, honesty is subverted by that technique?

Adm. R.: That's right. The smart boys try to do that. Of course, on a new type of material, they come again. For instance, you've got, say, an electronic device, something that's new, that's never been used before. The man who gets that first contract gets the know-how and how to make it. He's got the expense of the material and so on. Then, on a repeat order, he's sitting pretty because he's got all of that dope and on an honest bid he can generally underbid anybody else who doesn't have that information. That's one reason why on the first order a lot of people would sacrifice a little bit of profit.

Q: Well, where it's a pioneering field, I can see why this would be.

Adm. R.: That's right. There are a lot of games to be played in the purchase field. It was very interesting to go through that. But the thing that used to get me more than anything else was just what I said in the first place, people would come in, deliberately put in a low bid, and, if they were any kind of businessmen, know that they couldn't buy it for that -

Q: And then use political influence!

Adm. R.: Use political influence to get it and then get into trouble. We didn't want it because when a man gets into trouble we don't get our product. We don't get our material. And there's always a legal battle. We're doing him a favor when we turn him down.

So we got to putting in our contracts and a bid would be accepted only after inspection by inspectors in naval material and a determination made as to the fairness of the price.

Q: This whole area of contracts and the awarding of contracts was this an area of considerable concern to you? I mean there's so much possibility for dishonesty in the area.

Adm. R.: Well, as you may know, each bureau has its own purchasing department. There's a Supply Corps officer generally in charge of the contracts section. Our men that were in there were good men. They'd been well trained. I never found, or I never had any occasion to know of, any collusion between any of our contract people and prospective bidders. They were pretty honest people. There are so many checks and balances in there and so many people have to know something about it. Not only is a man honest, but these checks and balances keep him pretty much on a straight line.

Q: Would you care to comment on the system as you describe it in contrast with the system used in the Polaris program, where competitive bids weren't sought and they simply awarded contracts?

Adm. R.: In those cases what they do is they go out and make a survey of the field and find out the companies that are capable of making thepproduct. There may be only three or four, maybe only one, that would be capable of developing and manufacturing the product. Then you've got to consider how soon you've got to have this product. Do you have to have it right now, or can you wait three years?

Then you go out and you make a survey of these prospective companies. You have to find out whether they're financially able, whether they're going to need government assistance, progress payments, for example. You've got to find out what their capacity is, whether they're big enough to handle this whole thing. And you've got to find out how soon they can make it. What their situation is at the present time, whether they can go right to work on it and push it right through, or whether you're going to have to wait for it. Then you can go ahead and choose your one or two - maybe one or two, maybe only one, fits the proposition. In that case, negotiate a contract. I'd have no objection to that at all.

But if it's a pioneering thing, I'd have a cost plus fixed fee, because cost plus fixed fee gives the manufacturer a chance. He never knows what unforeseen developments he's going to have to take or what unforeseen problems there are going to be. Fixed fee means that he'd only get the same fee if he took a year as if he took six months, and he's going to do that thing just as fast as he can. Those contracts are not bad. I know after I got out of the service I was director of a small electronics company up in Massachusetts and they were getting burned on some of these contracts. They'd go into these development contracts and try to do them on a fixed-fee basis, and they got burned badly because they got into problems that not even the government anticipated they'd get into. They'd have to get change orders approved and everything else. Once or twice they pretty near went under. I made them quit doing that. There's so much to this contracting business, and that's where the chief of Naval Materiel – of course, when one of the bureau contracting sections gets in trouble they bring it right in to ONM and ONM takes a look at it and makes a decision. If that's not satisfactory to the other man, he can go to the Contracts Appeals Board, which generally always backed us up because our people gave them very good opinions. They were experienced men there.

We had a number of ex-FBI men working for us, and they still have that division which was more or less inspection work with the inspectors. We'd often have letters come in saying so and so is gypping the government, and doing this or doing that, and we'd put these FBI men on the trail – ex-FBI men – get them cleaned up right away. It was a very, very satisfactory outfit.

Q: They had real aptitude in that?

Adm. R.: Oh, boy, they knew what they were doing.

But we had no big scandals. We had some reports that somebody way down was taking money for passing material. All of that, as far as I know, they cleared up. We had to fire one or two people.

Never could prove anything, but it was suspicious enough so that we'd get rid of the man. We kept it clean - that's the main thing.

Q: You were there during a changeover in Chief of Naval Operations. Admiral Carney was there at first, and then Admiral Burke came in. Was there any noticeable difference in the way things ran? In your bailiwick, were there any repercussions?

Adm. R.: No. Over in our place they left us pretty much alone, both when I was in the bureau and when I was chief of Naval Materiel. I knew Mick Carney very well and I knew Arleigh Burke very well, and they never interfered at all. That was one nice thing about the Chief of Naval Operations. All they demanded was that they got service for the fleet, and as long as they got service for the fleet they never bothered us. And that's exactly what our side of the house was doing.

Is there anything else now?

Q: You seem to have a very particular aptitude in dealing with the labor element. Did this enter into the picture when you were in Naval Materiel?

Adm. R.: Yes, it did. The fact is we conducted labor relations of the Navy Department with labor. Most of this, of course, was with the AF of L and the CIO. We had very cordial relations with them. One thing that we did, I organized some parties with Secretary Schnitzler and President George Meany of the AF of L and CIO and, in order to get them interested in what we were doing -- there were talks of strikes and labor troubles and so on in different places -- we'd put on some exhibitions down at Norfolk and in various places, showing material that was produced by labor and then showing how it was used by the service. For instance, tanks we'd show how they were used, put on a little party with it, and guns, even special transportation material, and so on.

We'd organize this day's outing to take a number of the top labor people down by plane. One was to Norfolk and we put one or two others on in different places. We'd gather up these top labor people and give them a day at this station, showing them exactly what they had produced and how it was being used by the service. In other words, we wanted to get the tops to know about it so that they could let it filter down in their house papers and so on, and let them let their people, the workers and so on, that the Navy appreciated what was being put out, let them know how it was used, and that it was one of the most important things that they could do in their work.

This went over very well. We had these people in and we got some very fine publicity in labor's house papers about these trips and the fact that the Navy Department was appreciative of what labor was putting out. As I say, our relations were very good. In the period of strikes I contacted my friends over in the AF of L/CIO and if we had material that was tied up in a strike-bound plant, we never had any trouble getting it out. They would give orders to the strikers down there to let the material that the Navy had to have that was in that plant come through the picket lines. I think that was one of the most satisfactory things I've seen done, because we had one civilian there who knew these people just as well as I did and he could work with them, and we'd get the bureaus to come in and say "we've got certain stuff tied up in a certain plant, we can't get it out, and we've got to have it. What do I do?" All we had to do was go to these top labor people and ask them for it, tell them why we needed it, that it was not interfering with their strike at all, and we'd get it. It happened many times.

Q: That was in the days before they thought of striking against the government!

Adm. R.: That's right. I enjoyed working with them very much.

Q: What innovative steps did you take in the field of public relations, which seems to have been one of your fortes also?

Adm. R.: The only thing that I did with public relations was to be very fair with everybody I worked with, the press, labor, I was very frank and cooperated wherever I could.

We in the Supply Corps often thought, as far as public relations went, that we had a story to tell, and we never passed up a chance if there was a celebration of any kind in the city. For example, in San Francisco and Oakland, which are great places for parades, we always had a contingent in there from the Center - over in San Francisco as well as in Oakland. The State Fair in Sacramento, they gave us a spot up there and we had a miniature box factory in the fair one time.

Each year in all of our installations on Navy Day we took a leading part in working out exhibitions and tours through the supply activities, the main thing being that we impressed on people that we were part of the community, that we had jobs there for them, and they needed us just as much as we needed them.

I think public relations is one of the most important things that the Navy can do. I remember Admiral King one time - I tried to talk to him about public relations and all I got out of Admiral King was, "We've done our job and that speaks for itself."

Q: That pretty much personified the attitude of the Navy before World War II.

Adm. R.: Yes, but that doesn't work. You may have done a job but if people don't know about it it's not going to help you at all.

Q: You have to blow your own horn!

Adm. R.: You have to blow your own horn, and I encouraged it when I was Chief of the bureau. I used to write to the commanding officers of the various places where we had commands prior to Navy Day and prior to any occasion like that, encouraging them to get into the community and to take part and show the flag. I had a lot of fun out of that.

But, as I say, I have a lot of respect for labor. I think they're wonderful people and certainly as far as I'm concerned I've never had any trouble. They'd come through in fine shape.

Q: That's an enviable record, I think.

Adm. R.: Well, I don't know. They're all human just like the rest of us. As I look back, I had a lot of fun with Harry Bridges. I'd like to see him again. I've enjoyed the public relations end of it very much. I always encouraged my officers and civilians, too, if they ever had a chance to talk before groups, lodges, and so on, to go out and speak their piece. We at the center - it's still going, I think - had a Toastmasters' Club, where a lot of the boys would enjoy getting up and talking. And we used to have requests for speakers quite often from all over Oakland. I did a lot of speaking, too. I'm not much of a speaker, but I had a good speech writer who helped me out.

Q: Did you find that, generally speaking, your officers didn't have that specific ability?

Adm. R.: There were some who didn't have a specific ability, but they all tried. That was the main thing. With the Toastmasters' Club right in the center there, it gave them a chance to get up. They realized that they had to do it. As they were getting up and got more rank they were going to have to do something like that. These little clubs, like the Toastmasters' Club, give them a chance to get on their feet and do a little bit of talking.

Q: They get the experience.

Adm. R.: Also, we'd have conferences and I'd call on these men to get up and make a presentation, get on their feet and say their piece.

They didn't want to be kidded about not being able to talk and a lot of them went out of their way to learn how to talk. I found that that was a good way to get some of them started.

The press, I think, is one of the most important things. I think I told you about the time in Oakland when I got the city editor to come down.

Q: It came time for your retirement on the 1st of February 1956. Tell me something about the circumstances and then tell me something about what you did to busy yourself afterwards.

Adm. R.: I had a letter from Admiral Jimmy Holloway in the Bureau of Personnel in January of 1956, and he told me that I'd be 62 in November of 1956 and I'd have to retire. He wanted to know if I was going to stay on until I was retired or whether I wanted to get out early. No, I guess it was in November of 1955 that I got that letter, and I wrote back and told him that I hadn't decided what I was going to do and I'd let him know after the first of the year.

So in 1956 I had an offer from this little company, the National Radio Company of Malden. They asked me if I'd go on the board and represent them down in Washington.

Q: This is Malden, Massachusetts?

Adm. R.: Yes. I said I would if I got out, and there were a couple of other small concerns that wanted me to do some consulting for them. So I decided I might as well get out now and not wait until I had to, so I put in for retirement as of 31 January 1956. It came and I retired. They had a nice party for me over at the Army and Navy Club - the Country Club. There were no retirement ceremonies in those days.

Q: When had you been advanced to vice admiral?

Adm. R.: As of 2 October, when I took over the job. That went with the job.

I was retired and we got out of Falls Church and bought a house over in Arlington, on South Ives Street, and I got an office down town in the Washington Building, in conjunction with a friend of mine, Tom Weed, who was a retired colonel in the Army. He represented San Francisco. And Barry Sullivan, who was the representative of a number of people here. He was a civilian. The three of us had this office and a secretary. I went up to Malden once a month for board meetings.

In the meantime the Chamber of Commerce of Oakland called me up and wanted to know if I would represent the Chamber and the city of Oakland, the county of Alameda, and the port of Oakland.

Q: You mean their Washington representative?

Adm. R.: Their Washington representative. That was a combination of four jobs. The other three paid the Chamber of Commerce and I drew my pay right through the Chamber of Commerce. I represented all four activities. That was a very interesting time. I enjoyed it. In the meantime we bought a farm up in West Virginia, 300 acres. It had a small apple orchard, and we put in some more trees. We had about 4,000 trees up there. We had two ponds on it and we built a couple more, so we had four ponds altogether, and they were all stocked with fish. It was really a beautiful place. That gave us good weekends. We'd go up on Thursday or Friday and come back on Sunday night.

I wasn't very well satisfied with the radio company. I didn't like the management too well and, although I was on the board and tried to get them straightened out and lined up some government work, I didn't want them to rely on government work. We found out when I was chief of Naval Materiel that the smaller companies who depended on government work were not very healthy, because it was a case of have something and have nothing. While they had a contract they were going all right, but when the contract ran out, why, they had nothing till they got another one.

Q: No resources!

Adm. R.: No resources. This company was an old company. It had been started in 1914, but it was depending entirely on government work and as a result they were having troubles. I told them that they should have only about 20 percent - 20 to 30 percent - government work, and go in for commercial work. They had an excellent reputation in the trade and the material that they turned out. They turned out excellent radios. At one time they had a television, but that wasn't very successful and they dropped it before I was with them. So I talked to them, talked to the president, talked to the board, but they knew more about it than I did. They didn't try to develop the commercial business. They had excellent potential for radio parts, all sorts of parts. They put out an excellent radio, a terrific radio, but their marketing wasn't very strong on it. They sold a lot overseas. National Radio was well known in the services. But they insisted on sticking to government business and we rocked along there. Some years we made some money and some years we didn't. Finally, around 1968 or 1969, they were put under partial operation by a conservator and I got off the board right after that.

Q: Because the financial condition was shaky?

Adm. R.: It was shaky. They'd gotten into trouble with the government on some of their contracts and they didn't have a civilian backlog. They had some civilian work but not too much. They'd gotten in trouble with the Air Force and trouble with the Army on some contracts. Of course, in my position, I couldn't help them out there because, being a regular officer retired, I couldn't get into it. I told them what they could do but they didn't do it, so I got disgusted and got off the board.

They're still going, but they're still under a conservator. I don't know whether they'll come out of it or not.

In the meantime I worked on my jobs from the West Coast which gave me plenty to do. I enjoyed it because I was on the Hill a great deal.

Q: What sort of jobs would you be required to do for Oakland?

Adm. R.: Primarily going on the Hill. You'd be surprised how much a municipality, how much a county, how much a port has to do with

Congress. They're always having bills come through that either hurt them or give them some help. Also, they have a great deal to do with departments, such as Commerce and Labor. I worked on those bills, keeping in touch with our congressmen and senators. I would go over to the Department of Commerce and Labor in connection with questions that might come up in their operations out there. It kept me quite busy.

I enjoyed it because I'd been used to going on the Hill and I knew most of these people up there.

Q: And you are fond of Oakland as a community!

Adm. R.: Yes. I had one interesting case, as an example. They built a stadium out there in Oakland - a stadium compex. They had the stadium plus the Coliseum right next to it in the same complex. It was built by the city and county and they had a football team out there but no baseball team.

They called me up one day and said:

"Listen, can you help in doing anything about getting a baseball team out here?"

"Well," I said, "you're building a stadium there. Haven't you got any leads yet?"

"No. The fact is we've broken ground and made quite a start on the stadium and we think it's about time to see if we can get a baseball team."

I said, "I don't know anything about it, but I'll talk to some people." I knew the group that had the Washington ball club here and I talked to some of my friends there. They didn't have much to say. So next time I went up to Boston I dropped in to see Joe Cronin, who was President of the American League. He's an old San Francisco boy and I'd met him a number of times.

Q: Did you know him when he was here in Washington?

Adm. R.: No, I didn't know him when he was in Washington, but I met him up there a couple of times and then went back to see him this time. He said:

"Well, I'm the president of the league and I can't give you any advice at all. That wouldn't be quite ethical, but why don't you call up Charlie Finley."

"I know who he is," I said, "he has the Kansas City Athletics and he doesn't like it there."

He said, "Yes, that's right. I don't know anything about it. Don't quote me, but I just suggest you call him up."

Well, I got back to Washington and I called up Finley at his office in Chicago. I introduced myself over the phone and he said:

"Well, Kansas City is not too satisfactory. I might want to make a change. What you got to offer?" So I gave him a rundown on the Oakland Coliseum, told him how modern it would be. I had gone to the Washington ball park and got those people to give us all the information about building a ball park, faults that they may have found when they surveyed other places, too. This was going to be a real thing.

He said, "It's beginning to sound pretty good. Who should I see out there?"

I told him who he should see if he went out and I said, "They're building it now."

"Oh, they are," he said, "I didn't know that."

I said, "Yes, and if you will go out I'll see that you're taken care of and you can see the whole situation."

He said, "Sure, I will. Give me a call back and let me know when it will be convenient."

So I called the Coast and they got hot and bothered right away. Here was a prospect. They gave me a date and told me to have him call Robert T. Nahas, who was the head of the Coliseum, a fine chap who used to be Chamber of Commerce president. I called Finley back and told him. He called Bob, set a date, went out there, made up his mind like that, so the Oakland Oaks went from Kansas City to Oakland!

Q: That was quite an accomplishment.

Adm. R.: Well, I just opened the door. I found the right lead, that was all. But that's how the Kansas City team happened to go out to Oakland.

My friends here in Washington said, "You're crazy to get Finley out there. He's a rat. We wish he wasn't even in the American League." They talked about it. I don't know but I guess he's getting along all right out there. I think he's making money now, since he had his world championship last year. He's very eccentric.

That was one thing that I had to do. Anything that they could think of, they'd call me up and I'd have some fun trying to do it.

Through the years I worked along with them and then about 1971 I thought well, now there are things I'd like to do besides work. I've got my place loaded up here with stamps and firstday covers. I've been a first-day-cover collector for 30 or 40 years and I've got a pretty good collection. I'd like to get them in shape and get to work on them. So I resigned from the Oakland job, and it wasn't a month or so later that I got a call from the port. The port said:

"Well, you've resigned, but we really need somebody back there."

I said, "There are plenty of people." They said, "Won't you stay on with us?"

I said, "Well, I'm not going to do much work for you."

"Oh, well, stay on – "

Q: Stay on call?

Adm. R.: On call, and I said, "All right, I'll do it. It will be a lot of fun to keep in contact with you people." So I'm still with the port.

Q: How frequently do they call on you?

Adm. R.: Oh, once a month – let's see, a week ago Monday Wally Abernathy, the deputy manager of the port, was having a problem out there. The port is the largest container port on the West Coast, second largest to New York. New York is the only one in the States that handles more container ships. You know what a container ship is?

Q: Oh, yes.

Adm. R.: The trouble is Oakland only has 35 feet of water and these new container ships that are coming out draw 35 feet, and it's not good to have the ship sliding on the bottom.

Q: Not good at all!

Adm. R.: So they're trying to get 5 feet more and they've been having a battle. The good people don't want them to do any more dredging because it will hurt the ecology out there or something. The conservationists don't want them to do it. They want them to carry the soil that they dredge out clear out to sea and dump it, which is very expensive. They won't let them dump it inland. And, at the same time, they've got to get some money from the government to do the dredging. So we're trying to get $20,000 in this year's budget just to start the planning.

In doing a thing like this, you don't get it done in six months, you don't get it done in a year, and you don't get it done in three or four years. A job like that generally takes you four to five years before it can be accomplished.

Q: Well, at the rate the container ships are developing, you'll be behind the times?

Adm. R.: We'll be behind the times, so they'll undoubtedly modify that.

So, rather than to lose a whole year we're working with the Corps of Engineers to get $20,000 in to start their evaluation of this, and we're up before the appropriate committees of the House and the Senate, visiting all the congressmen and so on last week. So I probably won't hear from them again for awhile.

Q: How much are you budgeting to fight the Sierra Club?

Adm. R.: I don't know. People are so impractical. You know, I have a lot of fun with some of these congressmen. They don't realize what's involved. For instance, we have one congressman - or two of them rather, both of them pretty much conservationist-inclined - so I said: "Now, listen. You're going to have to back us. If you don't in your own districts, it's going to mean that these big container ships are going to Seattle or to Los Angeles. They won't go to Oakland. I can tell you that you're going to lose around 2,000 to 3,000 jobs right there on the waterfront, if that happens. You're going to have to do it."

When you start talking jobs, a congressman listens to you. Then they said they'd help and, believe me, those men have been really helping, too. But whether we'll get it in this budget, I don't know yet. The reason they don't want to give us the $20,000, I think, is because they don't want to have a new start. Of course, the $20,000 is only a drop in the bucket. It'll be around an 8- to 10-million-dollar job, and they're trying to cut costs all they can. But we've got a pretty good group lined up behind us now and they

may get the thing over. But that's the kind of thing that I do.
P.S. We got the new start and the $20,000.00.

Q: Well, its a very constructive job that you're still engaged in. I think that's great.

Adm. R.: I've enjoyed it.

Q: You know, you told me, you have said all along as you recounted the events in your career, that you learned from this job and you learned from that, and so forth. The cumulative knowledge is a very great and impressive thing, and I'm glad to know that it's still being used.

Adm. R.: Well, I enjoy it.

Q: Thank you very much, Sir.

Adm. R.: You're welcome, it was my pleasure.

Index to

Series of Interviews with

Vice Admiral Murrey L. Royar, U.S. Navy (Ret.)

Ainsworth, VADM W. L. (Puggie): Commanding Officer at Norfolk Navy Base, p. 194; p. 196-7.

HMS AJAX - British Light Cruiser: transports BuSanda Chief and Royar on European trip (1943), p. 140-1.

USS ALBANY: becomes Station Ship at Vladisvostok, p. 28, 38; incident involving the death of the Chief Engineer in Vladisvostok, p. 41.

Allison, Leonard B. (Stub): Industrial Relations man with Naval Supply Center, p. 222.

Arnold, RADM Ralph Judd: (Bear) - succeeds Royar as Chief of BuSanda, p. 286.

HMS ASBURY PARK: designation for the training center for British personnel involved in taking over craft of U.S. manufacture - details of this installation, p. 127-132.

Baggs, Lt. Comdr. Harold: Manager of the Traymore Hotel in Atlantic City - sent to represent the International Aid Division of the BuSanda at HMS ASBURY PARK, p. 128.

Bates, The Hon. Wm. H.: comes into Supply Corps (1941) as a navy ensign - later Representative in Congress from Massachusetts, p. 111-112.

Bauernschmidt, RADM George: p. 286.

Baugham, RADM George F. (Supply Corps), p 145-6.

Black Workers - Oakland Supply Center: p. 221-223.

Bonner Committee: chaired by Cong. Herbert C. Bonner - interested in retrenchment and the cutting of military supplies, p 258.

Bridges, Harry: Labor leader - calls a stevedore strike at Supply Center (1949), p. 209-216; p 242-3.

Brinser, RADM Harry L.: skipper of the COLUMBIA, 1917-18, p. 21 ff.

British Supply System: contrasted with that of U. S., p 186-189.

Buck, Walter: one-time Paymaster-General and Vice President of RCA, p. 61, 64.

Bureau System in the Navy: Royar comments on merits of the old system, p. 261 ff.

BU SANDA (Supplies and Accounts): 1934 Royar reports for duty in Washington, p 88-91; Royar takes over the Clothing Division, p 91-96; inaugurate program of expansion, 1937; p. 99; in Stock Division, Oct. 1937 - June 1938 - process of building wartime stocks, p 99-101; June, 1942 Royar promoted and put in charge of Maintenance Division, p 118 - duties, p 118; requisitions from foreign governments, p. 120-1; French efforts at obtaining supplies in Oran, p. 122-123; Russian efforts to obtain extra supplies, p. 123-124; priorities, p. 120, 123-4; in charge of travel and shipping of supplies for foreign governments, p 125-6; HMS ASBURY PARK, p 127 ff; North African Bases, p. 132-3; Mechanicsburg, p. 133; Norwegian Base on Travis Island, p. 133-4; Royar goes with Inspector General to Pearl Harbor, 1943, to investigate Supply Depot there, p. 136-8; trip to Midway, p. 139-40; trip to Europe with Chief of Bureau, p. 140-142 ff; Sicily, p 142; North Africa, p 143-4;

comments on pilferage in North Africa, p. 144; Germany, Belguim, England, 147 ff; Royar becomes General Inspector of Supply Corps, p. 144-5; Exeter, p 147 ff; Guam, p 154 ff. Royar becomes chief of Bureau, Oct. 10, 1951, p 245 ff. getting acquainted, p. 251-2; Operations SLIM TRIM, p 253-4, 257-8; selection and building of an East Coast Depot at Byron, Georgia, p 254-255, 258; Korean War problems, p 263 ff; Royar inspects MAAG offices in Western Europe, p 264 ff; Far East, p 268 ff; program for training supply officers from foreign nations, p 269-70; Bureau responsibility for material transportation, p. 270-1; freight transportation school set up in Oakland, p. 271-273; BuSanda reorganizes system for running shop stores, p. 272-3; problems that showed up with Busanda personnel stationed in Western Europe, p. 274-5 ff; Budget and BuSanda, p 278-9; Royar witnesses the Bikini hydrogen bomb tests to aid in future planning for supplies, p 283-5; BuSanda administration in Royar's time as Chief, p. 286.

Byrd, RADM Richard E.: expedition to Antarctic outfitted in Norfolk, p. 185-6.

Byron, Georgia: Eastern Supply Center established there - see entry under BuSanda.

Chan, George: Chauffeur to Naval Supply Center, Oakland, p. 247.

Cheatham Annex: p. 177-178; also see entries under Supply Depot, Norfolk.

Chesney, Earl: p. 282; served on staff of Royar when he was Chief of BuSanda - helpful with congressional relations, p. 282, 284.

USS CHICAGO (1931): commissioned from Mare Island - Royar Supply on board, p. 78; shakedown cruise, p 79-81; 82-3; rammed by merchantman SILVER PALM, p. 85.

Clearfield, Utah: BuSanda Depot in the far west, p. 254.

USS COLUMBIA: Royar ordered to her for duty, p. 15-16; becomes Paymaster on board, p. 16; matter of the missing side of beef, p. 17.

Convoys - North Atlantic - WW I: p. 16 ff.

Cope, Captain Elijah Henry, Supply Corps: in charge at the Washington Navy Yard (1940), p. 108 ff; p. 117-118.

Cumshaw: examples of cumshaw in Asiatic waters in 1920s, p. 51-53.

Curley, Mayor James: Mayor of Boston, p. 65-67.

Emmons, Gen. Delos C.: first commandant of the Armed Forces Staff College, p 170-1.

Flood, The Hon, Dan: Congressman from Pennsylvania, p. 281.

Forrestal, The Hon. James: concept of the newly established Department of Defense, p. 294-5; 297.

Foster, RADM E. D.: Chief of BuSanda (1948), p 204-6.

Fox, VADM Charles: becomes Chief of Naval Materiel, p. 251.

Franke, The Hon. Wm.: Assistant SECNAV - 1954, p. 293-4; p. 298.

Gaffney, RADM John J.: Commanding Officer, Naval Supply Depot, Pearl Harbor, p. 137; commended for his foresight in building supplies at Pearl Harbor, p. 137-8. Commanding, Supply Center, Oakland (1947), p. 198; p. 206-7.

Gaida, General: Czeck Commander in Siberia at end of WW I who wanted to set up a Republic, p. 35 ff; encounter with Red Russians, p. 37.

Gingrich, ADM John Edward: Chief of Naval Materiel - 1954, p. 292-3; retires in 1954 and recommends Royar as his successor, p. 292-3.

Gordon, Walter: former governor of Virgin Islands - lawyer in Oakland, p. 222-3.

Graves, Major Gen. Wm. S.: (U.S. Army) - commanded so-called 'lost army' in the Vladisvostok area, p. 29-31.

Gresham, Judge E. G.: Superintendent of Transportation at the Norfolk Supply Base - also police judge in Virginia Beach, p. 190; p. 194-5.

Guam: Royar makes trip to reopen the Bank of Guam, p. 154-156.

Halsey, Fl. Adm. Wm.: in 1938 commander of Cruiser Division - inveterate golfer, p. 102-3.

Harvard Business School: Royar detailed there in 1922, p. 60-67.

Honaker, RADM Walter: p. 286.

Inspector General, Supply Corps: p. 144 ff; base at Exeter, Eng. used as illustration, p. 147-9; comments on policy regarding surplus materials p. 149-150; 151-2; Royar given additional duties as General Inspector for the Atlantic Coast, p. 156.

IZARD, Comdr. Walter B. (Snake): Supply Officer at Cavite Naval Station (1921), p. 46-7.

Kent, Lt. Comdr. Don: worked with MAAG office in Europe and in purchase of supplies abroad, p. 266.

Kimball, The Hon. Dan: Secretary of the Navy - names Royar as Chief of BuSanda, p. 245-7; 250.

King, Fleet Admiral E. J.: story of his denial of a request from a foreign government, p. 120-1. On Public Relations and the Navy, p. 201, p. 310.

Leiser, Harry: in command of the Supply Corps Base at Exeter, England, p. 147-9; writer on staff of Norfolk Supply Depot, p. 202, 241.

Le May, General Curtis: p. 115-6.

Lundberg, Harry: Labor leader - head of Sailor's Union of the Pacific (1949) - helps Royar in the strike called by Harry Bridges against the Oakland Supply Center, p. 211-214.

MAAG: Royar on European trip to inspect MAAG offices, p. 264-6; incident on MAAG trip to Taipai, p. 267-8; inspection trip (1953) to Far East, p 268-270; p. 276-7.

Mare Island Navy Yard: Royar detailed as Assistant to Accounting Officer, p. 67-68; p. 241.

McIntire, Adm. Ross F.: p. 27-29, 32.

the Naval Supply Depot, Norfolk, at behest of Adm. Nimitz, p. 181 ff.

Upham, RADM F. Brooks: Captain of the DD COLUMBIA (1917) in North Atlantic convoys, p. 16 ff.

Vinson, The Hon. Carl: selection of east coast inland supply depot, p. 254-7.

Washington Navy Yard: in 1940 Royar assigned there as assistant to Capt. Cope, Supply Corps, p. 108-9; they develop their own system for purchasing supplies, p. 110-111; comments on young officers who were sent there for training, p. 111-114; BuSanda commends the supply Department at the Navy Yard, p. 117.

Wilkins, Lt. Comdr. John Howard: established coffee roasting plant for Naval Supply Center, Oakland, p. 232-235.

Wilson, The Hon. Charles: Secretary of Defense, 1953 annual meeting at Quantico, p. 290-1.

www.ingramcontent.com/pod-product-compliance
Lightning Source LLC
Chambersburg PA
CBHW080618170426

43209CB00007B/1458